HISTORY OF KANNADA LANGUAGE

HISTORY OF KANNADA LANGUAGE

(READERSHIP LECTURES)

R. NARASIMHACHARYA

GYAN

Published by

Gyan Publishing House
5, Ansari Road
Daryaganj, New Delhi-110002
Phone: 011-47034999, 9811692060
E-mail: books@gyanbooks.com

Distribution Network
gyanbooks.com
India, USA, Canada, UK, Australia, France

ISBN : 978-81-212-3521-1 (PB)
First Published, 1934

2nd Impression 2020

Printed at: Gyan Press, Delhi.

UNIVERSITY OF MYSORE

HISTORY OF KANNADA LANGUAGE

(READERSHIP LECTURES)

BY

Praktana Vimarsa Vichakshana Mahamahopadhyaya
Rao Bahadur

R. NARASIMHACHARYA, M.A., M.R.A.S.,

Hony. Correspondent of the Government of India Archaeological Department,
Director of Archaeological Researches in Mysore (Retired)
Author of Karnataka-Kavi-Charite Volumes I—III,
Nitimanjari Pts. I and II, Sasanapadyamanjari,
Nagegadalu, Nitivakyamanjari, etc.

PRINTED AT MYSORE
BY THE ASST. SUPDT., GOVT. BRANCH PRESS
1934

PREFACE

AT the request of the Mysore University I delivered ten Readership Lectures, five on the History of Kannada Language and five on the History of Kannada Literature. The lectures on the History of Kannada Language were delivered in Mysore at the close of November and the beginning of December 1926, and the same were repeated in Bangalore in January 1927. The lectures on the History of Kannada Literature were delivered in Mysore in March 1928 and were repeated in Bangalore in August of the same year.

In 1933 the University undertook the publication of the substance of the course on the History of the Kannada Language in the present work.

The conditions under which the book has been issued permitted only a limited time for revision and editing, to which circumstance must be attributed certain short-comings of which I am conscious.

My thanks are due to Mr. M. Venkatesa Iyengar, M.A., for supplying certain figures regarding population speaking Dravidian Languages. I have also to acknowledge the assistance rendered by my son Mr. R. Tirunarana Iyengar, B.A., in preparing the Index.

I have in conclusion to express my indebtedness to the authorities of the Mysore University for having given me an opportunity to deliver these Readership Lectures.

MALLESWARAM,
25th January 1934.

R. NARASIMHACHAR.

CONTENTS

CHAPTER I

CHAPTER II.

CHAPTER III.

GRAMMAR.

CHAPTER IV.

CHAPTER V.

ERRATA.

PAGE	LINE				
21	13	*for*	participles	*read*	nouns
23	19	,,	*ni*	,,	*nī*
24	34	,,	derivations	,,	derivatives
26	last	,,	participles	,,	particles
31	39-40	,,	[illegible]	,,	[illegible]
39	1	,,	Irula	,,	Iruḷa
40	3	,,	Siḍi	,,	Siḍil
55	22	,,	*lri*	,,	*lṛi*
57	20	,,	*ta*	,,	*ṭa*
58	18	,,	*Tamil Kannaḍa*	,,	*Tamil and Kannaḍa.*
62	33	,,	ಅಚ್ಚೆತ್ತಿ ಅಚ್ಚೆ ; ಅಚ್ಚೆ ಅಚ್ಚ	,,	ಅಚ್ಚೆತ್ತಿ ಅಚ್ಚೆ ಅಚ್ಚ
63	19	,,	ಏನುಗು	,,	ಏನುಂಗು
69	13	,,	Com-pound	,,	Compound
73	15	,,	ವಲವಟ್	,,	ಪಲವಟ್
81	15	,,	in	,,	on
84	last	,,	in	,,	on
88	34	,,	roots	,,	some roots
	35	,,	some or	,,	or
89	23	,,	ಫೋರ್ ಪೋಲು	,,	ಫೋರ್ ಪೋಲು
	24	,,	ಅಲಮುಗು	,,	ಅಲಮರು
93	14	,,	ಜು	,,	ಜ್ಜು
94	10	,,	ಅ, ಅನ,	,,	ಅ ಅನ.
98	6	,,	ಅಡೇನಿ	,,	ಅಡೇನಿ.
	20	,,	ಚೇಯಕ	,,	ಚೇಯಕ,
103	19	,,	ಕೊಟ್ಟುದುರು,	,,	ಕೊಟ್ಟುದುರು
	22	,,	ಕೊಟ್ಟೆನು,	,,	ಕೊಟ್ಟೆನು ;
107	22	,,	ಗುಜ್ಜಿಮು	,,	ಗುಜ್ಜ್ರಿಮು
110	24	,,	ಅರುವಮು	,,	ಅರುವಮು
111	35	,,	cupid	,,	Cupid
112	9	,,	ಕಂಬು ಕೊಂಬು	,,	ಕೊಂಬು
129	31	,,	88,	,,	88.

Page	Line				
129	34	*for*	27,	*read*	27.
130	3	,,	Jayasangraba.	,,	Jayasangraha.
	5	,,	Badāmi,	,,	Bādāmi.
140	23	,,	ಬ್ತು	,,	ಎಬ್ತು
141	18	,,	ಮರಕ್ಕಾರ್	,,	ಮರಕ್ಕಾಲ್,
145	5	,,	ಪ್ರೊಗು	,,	ಹೊಗು
	29	,,	old	,,	Old
	34	,,	Also	,,	also
151	8	,,	Timil	,,	Tamil
152	33	,,	i,	,,	i, 7

HISTORY OF KANNAḌA LANGUAGE

CHAPTER I

Languages, their classification. Draviḍian languages. Their affiliation to Indo-European and Scythian families. Draviḍian languages form an isolated group. The term Drāviḍa old. Drāviḍa, its different senses. Derivation of Drāviḍa. Draviḍians, their civilisation. Recent discoveries. Region of Draviḍian languages. Enumeration of Draviḍian languages. The Pancha-Drāviḍa. Where spoken. Number of speakers. General characteristics of Draviḍian languages. Affinity of Behistun tablets to Draviḍian languages. Draviḍian group different from Sanskrit. Influence of Sanskrit and the Aryan vernaculars on the Draviḍian group. Draviḍian influence on Sanskrit and the Aryan vernaculars. Difference between Gauḍian and Draviḍian languages. Lexical affinities in Draviḍian languages. Draviḍian tongues of Southern India. Tamil. Malayāḷam. Telugu. Kannaḍa. Antiquity of the name Kannaḍa. Wrong use of the name Karṇāṭaka. Derivation of Karṇāṭa or Kannaḍa. Antiquity of the Kannaḍa language. Kannaḍa closely related to Tamil. Dialects of Kannaḍa: Tōḍa, Kōta, Baḍaga, Tuḷu and Koḍagu. Lexical affinities in Kannaḍa and its dialects. Number of speakers of Kannaḍa and its dialects.

LANGUAGES were divided by the philologists of a previous generation into three families, namely, the Aryan or Indo-European, the Turanian or Scythian and the Semitic. This division has, however, been found to be not only incomplete, inasmuch as it does not take into account the Chinese language and the numerous languages of America and Africa, but also scientifically incorrect, as the distribution of languages by families is based on the supposition, expressed or implied, of ethnical union at some very remote period. But race and language are not convertible terms. The science of language and the science of ethnology ought not to be mixed up together; they should be kept quite independent of each other. "Any attempt at squaring the classification of races and tongues must necessarily fail."* Language is the test of social contact and not of racial kinsmanship. Tribes and races lose their own tongues and adopt those of others. The Aryan Brâhmans of Southern India speak Dravidian languages. The Kelts of Cornwall speak English; the non-Aryan population of Wales and Ireland either Keltic or Saxon; and the Jews the manifold languages of the countries they inhabit. "Race in physiology and race in philology are two totally different things. Races physiologically as distinct as the Mongols and the Turks may be found speaking allied tongues, while races physiologically related, like the Jews of Europe and the Bedouins of Arabia, may be found speaking unallied ones. So far as ethnology is concerned, identity or relationship of language can do no more than raise a presumption in favour of a common racial origin. If ethnology demonstrates kinship of race, kinship of speech may be used to support the argument; but we cannot reverse the process and argue from language to race. Language, in fact, is not one of the characteristics of race, not one of those fixed and permanent features which distinguish the different ethnological types of man."† But it is satisfactory to note that the attempt made in the infancy of linguistic science to reduce groups of languages to a mystical triad has long since been abandoned by the scientific student.

The principle of the classification of languages now adopted by philologists is the morphological, *i.e.*, the one based on their grammatical structure. According to the morphological classification, languages differ from

* Max Muller: *Science of Language*, I, 458.

† Sayce: *Introduction to the Science of Language*, II, 315-18.

one another in the structure of the sentence and the grammatical relation of its parts. The forms of grammar are the expression of the mental life and history of a people: so the formative part of a language must ever be the surest *differentia* of linguistic kinsmanship.* "The life and soul of a language, that which constitutes its substantial individuality, and distinguishes it from all others, is its grammar. It is the only decisive evidence of the relationship between languages."† Morphologically, then, languages have been divided into five groups, namely, isolating, agglutinative, inflectional, polysynthetic and incorporating. These names well express the peculiarities characterising the groups. Thus, in the isolating group like the Chinese, each root preserves its independence and is distinctly significant. Here the position of the word alone denotes the meaning of a sentence without the assistance of any signs of relationship. Every word remains a separate and distinct sentence. In the agglutinative group like the Finnish and the Dravidian languages, two roots coalesce to form a word, the one retaining its radical independence, the other sinking down to a mere termination. These languages show grammatical relations by prefixing, suffixing or infixing sounds and syllables which are no longer independent words, and yet are clearly distinguishable from the full words they modify and not inextricably blended with them. In the inflectional languages like Sanskrit, two roots coalesce so that neither the one nor the other retains its substantive independence. The root and the suffix become so inextricably blended as to make the history of the word quite obscure. The difference between an Aryan and a Turanian language, *i.e.*, between an inflectional and an agglutinative language, is aptly compared by Max Muller to the difference between good and bad mosaic. The Aryan words, he says, seem made of one piece, whereas the Turanian words show clearly the sutures and fissures where the

* Sayce: *Principles of Comparative Philology.*
† Max Muller: *Survey of Languages*, 7.

small stones were cemented together. In the polysynthetic group like the North American languages, the words that make up a sentence are stripped of their grammatical terminations, and then fused into a single word of monstrous length. And lastly, in the incorporating languages like the Basque, a few words are loosely attached to the verbal root, unimpaired and independent. "If inflexion is 'agglutination run mad,' incorporation is inflexion run madder still: it is the result of attempting to develop the verb into a complete sentence."*

The Dravidian languages.

The relationship of the Dravidian languages to the great divisions of human speech is thus stated by Dr. Caldwell:—

Affiliation of the Dravidian group of languages.

"The Dravidian languages occupy a position of their own, between the languages of the Indo-European family and those of the Turanian or Scythian group—not quite a midway position, but one considerably nearer the latter than the former. The particulars in which they accord with the Indo-European languages are numerous and remarkable, and some of them are of such a nature that it is impossible to suppose that they have been accidental; but the relationship to which they testify—in so far as they do testify to any relationship—appears to me very indefinite as well as very remote. On the other hand, the particulars in which they seem to me to accord with most of the so-called Scythian languages are not only so numerous but are so distinctive and of so essential a nature that they appear to me to amount to what is called a family likeness and therefore naturally to suggest the idea of a common descent."

On the other hand, the Indo-European relationship of the Dravidian languages has been advocated by Dr. Pope on the ground of "deep-seated and radical affinities between them and the Celtic and Teutonic languages." But Dr. Caldwell observes in reply that "of all the members of the Indo-European family, the Celtic is that which appears to have most in common with the

* Sweet: *The History of Language.*

Scythian group, and especially with the languages of the Finnish family,—languages which may possibly have been widely spoken in Europe previously to the arrival of the Celts." Dr. Pope has also expressed the opinion that the more the Dravidian languages are studied, the closer their affinity to Sanskrit will appear. Gover, Seshagiri Sastri and R. Svaminatha Iyer have also advocated the Indo-Europern relationship.

The affiliation of the Dravidian languages to the Scythian family advocated by Dr. Caldwell appears to have received, more or less, the approval of scholars such as Max Muller, Whitney, Cust, and a few others, though other scholars have condemned it.

Max Muller, who has included the Dravidian group in the Turanian (Scythian) languages, describes the latter as follows :—

"The most characteristic feature of the Turanian languages is what has been called agglutination or 'gluing together.' This means not only that, in their grammar, pronouns are glued to the verbs in order to form the conjugation, or prepositions to substantives in order to form declension, . . . but that in them the conjugation and declension can still be taken to pieces; and, although the terminations have by no means always retained their significative power as independent words, they are felt as modificatory syllables and as distinct from the roots to which they are appended."

Whitney has the following remarks on the subject :—

"The Dravidian tongues have some peculiar phonetic elements, are richly polysyllabic, of general agglutinative structure, with prefixes only, and very soft and harmonious in their utterance; they are of a very high type of agglutination like the Finnish and Hungarian. . . . Excepting that they show no trace of the harmonic sequence of vowels, these languages are not in their structure so different from the Scythian that they might not belong to one family with them, if only sufficient correspondences of material were found between the two groups. And some have been ready, though on grounds not to be accepted as sufficient, to declare them related."

Cust says that the Dravidian family may be considered to represent the agglutinative method, notwithstanding that Pope, up to this day, maintains that the Draviḍian family belongs to the same morphological order as the Aryan.

It will thus be seen that scholars are generally agreed that the Draviḍian languages are agglutinative. The harmonic sequence of vowels, of which, according to Whitney, the Draviḍian languages show no trace, is, however, found to exist to an appreciable extent in Telugu, though not to the same extent in the other Draviḍian tongues also. Agglutination and vocalic harmony are two characteristics common to the Draviḍian group and some of the languages of the so-called Scythian family. Added to these, there are a few coincidences in grammar. These similarities are, according to some scholars, quite inadequate to warrant the affiliation advocated by Caldwell. The same is the case with the forms and words given by him under Aryan and Semitic affinities to prove an ultimate connection of the Draviḍian group with these families of languages. Further, the name Scythian is not at all satisfactory, as under that heading various languages of the world belonging to different morphological groups are lumped together. Other names used for Scythian are Allophylian and Ural-Altaic.

Draviḍian languages form an isolated group.

Sir George Grierson and Dr. Sten Konow think that the name Scythian is very unsatisfactory and that the Draviḍian languages are related neither to the so-called Scythian family nor to the Indo-European family. They say :—

"The denomination Scythian is a very unhappy one. The Scythian words which have been handed down by Greek writers are distinctly Eranian, *i.e.*, they belong to the Indo-European family. But, nevertheless, the word has been used as a common designation of all those languages of Asia and Europe which do not belong to the Indo-European or Semitic families. Moreover, those languages cannot by any means be brought together into one linguistic family. The monosyllabic languages of China and neighbouring countries are just as different from the dialects spoken in the Caucasus or from the speech of the Finns and

Magyārs as is the Indo-European family. The points in which they agree are such features as recur in almost all languages and they are by no means sufficient to outweigh the great and fundamental characteristics in which they differ from each other. With regard to the Draviḍian languages, the attempt to connect them with other linguistic families outside India is now generally recognised as a failure, and we must still consider them as an isolated family. The attempts made to show a closer connection with the Indo-European family have proved just as futile."

The Committee of Publication of *The Journal of American Oriental Society* (Vol. VII, 271), express the same opinion in the matter. They say:—

"The dialects of the Scythian family are remarkable for their great discordance with one another, for the slenderness of the ties which connect them, and the immense variety of elements and forms which they exhibit; hence the facility of going astray in an incautious ramble through such a wilderness of lexical and grammatical materials is extreme, and a careful comparative study of the different idioms, and a wary determination and selection of features among them, which can be pronounced of general occurrence and genuinely ancient, ought to precede any detailed comparison with another family of languages . . . His (Caldwell's) whole parallelism of Draviḍian words and forms with Indo-European and Semitic for the purpose of proving an ultimate connection of the former with the two latter also contains the merest assonances and chance coincidences of no account as historical evidence.

The most cogent arguments in favour of the relationship of the Draviḍian and Scythian languages which the comparison instituted between them brings to light are, in our view, the correspondences of general form and spirit, apprehension of grammatical relations and treatment of linguistic materials, which they undeniably present. And if the Science of Comparative Philology is strong enough to pronounce with confidence that such correspondences as are here displayed cannot be the result of analogous qualities of race, equal grade of capacity and culture, then the whole question is settled. But we are not certain that she has yet so far mastered the immense field of human speech as to be able to do this, and certainly there are few men living who are entitled to be accepted as her mouthpieces in making the decision. We shall prefer, then, to consider the question of Dravidian affiliation as one not yet authoritatively settled."

We are thus led to the conclusion that the Draviḍian languages form an isolated family.

The term Drāviḍa old.

The term Drāviḍa is very old, being found in such ancient works as the Mahābhārata and those of Parāśara, Manu, Varāhamihira and Kumārila-bhaṭṭa.

Drāviḍa, its different senses.

It appears to be used in three senses—territorial, ethnological and linguistic. According to the Mahābhārata it denoted a tract of country in Southern India. It is also loosely applied to the south of the Peninsula. Ethnologically it denotes the Draviḍian race. It had also the special meaning of a Tamil speaking Brāhman, which was subsequently extended to other Brāhman communities of the Peninsula, namely, the Āndhras, the Karṇāṭas, the Mahrāṭṭas, and Gujarātis, as evidenced by the term Pancha-Drāviḍa as used by Indian Pandits. These communities were grouped together, because they all observed more or less the same customs, practices and rituals known as *Drāviḍāchāra* which differed from those of the Brāhman communities of the north known as the Pancha-Gauḍa. Linguistically the word has both a general and a special signification. When used in a general sense, it designates all the Draviḍian languages, and when used in a special sense, it designates Tamil alone. Similarly. Gauḍa, too, is the name of country, people and language. The Pancha-Gauḍa include the five dialects derived from Sanskrit of the north, at the head of which stands the Bengāli, just as the Pancha-Drāviḍa include the five dialects of the south at the head of which stands Tamil.

Derivation of Drāviḍa.

The name Draviḍian is derived from the Sanskrit Drāviḍa, which is derived from an older Dramiḷa, Damiḷa, and is identical with the name of Tamil. In the old Pāli of the Mahāvamśa, the Tamils are called Damiḷa. The same is the case in the Canon of the Śvētāmbara Jainas. Daviḷa and Daviḍa in the Prākṛit literature of the Jainas and of the Sanskrit plays seem to be a later stage, due to the Prākṛit change of *m* to *v*. The oldest texts have Damiḷa. Damiḷa and Daviḍa were Sanskritised to Dramiḷa, Dramiḍa, and Draviḍa, respectively. Varāhamihira of the sixth century probably used Dramiḍa, though printed editions of his *Bṛihatsamhitā* read Draviḍa. Kern says some manuscripts read Dramiḍa. Tārānātha in his *History of Buddhism in India* mentions the Dramiḷas. Dramiḷa also occurs in old Malayāḷam versions of the Purāṇas, and in inscriptions such as the pillar inscription of king Mangaḷēśa (597-608) from Mahākūṭa near Bādāmi. Classical authors know the word under forms such as Damirice, Dimirica. A commentator on the Brahma-sūtras referred to by Rāmānuja is known as Dramiḍa; and a Sanskrit metrical abstract of the Tamil *Tiruvāymoḻi* of Saṭhakōpa is styled Dramiḍōpanishatsangati. Among the Jainas, Draviḷa-gaṇa or Tivuḷa-gaṇa is the designation of a section of the community. The occurrence of the archaic letter *ḻ* in these words as in the word Tamiḻ deserves notice. Dramiḍa was again borrowed by Tamil under the form Tiramiḍa.

Draviḍians, their civilisation.

The Draviḍian race is not found outside India. It is commonly considered to be that of the aborigines of India, or at least, of Southern India. According to some statements made in early Tamil literature, the original home of the Draviḍians was Lemuria, a continent now submerged in the Indian Ocean. Another theory is that the original home of the Draviḍians was Asia Minor where they lived with the ancient Accadians and migrated to India from the north-west entering Sindh, probably by the Bolan Pass, as testified to by the affinities of the Behistun tablets of Persia and the Brāhūī of Balūchistān to their own languages. They then spread over nearly all India.

Dr. Caldwell gives the following account of the prē-Aryan civilisation of the Draviḍians as indicated by the words in use amongst the early Tamilians :—

"They had 'kings' who dwelt in 'strong houses,' and ruled over small 'districts of country.' They had 'minstrels' who recited 'songs' at 'festivals,' and they seem to have had alphabetical 'characters' written with a style on palmyra leaves. A bundle of those leaves was called a 'book.' They acknowledged the existence of God, whom they styled *kō*, or king—a realistic title, little known to orthodox Hinduism. They erected to his honour a 'temple' which they called *kōil*, God's-house. They had 'laws' and 'customs,' but no lawyers or judges. Marriage existed among them. They were acquainted with the ordinary metals, with the exception of 'tin,' 'lead' and 'zinc,' with the planets which were ordinarily known to the ancients, with the exception of 'Mercury' and 'Saturn.' They had 'medicines,' 'hamlets' and 'towns,' 'canoes,' 'boats' and even 'ships' (small 'decked' coasting vessels), no acquaintance with any people beyond sea, except Ceylon, which was then, perhaps, accessible on foot at low water; and no word expressive of the geographical idea of 'island' or 'continent.' They were well acquainted with 'agriculture,' and delighted in 'war.' They were armed with 'bows' and 'arrows,' with 'spears' and 'swords.' All the ordinary or necessary arts of life, including 'spinning,' 'weaving' and 'dyeing' existed amongst them. They excelled in 'pottery' as their places of sepulture show."

This account affords sufficient proof that the elements of civilisation already existed amongst the Draviḍians before they came into contact with the Aryans.

Long before the Christian era, the Draviḍian South had developed a considerable culture of its own, and its inhabitants had consolidated themselves into powerful kingdoms, some of which carried on a thriving trade with Western Asia, Egypt, and later with the Greek and Roman empires. The occurrence of the word for peacock, *tuki* or *tūki*, which is none other than the ancient Tamil-Malayāḷam word *tōkai*, in the Hebrew text of *The Books of Kings* and *Chronicles* in the list of the articles of merchandise brought from Ophir in Solomon's ships, about 1000 B.C., also affords important confirmation of the antiquity of the Draviḍian languages spoken in India before the advent of the Aryan tribes.

Recent discoveries.

Recent discoveries tend not only to confirm the connection of the Draviḍians with the Accadians or Sumerians but also to change entirely our present conceptions with regard to the nature and antiquity of Dravidian civilisation. In the north-west of India, first at Harappa on the old bed of the Rāvi or Irāvati which under the name Parushṇi played a prominent part in the history of the Rigvēdic period, in the south of the Punjab, on a dry bed of the Indus, and then at Mohanjo-Daro near Dokri in the Larkhana District, some 400 miles away in Sindh, excavations had laid bare two cities which displayed evidences of a very considerable culture going back to a period long before the establishment of Buddhism. In those cities had been found, amongst other things, certain engraved and inscribed seals, bearing inscriptions in a hitherto unknown pictographic script, which were practically identical with the proto-Elamite tablets discovered at Sūsa. The graphs were in many cases the same, indicating that the same language must have been spoken in Elim in the west and in North-West India. Dr. Sayce, on the occasion of the presentation to him of the Triennial Gold Medal by the Royal Asiatic Society of Great Britain and Ireland on 12th May 1925, observed :—

> " Some of the discoveries now being made were of a revolutionary character and were tending to change entirely our conception based on many of the assumptions and beliefs which had been held with regard to the origin of civilisations. Among these later discoveries, was one which was to him of especial interest as bringing India into contact with the cuneiform world.
>
> They were coming to date the approximate time of the Sūsan placques (see above) as belonging to what was known as the three dynasty period, *viz.*, about 2300 B.C., and it would seem that at that period there was close intercourse between North-West India and Elim. This was an extraordinary result of exploration, and brought India within the domain of our cuneiform studies in the most unexpected way."*

Dr. Hall of the British Museum bases the following remarks of his on the similarity of the finds of Harappa, Mohanjo-Daro, as also those at Aḍittanallur in the Tinnevelly District, to those in Balūchistān, Babylon, Ur (Chaldea), Sumer and Crete :—

* *Journal of the Royal Asiatic Society*, 1925, 593-94.

"With our present evidences, the Draviḍians look like being a Mediterranean people, coming out of Crete, and passing through Asia Minor and Mesopotamia, where they were in close touch with the Sumerians and the Elamites: and possibly these latter were related to them and the Cretans. Then they came by the southern part of the Iranian plateau into Sindh, whence they spread into the interior of India. This must have happened long before 3000 B.C. Even if the Cretan connection cannot be satisfactorily demonstrated, Sumerian affinities are certain. India is thus linked more closely than ever to the western world, through both the Aryans and the Draviḍians."

Further discoveries might even demonstrate that Dr. Hall's theory, noted above, is true, and that the Sumerians were but Draviḍians from India. In that case it would be established that civilisation first arose in India, and was associated probably with the primitive Draviḍians. Then it was taken to Mesopotamia, to become the source of the Babylonian and other ancient cultures which form the basis of modern civilisation.*

According to Sir John Marshall,† we have by these sensational discoveries taken back at a single bound, our knowledge of Indian civilisation some 3,000 years earlier and have established the fact that in the third millennium before Christ and even before that, the peoples of the Punjab and Sindh were living in well-built cities and were in possession of a relatively mature culture with a high standard of art and craftsmanship and a developed system of pictographic writing. There can now no longer be any doubt that the Punjab and Sindh antiquities are closely connected and roughly contemporary with the Sumerian antiquities of Mesopotamia dating from the third or fourth millennium before Christ. Though the civilisation of the Indus will probably be found to have had its own distinctive characteristics, it will also be found to have formed part and parcel of a much wider sphere of culture which embraced not only Southern Mesopotamia and India, but

---

* *Modern Review*, December 1924.

† Annual Report of the Archæological Survey of India, 1923-24.

probably Persia, and a large part of Central Asia as well, and which may even have extended as far west as the Mediterranean, where the early Ægean civilisation presents certain somewhat similar features. Whatever the history of the Sumerians in Mesopotamia may have been, a culture closely akin to theirs must have been widely disseminated in the valley of the Indus, and have undergone a development reaching back incalculable centuries on Indian soil. If, therefore, those scholars are right who consider the Sumerians to have been an intrusive element in Mesopotamia then the possibility is clearly suggested of India proving ultimately to be the cradle of their civilisation, which in its turn lay at the root of Babylonian, Assyrian and Western Asiatic, culture generally.

With the revolutionary discoveries in Sindh and the Punjab the history of Indian culture has now suddenly been taken back an extra 3,000 years, and the last mists of the legend that art began with the Greeks and religion with the Jews have been finally scattered.*

The Sumerian or Accadian language which was non-Semitic and earlier than the Assyrian or Babylonian, was beginning to be a dead language as early as 2000 B.C. The Sumerian civilisation must have been an old-established one long before 3800 B.C., the date of the reign of Sargon I (a Semite) who united Sumer and Accad into one kingdom. The Sumerians must have been in possession of writing before 8000 B.C. which is about the date of the earliest of their written documents that have yet been discovered.†

The language has, like the Dravidian group, the characteristics of agglutination and vowel harmony.

Region of the Dravidian languages.

The region where the Dravidian languages are spoken is the whole of Peninsular India from the Vindhya mountains and the river Narmada in the north to Cape Comorin in the south, excluding Orissa

* *Times Literary Supplement*, 1926.
† Sweet: *The History of Language.*

in the east and the Gujarāti and the Mahrāṭhi districts in the west, and the northern half of Ceylon. Further to the north, Draviḍian dialects are spoken by small tribes in the Central Provinces and Chōta Nāgpur, and even up the banks of the Ganges at Rājamahāl. Finally there is a Draviḍian dialect in the far north-west in Balūchistān.

Enumeration of languages.

The best known Draviḍian languages are Tamil, Malayāḷam, Kannaḍa, and Telugu. They have all been used for a long time as literary languages with alphabets, grammars and literatures of their own. Each of the languages consists of two forms of speech—the literary, the one found in literature, and the colloquial, the one used in every-day speech—which differ considerably from each other. There are, besides, in Southern India, Tuḷu, Koḍagu, Tōda, Kōta and Baḍaga which may be looked upon as dialects of Kannada, as they are more closely related to that language than to any other of the Draviḍian group. Further, the languages in the north belonging to the Draviḍian family are Kurukh or Orāyon, Mālto or Rājamahāli, Kūī or Khonḍ, Gōnḍi, and Brāhūī. Barring the four literary languages mentioned above, all the others are uncultivated. They have not even an alphabet of their own. A few minor dialects of the north belonging to the same family are Kōlāmi, Nāiki and Bhīli. There are likewise a few minor dialects of the south such as Kuṟumba and Iruḷa.

The Pancha-Drāviḍa

Tamil, Malayāḷam, Kannaḍa and Telugu, together with the uncultivated Tuḷu, are now known as the Pancha-Drāviḍa. Indian Pandits, however, include Mahrāṭhi and Gujarāti in the Pancha-Drāviḍa in place of Malayāḷam and Tuḷu, but philologists, recognising that Mahrāṭhi and Gujarāti, like other Indo-Aryan vernaculars of the north such as Bengāli and Sindhi, are mainly derived from Sanskrit, place them in the Gauḍa group of languages. The reasons for the Indian Pandits including

Mahrāṭhi and Gujarāti in the Pancha-Drāviḍa may be the existence of a few special points of similarity between these languages and the Draviḍian group as indicated below :— .

1. "In northern vernaculars the masculine and neuter genders have been confounded, and in some, such as Bengāli and Oriya, the difference between masculine and feminine nouns is also blotted out. In Mahrāṭhi and Gujarāti, on the other hand, three genders are distinguished and the neuter is a living gender just as in Draviḍian tongues.

Northern Indo-Aryan vernaculars have developed in a country where the home speech was Kolārian, while the substratum over which Gujarāti and Mahrāṭhi have spread was Draviḍian." *The Aryan Gods of the Mitāni People*, by Dr. Sten Konow.

2. Another reason seems to be that the palatals in Mahrāṭhi are pronounced as in Telugu, *i.e.*, they retain the pronunciation as real palatals before *i, ī, e, ē, ai* and *y* while in other cases *ch* is pronounced as *ts* and *j* as *dz*.

3. It may also be stated that in the opinion of some scholars the waves of Aryan immigration gradully submerged Draviḍian blood and speech in Gujarāt and the same influences obliterated the language in Mahārāshṭra.

4. One more reason is the existence in Mahrāṭhi and Gujarāti of the inclusive and exclusive forms of the plural of the personal pronoun of the first person as in the Draviḍian languages.

From the above it may perhaps be inferred that Mahrāṭhi and Gujarāti were once Draviḍian.

Where spoken

Tamil is spoken throughout the country below the Ghāts from Pulicāt to Cape Comorin and from the Ghāts to the Bay of Bengal, as also in the south of Tranvancore and the northern and the north-western parts of Ceylon.

Malayāḷam is spoken along the Malabar coast on the western side of the Ghāts from about Chandragiri near Mangalore to Trivandrum.

Telugu is the language spoken all along the eastern coast of the Peninsula from about Pulicāt to Chicācōle, and inland it prevails as far as the eastern boundary of the Mahrāṭṭa country and Mysore including within its range the Ceded Districts and Karnūl, a considerable part of Hyderābād, a portion of the Nāgpur country and Gondvāna.

The region in which the Kannaḍa language is now spoken comprises the west of the Nizam's Dominions, parts of Central Provinces and Berar, the southern districts of the Bombay Presidency, the whole of Mysore and Coorg, and the Madras districts bordering these countries on the north, west and south.

In the *Linguistic Survey of India* the region is thus defined :—

"Kanarese is the principal language of Mysore and the adjoining parts of Coimbatore, Salem, Anantapur and Bellary. The frontier line thence goes northwards through the Dominions of His Exalted Highness the Nizam as far as Bidar, where it turns almost due west on to about the 78th degree and further southwards so as to include the south-eastern portion of Jāt and Daphlapur. Kanarese is also spoken in the extreme south-east of Satâra in Taluqa Tāsgaon ; to some extent in the Aundh State in the Satāra Agency ; and in the south of Belgaum, and further to the west, in Kolhāpur in almost so far west as the town of Kolhāpur. The line thence turns southwards, following the Ghāts to about Honāwar where it goes down to the sea. In North Kanara, Kanarese is the official language all over the district. It is the principal language of South Kanara with the exception of the southernmost corner. The frontier line thence coincides with the southern frontier of Mysore. Kanarese dialects are also spoken in the Nilgiris and the language has lastly been brought by immigrants to Madura and to Central Provinces."

Tuḷu is spoken in a very limited area, the Chandragiri and Kalyāṇapuri rivers in the Canara District being regarded as its ancient boundaries, and it does not appear ever to have extended much beyond them. Koḍagu is the language of Coorg; and Tōda, Kōta and Baḍaga, as also Kuṛumba and Iruḷa, are the languages of certain tribes inhabiting the Nilgiris.

Kurukh or Orāyon is spoken in the western portion of the Bengal Presidency and the adjoining parts of the Central Provinces ; Mālto or Rājamahāli in the Rājamahāl Hills in the north-east of the Sonthal Parganas ; Kūī or Khoṇḍ in the hills of Orissa and the neighbouring districts ; Gōṇḍi in the plateau of the Central Provinces from

Wārdha in the west and south to Bālāghāt and Maṇḍla in the east and north; Kōlāmi in East Berar and the Wārdha district of the Central Provinces; Bhīli in the Pusad Taluqa of the Bāsim district; and Nāiki, the dialect of the Darwe Gōṇḍs, in Chanda.

Brāhūī is spoken in the Sarawān and Jhalawār Provinces of Balūchistān and also in parts of Sindh.*

Number of speakers.

The total number of speakers of these languages is, in round numbers, about seventy-two millions.

General characteristics of the Draviḍian languages.

We shall now proceed to say a few words about the general characteristics of the Dravidian languages. As Tamil has developed the common Draviḍian principles with great consistency, it may be taken as a good representative of the Draviḍian languages.

Pronunciation.—There is a tendency to pronounce a short vowel after every final consonant.† There are a short and a long *e* and *o*.

Harmonic sequence of vowels.—This requires the vowel of the suffix to be so changed as to harmonise with the radical vowel; and conversely the vowel of the suffix also reacts on the vowel of the root so that the latter is altered into harmony with the former. This rule is particularly observed in Telugu and Tuḷu, though there are traces of it in Tamil and Kannaḍa also. In Telugu *i* is used when a neighbouring syllable contains *i*, *ī* or *ai*, and *u* in other cases: kattiki, kattulaku, kattulu; ā-manishinni, mīrunnu; kalugudunu, kaligitini. This law of vocalic harmony is a characteristic feature

* I may add here that two more Draviḍian tribes of Balūchistān, namely, the Oritæ and the Arabitæ, are mentioned by classical writers. One is tempted to recognise a connection between Arabitæ and Arava, the name applied to Tamil by the Telugus and the Kannaḍigas.

† Kumārilabhaṭṭa of the 7th century quotes in his *Tantravārtika*, *chōr* (śōru), *pāmp* (pāmbu) and *vair* (vayiru) without final *u*. This is perhaps due to his insufficient acquaintance with the Tamil language.

2

of many of the Ural-Altaic forms of speech.* Distinct traces of it are also found in the Muṇḍa languages. Its occurrence in Telugu is supposed to be due to Muṇḍa influence.

Convertibility of surds and sonants.—Hard and soft consonants are interchanged, especially in Tamil and Malayāḷam. A consonant when initial or double is hard, but when medial soft.

Phonetical changes of vowels and consonants.—*Ai* in Tamil becomes *e* in Kannaḍa and *a* in Telugu and Malayāḷam: talai, tale, tala. Gutturals in Kannaḍa change into palatals in Tamil and Telugu: kivi, sevi chevi; key, śey, chēyi; *v* in Tamil changes to *g* in Telugu: aruvar, aruguru; *y* in Tamil changes to *s* in Kannaḍa: peyar, pesar; vayiṟu, basiṟu; etc., etc.

Inflection of nouns.—Gender: Nouns are divided into high-caste and casteless or rational and irrational. Gender is denoted by pronominal suffixes in high-caste nouns—*an*, *aḷ*, *ar* (epicene plural). Brāhūī does not distinguish the genders even in the case of rational beings. Most other languages of the family—Kurukh, Mālto, Kūī, Gōṇḍi, Kōlāmi, and Telugu—have no feminine singular, but use the neuter instead. The same is the case in Kuṟumba, a dialect of Kannaḍa. Kūī and Gōṇḍi use the neuter even for the feminine plural.

Number: There are only the singular and plural numbers, but no dual. Demonstrative pronouns are added to denote number, as also the suffixes *kaḷ*, *gaḷ* and *lu*.

Case: Cases are formed by the addition of post-positions which are the same in the singular and plural. These post-positions are not independent words. They are added to the simple base in the nominative and to the oblique base formed by the addition of *ad* or *at*, marad or marat, in the other cases. The accusative and dative cases are generally distinguished, but not in some

* It is found in Finnish, Turkish, Hungarian, etc., but not in the language of the Lapps.

languages of the group, which is due to the influence of the Aryan vernaculars.

Adjectives.—Adjectives are not capable of inflection. The genitive of ordinary nouns is an adjective. Many adjectives are in the form of relative participles—ṡiṟiya, periya, uyarnda.

Numerals.—Nine is formed from the numeral ten by prefixing one—ombadu. ombattu; but tommidi in Telugu. Numerals are used partly as nouns and partly as adjectives.

Pronouns.—Generally in pronouns *n* denotes the singular and *m* the plural; but in the second person plural *r* is likewise used: Tamil nīr, Tuḷu īr, Kūī īru, Telugu mīru (old form īru). Reflexive pronouns are used in the beginning of words to form terms of relationship: tandai, tangai, tande. tange. There are two plurals of the first person, one inclusive and the other exclusive of the person addressed* :—

		Exclusive	*Inclusive*
Tamil	...	nāṅgaḷ	yām, nām
Malayāḷam	...	ñāṅṅaḷ	nām
Kurukh	...	em	nām
Kūī	...	āmu	āju
Telugu	...	ēmu, mēmu	manamu
Kannaḍa	...	nām	ām.

There are no relative pronouns but only relative participles. The plural is used as an honorific form in the singular.

Verbs.—Many bases are both verbs and nouns: kuṭṭu, tappu, malar, taḷir, paḷi. There is a negative conjugation. There are two negatives illa and alla, the one denying existence and the other denying quality or nature.

There are appellative verbs, *i.e.*, verbs formed from nouns: ṡēvaganen, sēvakanem, sēvakuḍanu. There is no passive voice.

* These two forms occur in the Muṇḍa languages also. They likewise occur in other families which have nothing to do with the Muṇḍas and the Drāviḍas. *e.g.*, in the Nūba languages, the Algonquin languages, etc.

According to Cust the distinctive features of the Dravidian family of languages briefly are, that in its gender it distinguishes between rational and irrational objects; it has an oblique form for many of its nouns; it specialises the meaning of a root by the use of formatives; it modifies the root itself to convey different meanings, and relations; it has a negative voice.

Affinity of Behistun tablets to Dravidian languages.

The important points of resemblance between the Dravidian languages and the Behistun tablets* are: the occurrence of cerebral letters; agreement with Tamil in regarding the same consonant as a surd in the beginning of a word and as a sonant in the middle, and in pronouncing the same consonant as a sonant when single and as a surd when doubled; formation of the genitive case by the suffixes *na, nina* and *inna, cp. ni* in Telugu and *in* in Tamil; the dative suffix *ikki, ikka, cp.* Malayāḷam ninakku; formation of the accusative by suffixing *un, in* or *n, cp. nu* or *ni* in Telugu; the ordinal suffix *im, cp. ām* in Tamil; the pronoun of the second person singular *ni* and the oblique form *nin*; and the use of the relative participle.

Dravidian group different from Sanskrit.

The general characteristics of the Dravidian languages given above distinguish these forms of speech from Sanskrit. A few more distinguishing features are:—

In the Dravidian languages all nouns denoting inanimate substances and irrational beings are of the neuter gender. The distinction of male and female appears only in the pronouns of the third person, in adjectives formed by suffixing the pronominal terminations, and in the third person of the verb. In all other cases, the distinction of gender is marked by separate words signifying "male" and "female." Dravidian

---

* Behistun in Western Media. The inscriptions discovered here which are in the old Persian, in the Babylonian and in the language of the Scythians of the Medo-Persian empire, record the political autobiography of Darius Hystaspes.

nouns are inflected, not by means of case terminations, but by means of suffixed post-positions and separate particles. Dravidian neuter nouns are rarely pluralized. Dravidian languages use post-positions instead of prepositions. It is characteristic of these languages in contradistinction to Indo-European, that wherever practicable, they use as adjectives the relative participles of verbs, in preference to nouns of quality or adjectives properly so called. Unlike the Indo-European, they prefer the use of continuative participles to conjunctions. It is a marked peculiarity of the Dravidian languages that they make use of relative participial nouns instead of phrases introduced by relative pronouns. These participles are formed from the various participles of the verb by the addition of a formative suffix. Thus "the person who came" is in these languages literally "the who came." Finally, in the Dravidian languages the governing word is invariably placed after the word governed, in consequence of which the nominative always occupies the first place in the sentence, and the one finite verb the last.

Further, Tamil rules of prosody are mostly different from those of Sanskrit, and the possession of peculiar sounds like *ḻ*, *ṟ*, *n* (final) and *h* (āydam) is an indication of the physiological characteristics of the Tamil people differentiating their language from the Aryan tongues. Moreover, in the Aryan languages the plural has a different set of case-terminations from the singular, by the use of which the complex idea of plurality and case-relation is indicated. There is no inflection of any case as such, irrespective of number, nor for number as such, irrespective of case. In the Dravidian languages plurality is expressed by a sign common to all the cases which is affixed directly to the singular, or crude form of the noun. To this sign of plurality are added the case terminations, which are fixed and unalterable, expressing the idea of case, and nothing more, and are the same in both numbers. Again, in the Aryan languages, case-relations of the singular are expressed by one set of forms and those of the plural by another; but in the

Draviḍian tongues the same case signs are employed, without alteration both in the singular and in the plural. There is only one declension properly so called. The conjunctive case is not found in the Aryan languages. In the Draviḍian languages the pronominal signs are annexed, not directly to the root as in the Aryan but to the tense particles. The Draviḍian languages are destitute of any common term for brother, sister, uncle, aunt, etc., and use instead a set of terms which combine the idea of relationship with that of age; *e.g.*, aṇṇa, (elder brother), tamma (younger brother), akka (elder sister), tange (younger sister), chikkappa (younger paternal uncle), doḍḍamma (elder maternal aunt), etc.

Influence of Sanskirt and the Aryan vernaculars on the Draviḍian group.

With regard to the cultivated Draviḍian languages of Southern India, the influence of Sanskrit has extended only to the vocabulary and not to the grammar. It has been said that the accession of culture from a superior race to an inferior is sometimes dangerous to the purity of a language; and accordingly the Draviḍian languages have suffered in this way by the large infiltration of Sanskrit. The amount of Sanskrit in Tamil is much less than in the other languages. Sanskrit has no doubt supplied these tongues with words for expressing abstract ideas of religion, philosophy and science; but in many cases Sanskrit words have been unnecessarily introduced with the notion of adding elegance and refinement to the speech. Caldwell says that the following remarks of Archbishop Trench respecting the character of the contributions which English has received from Anglo-Saxon and from Latin respectively, are exactly applicable to the relation and proportion which the native Dravidian element bears to the Sanskrit contained in these languages:—

"All its joints, its whole articulation, its sinews, and its ligaments, the great body of articles, pronouns, conjunctions, prepositions, numerals, auxiliary verbs, all smaller words which serve to knit together and bind the larger into sentences, these, not to speak of the grammatical structure of the language, are exclusively Anglo-Saxon (Draviḍian). The Latin (Sanskrit) may contribute its tale of bricks, yea, of goodly and polished hewn stones, to the spiritual buildings, but the mortar, with all that holds and binds these together, and constitutes them into a house, is Anglo-Saxon (Draviḍian) throughout."

But the Draviḍian languages of Northern India have been much influenced by the neighbouring Aryan vernaculars, and in some cases such as the Brāhūī, the influence has been very great owing to the segregation of these languages for centuries from the other Draviḍian tongues. It is, however, remarkable that these languages have still retained so many grammatical affinities to the other languages of the group. The Brāhūī has freely absorbed the alien vocabulary of Persian, Balūchi, Sindhi and other neighbouring languages and is no more an unmixed form of speech. Still its character as a Draviḍian language can easily be recognised. It has a short and a long *e* and *o*; *ni* for thou and *num* for you; a negative conjugation and a passive voice; aspirated letters and *f*. The first three numerals are Draviḍian, the higher ones being Aryan loan-words. Musit, three, may be compared with the Tuḷu mūji. The plural suffixes of the first and second person correspond to forms used in the other Draviḍian languages, but the singular suffixes are different. Kurukh and Mālto very closely agree with each other. They have no separate feminine singular, but use the neuter instead, just as is the case in Kūī, Gōṇḍi and Telugu. Their nouns have no separate oblique base, as is also the case in Brāhūī and often in Telugu. Their personal pronouns are most closely related to those used in the old dialects of Tamil and Kannaḍa. Their present tense is formed as in Kannaḍa. Only the first few numerals are Draviḍian, the rest being Aryan. Kūī and Gōṇḍi differ from other connected languages in using the neuter instead of the feminine in both numbers. They follow the same principles as Tamil and Kannaḍa in the formation of the plural, and mainly agree with

Kannaḍa in the formation of the present and past tenses. With regard to numerals, they resemble the other languages mentioned above. The minor dialects of the north, namely, Kōlāmi, Nāiki and Bhīli, use the neuter singular as a feminine like Telugu, Gōṇḍi, Kūī, etc., but the oblique base is formed as in Tamil and Kannaḍa. The plural suffixes agree with Kannaḍa dialects and Telugu, and the numerals are mainly the same as in Telugu. These three dialects very much resemble one another and show some interesting points of analogy with the Tōda dialect of the Nilgiris.

Dravidian influence on Sanskrit and the Aryan vernaculars.

Some scholars are of opinion that the Dravidian tongues have not only borrowed much from Sanskrit but have also lent much to it. It is even supposed that these languages have also influenced to some extent the grammar of Sanskrit and the Aryan vernaculars. The Dravidian family once extended over nearly the whole of India. The geographical names in most parts of India, in spite of Sanskritised forms and fanciful derivations, attest this fact to this day. Where peoples speaking different languages are in constant intercommunication with each other, they naturally borrow much from each other without examination or consideration. It may therefore be taken for granted that as the Aryans penetrated to the south and became acquainted with new objects bearing Dravidian names, they have, as a matter of course, adopted the names of those things together with the things themselves. Caldwell gives the following as the conditions on which any word contained in the Sanskrit lexicons may be concluded to be of Dravidian origin:—

1. When it is an isolated word in Sanskrit without a root and without derivations, but is surrounded in the Dravidian languages with collateral, related or derivative words;

2. when Sanskrit possesses other words expressing the same idea, whilst the Dravidian tongues have the one in question alone;

3. when the word is not found in any of the Indo-European tongues allied to Sanskrit, but is found in every Dravidian dialect;

4. when the derivation which the Sanskrit lexicographers give is fanciful, whilst Dravidian lexicographers deduce it from some Dravidian theme of the same or a similar signification from which a variety of words are found to be derived ;

5. when the signification of the word, in the Dravidian languages is evidently radical and physiological, whilst the Sanskrit signification is metaphorical or only collateral ; and

6. when Indian Dravidian scholars, notwithstanding their high estimation of Sanskrit as the mother of all literature, classify the word as a purely Dravidian one.

When any or several or all of these grounds exist, we may, according to Caldwell, safely conclude the word to be Dravidian, not a Sanskrit derivative. As judged by these conditions, the following among others are given as Dravidian loan-words :—

Akkā (a mother), attā (a mother, an elder sister), kuṭi (a house), kōṭa (a fort), nīra (water), palli (a village), mīna (a fish), ēḍa (a sheep or goat) *cp.* āḍu, marutta (a medicine man) *cp.* marundu, hēramba (a buffalo) *cp.* erumai, aṭṭa (boiled rice, food) from aḍu, ām (yes) *cp.* ām, valli (a creeper) *cp.* vaḷḷi, baḷḷi ; mukuḷa (a bud) *cp.* mugiḻ, muguḷ ; kuntala (hair) *cp.* kūndal, pāli (tip of the ear) *cp.* pāle (lobe of the ear), maṇḍa (the head) *cp.* maṇḍe, kāka (a crow) *cp.* kāge, māchala (a crocodile) *cp.* mosaḷe, mēka (a goat) *cp.* mēke, śīra (a large snake) *cp.* śērai, kēre ; tāḷa (palmyra) *cp.* tāḻ, varuka (a species of inferior grain) *cp.* baragu, varagu ; ulkā (a firebrand) *cp.* uḷku, taṭit, taḍit (lightning) *cp.* siḍil, teḍil (Tuḷu) ; Malaya from male, āli (a woman's female friend) *cp.* ālu (Telugu) a woman, a wife ; kali, gaṇḍa (a hero) ; śundi (a procuress, a bawd) *cp.* soṇdi, khalīna (the bit of a bridle) *cp.* kaḍiyaṇa, talpa (a float) *cp.* teppa, kaiya (spirituous liquor) *cp.* kaḷ, kharju (itch) *cp.* kajji, psā (hunger) *cp.* pasi.

Sanskrit has borrowed words of even Greek or Roman origin such as dīnāra dramma, hōra, etc.

So much for the Dravidian element in the vocabulary of Sanskrit. With regard to phonology, it is supposed that the cerebral letters in Sanskrit were taken from the Dravidian tongues. It is a general rule that a people which invades a foreign country, to some degree adopts the pronunciation of its new home, partly owing to climate and partly owing to intermixture with the old inhabitants. The cerebral letters form an essential feature of Draviḍian phonology and they are found in Sanskrit alone and not in any of the primitive languages related to Sanskrit. Further, the use of *l* in Sanskrit and the Aryan vernaculars where other Indo-European languages use *r* and *vice versa*, is probably due to Draviḍian influence, since in these languages the change of *r* to *l* is very common. Further features in the phonology of the Aryan vernaculars which may be attributed to Draviḍian influence are the softening of hard consonants after vowels in the Prākṛits, not only in single words but also in compounds ; the double pronunciation of the palatals in Mahrāṭhi as in Telugu ; and the change of *ch* to *s* and of *s* to *h* in many of these languages.

We observe Draviḍian influence of much greater importance in the inflectional system of the Aryan vernaculars. In the inflection of nouns post-positions are used as case-suffixes, which are the same in both numbers, not after the base but after an oblique form, the latter being also used as a genitive and this again as an adjective. The use of a separate oblique form is most extensive in languages such as Mahrāṭhi and Bīhāri, where the Draviḍian influence must have been very strong. The use of two different forms of the objective case is distinctly Draviḍian. It cannot, from an Aryan point of view, be explained why a post-position should, in this case, be added to a noun denoting a rational being, and not to other nouns as well. In the Draviḍian languages nouns are divided into two broad classes—rational beings and irrational beings, whether animate or inanimate. The Hindi rule for the use of a post-position in the objective case agrees with that prevailing in Tamil and Malayāḷam. The inclusive and exclusive plurals of the pronoun of the first person are also found in several of the Aryan vernaculars.

The Draviḍian tendency of using the participles without any addition as conjunctive participles in subordinate sentences, also with pronominal suffixes to indicate the person of the subject, has also pervaded the Aryan vernaculars. Verbal tenses have been replaced by participles. Forms like kṛitavān, one who has done, are peculiar to later Sanskrit, *cp.* šeydavan. The suffix *vat* is Aryan, but it is not clear how an active form can be arrived at by adding the suffix to a passive participle. In the Draviḍian languages, on the other hand, the past participle is active as well as passive, and a noun of agency is formed from it in all dialects—šeydavan. There cannot be any reasonable doubt about kṛitavān having been influenced by šeydavan. In Sanskrit kṛitavān is an anomalous form without analogy in connected languages, while Tamil šeydavan is quite regular. The order of words in the Aryan vernaculars, with the governed before the governing word and the verb invariably at the end of the sentence, is also in agreement with Draviḍian principles.

Difference between Gauḍian and Draviḍian languages.

In the Gauḍian languages, *i.e.*, the Aryan vernaculars, the non-Sanskritic portion of the vocabulary is very small and even words of every day use are taken, either pure or corrupt, from Sanskrit, as also many grammatical features, whilst in the Draviḍian languages, though a small proportion of the words, either pure or corrupt, has been borrowed from Sanskrit, the major portion being non-Sanskritic, the words for ordinary use are not derived from Sanskrit, nor do the grammatical processes resemble those of Sanskrit. Further, the Aryan vernaculars have no relative participles, no negative voice, not one of the Draviḍian pronouns or numerals and no common words of primary importance. The non-Sanskritic words in them have no manner of analogy to the non-Sanskritic words in the Draviḍian languages.

Lexical affinities in the Draviḍian languages.

We have briefly shown the agreement in grammar and structure of the Draviḍian tongues. We may now proceed to a comparison of their lexicons. In comparing words together it is desirable to take pronouns and numerals, which constitute a link between grammar and vocabulary and have acquired a fixed and arbitrary meaning, and terms of relationship and every day use. A list of twelve such words in nine Dravidian languages, namely, Tamil, Malayāḷam, Kannaḍa, Telugu, Kurukh, Mālto, Kūī, Gōṇḍi and Brāhūī, is appended. It will be seen from the list that there is some dissimilarity in a few words, especially of Mālto and Brāhūī; but this is accounted for by the influence exercised on these languages by the neighbouring Aryan vernaculars.

	nglish	Tamil	Malayāḷam	Kannaḍa	Telugu	Kurukh	Mālto	Kūī	Gōṇḍi	Brāhūī
1	One	onṟu	oru	ondu	okaṭi	oṇṭā	ort	ro (ṇḍi)	uṇḍī	asiṭ
2	Two	iraṇḍu	raṇḍu	eraḍu	reṇḍu	eṇḍ	iwr	ri (ṇḍi)	raṇḍ	iraṭ
3	Three	Mūnṟu	mūnnu	mūṟu	mūḍu	mūṇḍ	tīn	mūñji	mūnd	musiṭ
4	I	nān	ñān	nānu	nēnu	ēn	ēn	ānu	nannā	ī
5	We	(Excl.) nāṅgaḷ	ñāṅṅaḷ	nāvugaḷu	mēmu	ēm	ēm	āmu	mammāṭ	nan
		(Incl.) nām	nām	nāvu	manamu	nām	nām			
6	Thou	nī	nī	nīnu	nīvu	nīn	nīn	īnu	immā	nī
7	You	nīṅgaḷ	niṅṅaḷ	nīvu	mīru	nīm	nīm	īru	immaṭ	nun
8	Eye	kaṇ	kaṇṇu	kaṇṇu	kannu	khann	qanuth	kānu	kan	khan
9	Ear	kādu, śevi	chevi	kivi	chevi	khebdā	qethwuth	kriu	kavī	khaf
10	Nose	mūkku	mūkku	mūgu	mukku	muī	musoth	muṅgēli	mussōṟ	bāmuṣ
11	Tooth	pal	pallu	hallu	pallu	pall	paluth	pālkā	pal	dandān
12	Come	vā	vā	bā	rā	barā	bara	bāmu	varā	bar

Dravidian tongues of Southern India.

We may now proceed to consider in some detail the Dravidian tongues of Southern India. As stated before, four of these, *viz.*, . Tamil, Malayāḷam, Kannaḍa and Telugu, are cultivated, while the rest, namely, Tuḷu, Koḍagu, Tōda, Kōta and Baḍaga, which are all dialects of Kannaḍa, are uncultivated, inasmuch as they have not even a written character of their own. To these have to be added the minor dialects Kuṟumba and Iruḷa.

Tamil.

Of these languages, Tamil is supposed to be the oldest and most highly organised, exceedingly rich in vocabulary and cultivated from a very remote period. Some scholars, however, are of opinion that Tamil is not the oldest Draviḍian language, as Telugu and other languages have preserved older forms and represent a more ancient state of development. They think that the use of conjunctive participles instead of the ordinary verbal tenses in Malayāḷam also affords evidence of a more ancient stage of development of that language than is the case with Tamil. It has been stated that the name Tamil has been Sanskritised into Dramiḍa or Draviḍa, though it is not easy to account for the presence of *r* in the first syllable. Tamil Pandits say that the word Tamiḻ means "sweetness" and that it has appropriately become the name of their sweet language.* They consider that the theory that Tamil is derived from the Sanskrit Draviḍa is not at all tenable, since a language which was in existence before the advent of the Aryans could not have got its name from the new comers. The Telugus and the Kannaḍigas call the language Aravam, un-sonorous, probably because it is totally destitute of aspirates. Another name applied to it by the Kannaḍigas is

* In the Tamil lexicon called *Piṅgalandai* sweetness and mercy are given as the meanings of the word *tamiḻ—inimaiyum nīrmaiyum tamiḻ enal āgum.* The word appears to occur only once in Tamil literature in the sense of sweetness—in the *Śintāmaṇi* of Tiruttakkadēvar.

Tigula, meaning probably rude or rough. The Portuguiese called Tamil and Malayāḷam, Malabar, and Tamil, too, was known by that name long in Europe. In the very first book ever printed in Tamil characters at Ambalakkāḍu on the Malabar coast in 1577-9, the language of the book is styled Malavar or Tamul. Tradition refers the commencement of literary activity in Tamil to the sage Agastya, who is said to have been taught Tamil by Śiva or Subrahmaṇya, to have brought the alphabet from the north, to have composed the first grammar of the language known as *Pēragattiyam*, and to have caused another grammar named *Tolkāppiyam* to be written by one of his pupils. It is stated that from the sound of the right side of Śiva's drum arose Sanskrit and from the sound of the left side, Tamil, and that Śiva gave Sanskrit to Pāṇini and Tamil to Agastya. In a Sanskrit work called *Śambhurahasya*, which is in the form of a dialogue between Śiva and Subrahmaṇya, Śiva says : " Endowed by me with knowledge, the sage Agastya wrote Tamil grammar ; so Tamil being *ārsha*, *i.e.*, derived from a *ṛishi* author, does not fall under the head of *apabhraṁśa* (corrupt language) just as is the case with Āndhra, Karṇāṭa, Ghaurjara and other languages which are not *ārsha*."* Another tradition says that Agastya, having had a quarrel with the Sanskrit Pandits of Kāśi, came to the south and established the Tamil language. Invention of a language by an individual is, however, opposed to the principles of philology. Language is social and national, not individual. It is a social product, springing up with the first community and developing with the increasing needs of culture and civilisation. A grammar pre-supposes previous literature.† *Tolkāppiyam* has

* ಮಾಮುದ್ದಿಶ್ಯ ತಪಶ್ಚಕ್ರೇ ಪುರಾಗಸ್ತ್ಯೋ ಮಹಾಮುನಿಃ ।
ಮಯಾ ಪ್ರದತ್ತವಿಜ್ಞಾನೋ ದ್ರಾವಿಡೀಂ ವ್ಯಾಕೃತಿಂ ವ್ಯಧಾತ್ ।
ನಾಪಭ್ರಂಶತ್ವದೋಷೋಽಸ್ತಿ ದ್ರಾವಿಡೀನಾಂ ಗಿರಾಂ ತತಃ ।
ಅನಾರ್ಷಮಾಂಧ್ರಕಾರ್ಣಾಟಘೌರ್ಜರಾದ್ಯಂ ಚ ಭಾಷಿತಂ ।
ಅಪಭ್ರಂಶಂ ವಿಜಾನೀಯಾತ್ ।

† ಇಲಕ್ಕಿಯಮಿನ್ರಿ ಯಿಲಕ್ಕಣಮಿನ್ರೇ । ಇಲಕ್ಕಣಮಿನ್ರಿ ಯಿಲಕ್ಕಿಯಮಿನ್ರೇ ।
ಎಳ್ಳಿನಿನ್ರೆಣ್ಣೆಯೆಡುಪ್ಪದು ಪೋಲ । ಇಲಕ್ಕಿಯತ್ತಿನಿನ್ರೆಡುಪಡುಮಿಲಕ್ಕಣಂ ।
—ಪೇರಗತ್ತಿಯಂ.

quotations from older authors. If Agastya wrote a grammar at all, he must have based it on the works of previous authors. The indegenous words *eḻuttu* (a letter) and *śuvaḍi* (a book) in Tamil prove that Agastya did not bring the alphabet. The story of Agastya has to be taken to mean that he was an early sympathetic cultivator of the language. Tamil has a copious vocabulary, relatively independent of Sanskrit, and a wide range of literature. It is, as will be seen further on, more closely related to Kannaḍa than to any other member of the Dravidian group.

Malayāḷam.

Malayāḷam is composed of the two words *mala*, a mountain, and *āḷam*, a verbal derivative from the root, *āḷ*, to possess, to rule, which likewise occurs in this connection in the forms *āḷma* or *āyma*, a softened form of *āḷma* corresponding to the Tamil *āṇmai*. The whole word means "the mountain region," and then the language of that region. Caldwell considers Malayāḷam to be a very ancient offshoot of Tamil, differing from it chiefly at present by its disuse of the personal terminations of the verbs, and the larger amount of Sanskrit words it has incorporated into its vocabulary. Personal terminations began to be dropped after the 13th century, and by the end of the 15th they had gone completely out of use. Tuñjattu Eḻuttachchan, a noted writer of the 16th century, seems to have introduced the present alphabet, which appears to have been derived from the Grantha, the character in which Sanskrit is written in the Tamil country. The proportion of Sanskrit words adopted by the Draviḍian languages is least in Tamil, greatest in Malayāḷam. Malayāḷam has a close relationship to Tamil.

Telugu.

In point of euphonic sweetness Telugu is said to occupy the first place among Draviḍian idioms. It was called by the Europeans gentoo, a corruption of the Portuguese *gentio*, a heathen. The term was originally, *i.e.*, in 1648, applied to all Hindus as opposed to the Moors or Muhammadans, and came in time to mean the Telugus alone, Telugu is called Āndhra by Sanskrit writers. The term Āndhra occurs as the name of an Indian people in the Aitarēya Brāhmaṇa, the Rāmāyaṇa, the Mahābhārata and in the Aśōka inscriptions of the third century B.C. Pliny calls them Andarae. The Āndhra language is mentioned by the Chinese pilgrim, Hwen Thsang, about the middle of the seventh century, who says that it differed from that of Central India, whilst the forms of the written characters were for the most part the same. The name Telugu, which also occurs in the forms Telungu, Telinga, Tailinga, Tenugu and Tenungu, is said to be derived from Trilinga, "the language of the three lingas," *i.e.*, of the country of which three famous linga temples formed the boundaries. According to tradition Śivā as a linga descended on three mountains, namely, Kālēśvara, Śrīśaila and Bhīmēśvara, which marked the boundaries of the Telugu country. The Prākṛit form of Trilinga is Telinga. The Telugu country was called Telingāna by the Muhammadans. Besides Trilinga the Telugu country had likewise the name Trikalinga given to it. Telugu Pandits derive the name Tenugu from *tēne*, honey, and say that the name indicates the mellifluous character of the language. In the Tamil country Telugu is known as Vaḍugu, and the Telugus as Vaḍugar from *vaḍa*, north, the Telugu country lying to the north of the Tamil. According to tradition the first Telugu author was the sage Kaṇva who lived at the court of Āndhrarāya and wrote Telugu grammar. Atharvaṇāchārya, who lived at the beginning of the thirteenth century, names, besides Kaṇva, Bṛihaspati, Hēmachandra, Pushpadanta, Rāvaṇa, Gautama and Dharmarāja as writers on Telugu grammar in his *Trilingaśabdānuśāsana*. None of these grammars has come down to us. In Tamil we have only one sage Agastya as the formulator of the rules of grammar, but here we have a good number of them besides Rāvaṇa, the demon king of Lanka.

Unlike Tamil and Telugu, Kannaḍa has no sage's name associated with its literary origin. But the name Karṇāṭa or Kannaḍa is very old.

Kannaḍa.

It occurs as early as the sixth century in Varāhamihira's *Brihatsamhitā*, and its mention in Sōmadēva's *Kathāsaritsāgara*, probably due to its being mentioned in his source, *viz.*, the *Paiśāchi Bṛihatkathā* of Guṇāḍhya, carries it further back to the earliest centuries of the Christian era. It also occurs in the form Karunāḍar in the Tamil poem named Śilappadikāram which is supposed to go back to the second century A.D. and in the form Karunāḍagan in the Vēḷvikuḍi plates (c. 770) of the Pāṇḍya king Śaḍaiyan Parāntaka. The Sanskrit poet Rājaśēkhara (c. 900) refers in his *Kāvyamīmāmsā* to the mannerisms of the Karṇāṭas in reading their books.

Antiquity of the name.

According to Caldwell, the term Karṇāṭaka was at first a generic denomination of the plateau of the Southern Dekhan. He goes on to remark :—

"Karṇāṭaka has now got into the hands of foreigners who have given it a new and entirely erroneous application. When the Muhammadans arrived in Southern India, they found that part of it with which they first became acquainted—the country above the Ghāts, including Mysore and part of Telingāna—called the Karṇāṭaka country. In course of time, by a misapplication of terms, they applied the same name, the Karṇāṭak or Carnāṭic, to designate the country below the Ghāts, as well as that which was above. The English have carried the misapplication a step further, and restricted the name to the country below the Ghāts, which never had any right to it whatever. Hence the Mysore country, which is properly the Carnāṭic, is no longer called by that name by the English, and what is now geographically termed "the Carnāṭic" is exclusively the country below the Ghāts on the Coromandel Coast, including the whole of the Tamil country and the District of Nellore only in the Telugu country."

Wrong use of the name Karṇāṭaka.

The derivation of Karṇāṭa or Kannaḍa is uncertain. Dr. Gundert proposed *Kar-nāḍu*, " the black country," as the original form of Karṇāṭa, in allusion to the black cotton soil which characterises the plateau of the Southern Dekhan in which the language is spoken.

Derivation of Karṇāṭa or Kannaḍa.

Other scholars have suggested that Karṇāṭa is derived from *Karu-nāḍu* "the elevated country," with reference to the height of the plateau above the sea level. Indian grammarians have expressed the opinion that Kannaḍa is a *tadbhava* or corrupt form of Karṇāṭa, though it is more likely that the latter is a Sanskritised form of the original Kannaḍa. We may compare with this Punnāṭa, the Sanskritised form of Punnāḍu, a kingdom which existed in the south of Mysore in the early centuries of the Christian era. Ptolemy names it Paunnata in the second century. The original form of Kannaḍa was most probably Kannāḍu (compare Punnāḍu) which was subsequently changed into Kannaḍu and lastly into Kannaḍa. The form Kannaḍu as the name of the language is even now heard in some parts of the Kannaḍa country. The suggested derivation from Kar-nāḍu, the black country, may seem appropriate to outsiders, but the Kannaḍigas themselves are not likely to designate their language "the black country language." The Tamils and Telugus derive their respective languages from words which bear the signification of sweetness, though outsiders may suppose that it is an afterthought. It is not therefore too much to presume that the Kannaḍigas also must have applied some good attribute to their language, and this attribute, I think, is fragrance as indicated by the derivation from Kammitu (fragrant) + nāḍu (country), which words when compounded become Kannāḍu. Kannāḍu, *i.e.*, Kannaḍa, thus means the language of the fragrant country, and the epithet fragrant may be considered appropriate to the Kannaḍa country abounding as it does in sandal forests and lotus ponds, the latter being invariably described by Kannaḍa poets as one of its most characteristic features.

With regard to the antiquity of the Kannaḍa language, one or two points may be mentioned.

According to Jaina tradition, Brāhmi, the daughter of Ṛishabhadēva, the first Tīrthankara, invented eighteen alphabets including, among others, Kannaḍa. Recently a curious inscription of about the ninth century was found in a Jaina temple in the Deoghar Fort containing specimens of different alphabets mostly Draviḍian.* Among the papyri belonging to the second century A.D., discovered at Oxyrhyncus in Lower Egypt, there is one which contains a Greek play or farce, based upon the story of a Greek girl carried off to the coast of India and rescued by her brother, in which there occur some Indian words which, according to Dr. Hultzsch, are Kannaḍa.†

Antiquity of Kannaḍa language.

Kannaḍa is closely related to Tamil. They alone have a regular feminine gender. The various suffixes of the plural of rational and irrational nouns are essentially the same in both and they are more consistently distinguished than in most other connected forms of speech. Both languages agree in the principles for the formation of the oblique base. There are also a few points of difference between the two languages. Kannaḍa agrees with Telugu in the formation of the oblique cases of the singular of the pronouns I and thou and in possessing a present participle. But it differs more widely from Telugu than it does from Tamil.

Kannaḍa closely related to Tamil.

A word or two may now be said about the uncultivated Draviḍian languages of the South, namely, Tuḷu, Koḍagu, Tōda, Kōta and Baḍaga, which may be looked upon as dialects of Kannaḍa by reason of their closer relationship to that language than to any other of the Draviḍian tongues, as indicated in the following statements: "Tuḷu does not differ widely from Kanarese;" "Koḍagu may be regarded as standing about midway between Old

Dialects of Kannaḍa.

* Report on the Hindu and Buddhist Monuments, Northern Circle, 1918, p. 19.

† Mysore Archæological Report for 1904.

Kanarese and Tuḷu"; "Kōta may be considered as a very rude dialect of Kanarese"; "Baḍaga is an ancient dialect of Kanarese"; "the language (Tōda) seems to have been originally Old Kanarese, and not a distinct dialect."

Tōda, the language of the Tōdas or Todavar of the Nilgiris, is peculiar in having the sound *f*; *e.g.*, pūf, insect. It has very few case-signs, there being no difference in it between the nominative, genitive and accusative. The earliest mention of the Todavar has been met with in an inscription, No. 83 of the Chāmarājanagar Taluk of the Mysore District, dated 1117, which states that Puṇisa, the general of the Hoysaḷa king Vishṇuvardhana, frightened them during his conquest of the Nilgiris. Kōta, the language of the Kōtas of the Nilgiris, is said to have been carried thither by a persecuted low caste tribe at some very remote period. In this language the sign of the genitive case is *a*, of the dative *ke* and of the locative *olge*; and the infinitive is formed by adding *alik* to the root; *e.g.*, *tin*, eat, *tinalik*, to eat. All this shows how closely it is allied to Kannaḍa. Baḍaga, the language of the Baḍagas, who form the most numerous class of people inhabiting the Nilgiris, is a more ancient form than ordinary Kannaḍa and agrees in several particulars with the language of old literature. The sounds *ṟ* and *ḻ* are still found in the language, though in several cases *ḻ* is used in the place of *ḷ*; *e.g.*, aṟi, to know; ēṟu, to ascend; kuṟi, a sheep; keṟe, a tank; irḻu for iruḷu, night; tingḻu for tingaḷu, the moon; avḻa for avaḷu, she; makkḻa for makkaḷu, children. A peculiarity about the use of *ḻ* is that it occurs generally as a subscript of the first or second syllable of a word instead of forming the next syllable as in Kannaḍa and other allied forms of speech; *e.g.*, kḻee, for kīḻu, to pull out; bḻū for bīḻu, to fall; mḻūgu for muḻugu, to sink; hogḻu for hogaḻu, to praise; hḻā for hāḻu, ruin; hḻayē for haḻe, old; hḻoye for hoḻe, a river; gḻuyi for guḻi, a pit. The personal pronoun of the first person singular is nām, I; the dative suffix is *ga*, holaga (hoḷakke), to the field; the past tense of the verbs agrees with Old Kannaḍa: māḍidem, I did. The Baḍagas are mentioned in ancient Tamil literature in verse 253, attributed to the old poet Nákkīrar, of the anthology known as *Aga-nānūṟu* in connection with the Mysore king (Erumaiyūrān—he of Mahishapura or Mysore) who is stated to be related to them. Tuḷu, though destitute of a literature, is one of the most highly developed languages of the Draviḍian family. The name Tuḷu which means mild, meek, humble, refers to the people rather than to the language. The Tuḷus have the reputation of being the most conservative portion of the Draviḍian race. Tuḷu does not differ much from Koḍagu. The dialect from which it differs most is Tamil. Koḍagu is the language of the Coorgs, the people of Coorg or Koḍagu. The name is derived from *kuḍa*, west, and means the western country. The earliest mention of the Coorgs or Koḍagas is found in an iscription, No. 20 of the Huṇsur Taluk of the Mysore District, dated 1174, which records that the Changāḷva ruler Pemma Vīrappa, aided by the Koḍagas of all the Nāḍus, attacked Beṭṭarasa, the general of the Hoysaḷa king Ballāḷa II, sent to put down the Changāḷva king Mahādēva whom he killed in battle, but was defeated. Koḍagu has preserved its form comparatively free from change owing to the retired position of the people who speak it.

Lexical affinities in Kannaḍa and its dialects.

Two lists of words are given below, one to show the glossarial affinities of Kannaḍa and the three dialects of the Nilgiris noticed above, namely, Tōda, Kōta and Baḍaga, as also the two minor dialects of the same place Kuṟumba and Iruḷa; and the other to show the glossarial affinities of Kannaḍa and the two dialects Tuḷu and Koḍagu. It will be seen that there is scarcely any dissimilarity in the words compared barring that due to a few dialectic interchanges.

LIST I.

	Kannaḍa	Tōda	Kōta	Baḍaga	Kuṟumba	Irula	English
1	Ondu	odd	odde	ondu	ondu	ondu	One
2	Eraḍu	eḍ	eḍe	eraḍu	eraḍu	irṇḍu	Two
3	Mūṟu	mūdu	mūnde	mūṟu	mūru	muru.	Three
4	Nānu	an, anu	ane	na, nānu	nā, nanu	nānu, nā	I
5	Nāvu	em, am	enge	engla	enga	navu	We
6	Nīnu	ni	ni, niye	ni	ni	ni	Thou
7	Nīvu	nīv	nīnge	nīngla	nīnga	nīv	You
8	Iṟumpe	erb	irbē	irūpu	irūpu	irūmbu	Ant
	Iruve						
9	Kaṇṇu	kaṇṇ	kaṇṇu	kaṇṇu	kaṇṇu	kaṇṇu	Eye
10	Mīnu	mīn	mīnē	mīnu	minu	mīnu	Fish
11	Pāvu	pāb	pābe	pāmbu	hāvu	pāmbu	Snake
	Hāvu						
12	Bā	vā	vāge	ba	ba	barave	Come

LIST II.

Kannaḍa	Tuḷu	Koḍagu	English
Kuṟi	kuri	kori	Sheep
Siḍi	teḍil	cheḍil	Thunderbolt
Nālage	nālayi	nālayi	Tongue
Kittiḷe	kittiḷi	kittuli	Orange
Mūṟu	mūji	mūnd	Three
Kiṟidu	kird	cheriya	Small
Paḷti, hatti	parti	parati	Cotton
Ombattu	ormba	oyimbadu	Nine

Number of speakers.

The numbers of the races speaking Kannaḍa and its dialects are estimated at about eleven and a half millions.

CHAPTER II.

History of the Kannaḍa language. Scope of History of language. State of Draviḍian philology in Southern India. Indian and European scholars. The range of Kannaḍa about a thousand years ago. Its influence in the Telugu country. Kannaḍigas: their civilisation. Phonology. The alphabet. Derivation from the Aśōka alphabet. Points of agreement and difference between the Kannaḍa and Tamil alphabets. Phonetic system. Help of Tamil in determining words containing ṟ and ḻ. Euphonic combination. Vocalic harmony. Dialectic interchange. Interchange of vowels Interchange of consonants.

History of the Kannaḍa language.

AFTER these introductory and preparatory remarks, we may proceed to examine the Kannaḍa language in some detail and try to give a brief account of its history. We have already said something in a general way about the antiquity of the language, its inclusion as an important member in the Draviḍian group of languages and its affinities to the other main members of the group in grammar. We shall now proceed to make a detailed examination of the language, and since the study of a language without reference to any other serves no useful purpose, we shall, as far as possible, compare and contrast the language with its sister languages in respect of the points that are brought under examination.

Scope of History of language.

Language has been defined as the expression of thought by means of speech sounds. As language is constantly undergoing change, we can speak of a history of it; and it is the business of an historical investigation to trace the changes in the language. These changes take place gradually so that the speakers of the language are unconscious of them; and this accounts for the uniformity of the language which otherwise would become unintelligible. The history of a language deals mainly with its grammar and vocabulary together with the changes that have taken place in it. The grammar of every language is full of irregularities, exceptions, anomalies and inconsistencies owing to imperfect correspondence between grammatical form and grammatical function. In a perfect language every grammatical category would correspond exactly to some logical category, and there would be no room for a history or science. The peculiar charm of the study of languages lies precisely, as has been rightly said, in the mixture of the rational and the irrational, the arbitrary and exceptional with the symmetrical and regular, which they all present.

State of Draviḍian philology in Southern India.

Before dealing with the history of the Kannaḍa language, a few remarks may be made on the state of Draviḍian philology in Southern India. It may generally be stated, with due deference, that Indian Pandits can scarcely be of much help to us in this department of research. Some of them believe that Sanskrit, *the language of the gods*, is the primeval form of speech from which all other languages, no matter in what part of the world they are spoken, are derived. There are others who do not, however, go so far, but believe that all the languages—Gauḍian, Draviḍian and Kolarian of India, at any rate, are derived from Sanskrit. They are, of course, right in their derivation of the Gauḍian languages from Sanskrit. The presence of Sanskrit words more or less in the vocabularies of several of the Draviḍian languages has led them to believe that this group of tongues is also derived from Sanskrit, though a slight examination into the vocabulary of any one of these languages would have clearly shown that the non-Sanskritic portion is very greatly in excess of the Sanskrit. The fact is that comparative study of languages is a thing with which the Indian Pandit is not familiar. A Pandit may have devoted his whole life-time to mastering the intricacies of the grammar of one language without giving so much as a thought to any striking resemblance that may present itself to him in the grammar of some other language. There is no lack of Pandits in all the Dravidian languages. There are even some who have made two or three of them the subject of their special study and possess equal proficiency in them. Their high proficiency in these languages, which would otherwise have proved of inestimable value, is not of much service to philologists owing to their unfamiliarity with the principles of comparative philology. An exception that I have come across is Pandit S. Krishnamacharya, the author of a Kannaḍa grammar styled *Hosagannaḍa-nuḍigannaḍi*, which he wrote in about 1830. He notices in this work the relationship between Tamil and Kannaḍa and formulates some rules according to which, in his opinion, Tamil words undergo alteration in Kannaḍa.

Indian graduates well trained in the Western modes of thought, who may be supposed to possess a critical scholarly habit of mind, may rightly be expected to do something for the advancement of Draviḍian philology. But with one or two exceptions, no Indian scholar has as yet produced a work of any importance tending to promote an intelligent and critical study of the Draviḍian forms of speech. The late Professor M. Seshagiri Sastri, M.A., of the Madras Presidency College, did some notable work in this line, but he believed, like Dr. Pope, that the Draviḍian tongues were derived from Sanskrit. It was, however, reserved for Europeans to do much useful work for us in the field of Draviḍian languages. European scholars, though tolerably well versed in one of the languages of the Draviḍian group, are likely to go wrong in making generalisations, owing to their imperfect acquaintance with the others. But they have done a world of good by writing valuable works on the languages which they had made their special study. Thus Rice and Kittel have earned the gratitude of the Kannaḍigas; Beschi, Pope, Ellis and Percival, of the Tamils; Campbell and Brown, of the Telugus; and Gundert, of the Malayāḷis. Caldwell and Sten Konow have done very useful work for the Draviḍian group as a whole. By writing his *Comparative Grammar*, Caldwell has done very valuable service to the Draviḍians. His work marks an era in the history of the Draviḍian languages and has given an impetus to the critical and comparative study of those tongues. Sten Konow's articles on the Draviḍian languages in the *Linguistic Survey of India* are of considerable value for the critical study of this group. Similarly, we are indebted to Europeans for works on the dialects of Kannaḍa; to Brigel, Hodgson, Major Cole and Pope for their grammars of the Tuḷu, Baḍaga, Koḍagu and Tōda languages respectively. The same is likewise the case, with one or two exceptions, with regard to the Draviḍian dialects of Northern India.

The range of Kannaḍa about a thousand years ago.

Regarding the range and principal seats of the Kannaḍa language a thousand years ago, *i.e.*, at about the beginning of the 9th century, we have the following interesting particulars given in the *Kavirājamārga* of the Rāshṭrakūṭa king Nṛipatunga or Amōghavarsha I (815-877):—

"The region in which Kannaḍa was spoken extended from the Kāvēri as far as the Gōdāvari. The Kannaḍa spoken in the district lying within Kisuvoḷal, Kopaṇa, Puligeṟe and Onkunda was the pure well of Kannaḍa undefiled."*

The range given above includes a considerable part of what is now regarded as a purely Mahrāṭṭa country.

---

* ಕಾವೇರಿಯಿಂದಮಾ ಗೋ
ದಾವರಿವರಮಿರ್ದನಾಡದಾಕನ್ನಡದೊಳ್ ।
ಧಾವಿಸಿದ ಜನಪದಂ ವಸು
ಧಾವಳಯವಿಲೀನವಿಶದವಿಷಯವಿಶೇಷಂ ॥
ಅದಱೊಳಗಂ ಕಿಸುವೊೞಲಾ
ವಿದಿತಮಹಾಕೊಪಣನಗರದಾಪುಲಿಗೆಱೆಯಾ ।
ಸದಭಿಸ್ತುತಮಪ್ಪೊಂಕುಂ
ದದ ನಡುವಣ ನಾಡೆ ನಾಡೆ ಕನ್ನಡದ ತಿರುಳ್ ॥

But this ought not to incline us to doubt the accuracy of Nṛipatuṅga's statement concerning the northern limit. In the 9th century Kannaḍa was spoken over a considerable part of the Mahrāṭṭa country, but subsequently it has had to yield its place to the encroaching Mahrāṭhi idiom since the rise of the Mahrāṭṭa empire. Kolhāpūr, now considered a purely Mahrāṭṭa District, was not so in ancient times, as is abundantly proved by the Kannaḍa inscriptions in the Mahālakshmi temple situated in the heart of the Kolhāpūr town, by the large number of Kannaḍa manuscripts in the Jaina Maṭha at Kolhāpūr, by the Kannaḍa local names in the Kolhāpūr territory, as, for instance, Sirol (Siri-voḷal), and by the fact that the head of the Lakshmīsēna-maṭha at Kolhāpūr issues his circulars to this day in Kannaḍa to his numerous disciples in the Karahāṭaka-prānta, which is identical with the Satāra District, the name Karahāṭaka or Karhāḍa being now restricted to the town of that name. Further, the Political Agent at Kolhāpūr is, to the present day, always addressed as the Political Agent not of the "Dakshiṇa-Mahārāshṭra" or "Southern Mahrāṭṭa Country," but of the "Karavīra Ilākha and the Karṇāṭaka-prānta." The official designation, Southern Mahrāṭṭa Country, which includes the three Kannaḍa Districts of Belgaum, Bijapur, and Dharwar, together with the Kolhāpūr, Miraj and other Indian States, is a misnomer. It is true that in one of the earliest inscriptions of Pulakēśi II (609–642) this part of the country is included in Mahārāshṭra; but this term, meaning literally "the great country," did not imply any of the racial and linguistic peculiarities which are now attached to the terms Mahrāṭṭa and Mahrāṭhi, derived from it. In the whole area of the so-called Southern Mahrāṭṭa Country, not a single Mahrāṭhi inscription has been discovered, of a greater age than two or three centuries, while all the old inscriptions hitherto found are either in Sanskrit or Kannaḍa, or in the two languages combined. This fact speaks of itself as to what the vernacular of the country was in early times. At present, the people and the language of the British Districts - are essentially Kannaḍa, and the Kannaḍa people and language have been displaced, to a certain extent, by the Mahrāṭhi people and language in the Indian States, only because those States were established by the aggressions of Mahrāṭṭas from the north, whose local influence proved to be greater than that of the rulers whom they dispossessed. The town and District of Sholapur contain numerous Kannaḍa inscriptions, though the district now counts officially as a Mahrāṭhi one. Names such as Vappuvaṇṇa and Lasthiyavva among the Silāhāras of Ṭhāṇa betray their Kannaḍa origin. The influence of Kannaḍa in ancient times in what is now known as the Telugu country is evidenced by the Kannaḍa titles applied in old Telugu inscriptions to Telugu kings and chiefs; *e.g.*, in a Telugu Vaidumba inscription of about the 9th century, the name of a general is given as Manujaradēva;* the Eastern Chāḷukya king Guṇaga-Vijayāditya (844-888) had the title *Guṇake-nalla ;* and some of the Reḍḍi chiefs bore the titles *Jagad-obba-gaṇḍa* and *Jagada-Gōpāla.*† It may also be incidentally noted that in the Indrakīlaparvata Telugu inscription of about the 9th century at Bezwada occurs the form *saṁvatsaraduḷ* with the archaic Kannaḍa locative suffix *uḷ* instead of the corresponding Telugu suffix *lō*.

Ādi-Pampa (941) says that he wrote his *Vikramārajuna-vijaya* or *Bhārata* in the pithy Kannaḍa of Puligeṟe, which is one of the four seats of pure Kannaḍa named by Nṛipatunga. Ranna (993) also states that the Kannaḍa of the two (which make together a six-hundred) was pithy Kannaḍa‡ and that he wrote in it. The two referred to by Ranna are the Beḷvola three-hundred and the Puligeṟe three-hundred, § so that

* Madras Epigraphical Report, 1923, p. 98.

† *Ibid*, p. 124.

‡ ಎರಡಱುನೂಱಱ ಕನ್ನಡಮಾತಿರುಳ ಕನ್ನಡಂ.

§ ಬೆಳ್ವೊಲ ಮೂನೂಱುಮಂ ಪುಲಿಗೆಱೆ ಮೂನೂಱುಮಂತೆರಡಱುನೂಱುಮಂ.—*Epigraphia Indica*, XV, p. 339.

Puligeṟe again appears as the region of pure Kannaḍa. The expression Eraḍ-aṟu-nūṟu, as the name of a province, which was an ornament of the Kuntaḷa country, occurs in the Kalās inscription of 930,* and the same appears as Dvi-triśatam, the two three-hundreds, in the Nīlgunda inscription of 982.†

Nṛipatunga also makes the following interesting remarks about the intelligence and culture of the Kannaḍigas inhabiting the region of pure Kannaḍa already mentioned as lying within Kisuvoḷal, Kopaṇa, Puligeṟe and Onkunda :—

"Skilled are the people of that region in making speeches with apt words and also in understanding and pondering over (others') speeches. Naturally intelligent, they are, even without special study, versed in the usages of poetry. All are skilful in their speech. Even young children and the dumb learn wisdom and words respectively at a hint."‡

Kannaḍigas: their civilisation.

We learn from the Ceylonese Buddhist Chronicle *Mahāvaṃśa* that the Maurya emperor Aśōka sent in the 3rd century B.C. a Buddhist missionary named Rakkhita to Banavāsi, situated on the north-west border of the Mysore State, and another named Mahādēva, to Mahisha-Manḍala, probably Mysore. The late Dr. Fleet was of opinion that Mahiṣha-Manḍala did

---

* ಕುಂತಳಧರಾತಳಂ ; ತದ್ವಿಷಯಕ್ಕೆರಡಱುನೂಱು ಲಲಾಮಂ.—*Epigraphia Indica*, XIII, p. 326.

† *Ibid*, IV, p. 207. The term ಎರಡಱುನೂಱು has been taken in the sense of 1,200 and wrongly applied to Kopaṇa by some scholars without any literary or ephigraphical evidence for doing so.

‡ ಪದನಱಿದು ನುಡಿಯಲುಂ ನುಡಿ
ದುದನಱಿದಾರಯಲುಮಾರ್ಪರಾ ನಾಡವರ್ಗಳ್ ।
ಚದುರರ್ ನಿಜದಿಂ ಕುಱಿತೋ
ದದೆಯುಂ ಕಾವ್ಯಪ್ರಯೋಗಪರಿಣತಮತಿಗಳ್ ॥
ಕುಱಿತವರಲ್ಲದೆ ಮತ್ತಂ
ಪೆಱರುಂ ತಂತಮ್ಮ ನುಡಿಯೊಳೆಲ್ಲಂ ಜಾಣರ್ ।
ಕಿಱುವಕ್ಕಳುಮಾಮೂಗರು
ಮಱಿಪಲ್ಕಱಿವರ್ ವಿವೇಕಮಂ ಮಾತುಗಳಂ ॥

not refer to Mysore but to a province on the banks of the Narbadā. But Mahisha-rāshṭra or Maisa-nāḍu occurs as the name of the Mysore country in inscriptions and literature. *Maisa* is only a *tadbhava* or corrupt form of *Mahisha*, a buffalo. In the Tamil Anthology called *Aganānūṟu*, verse 115 composed by the ancient poet Māmūlanār, who has been assigned by some scholars to about the 2nd century A.D., names Erumai-nāḍu (erumai=a buffalo), which may be compared with Maisa-nāḍu mentioned above, and says that it was situated in the west. Verse 36 attributed to Nakkīrar, another ancient poet, tells us that in a battle that was fought at Talaiyālangāṇam the Pāṇḍya king Neḍuñjeḻiyan defeated the combined forces of these seven chiefs, namely, the Chēra, the Chōḷa, Tidiyan, Eḻini, Irungōvēṇmān, Porunan and Erumaiyūrān (he of Mahishapura or Mysore). And verse 253 of the same poet states that Erumaiyūrān was related to the Baḍagas. In another old Tamil work called *Śilappadikāram* it is stated that the Chēra king Śenguṭṭuvan, who, according to some scholars, ruled in the 2nd century A.D., while on an expedition to the north, stayed on the Nilgiris and witnessed with great pleasure the dance of the Kannaḍigas. We gather from the Ceylonese chronicles that a Chōḷa king named Elala conquered Ceylon in 205 B.C. with the help of a Mysore army.* An inscription of the Rāshṭrakūṭa king Dantidurga, of about the middle of the 8th century, states that the Karṇāṭaka army was capable of defeating the Pallava king of Kānchi, and the Kēraḷa, Pāṇḍya and Chōḷa kings.† The Kaḷabhras, mentioned in the Vēḷvikuḍi plates (c. 770) of the Pāṇḍya king Saḍaiyan Parāntakan as having gained possession of the Pāṇḍya country in about the 7th century, are believed to be Karṇāṭas. The Vaḍugar (Baḍagas) of Erumai-nāḍu (Mysore) formed the advance guard of the Mōriyar of Tamil Sangam literature or

---

* *The Lost Cities of Ceylon*, p. 26.

† *Indian Antiquary*, XI, p. 114.

Mauryas of Konkan who ruled in the 5th, 6th and 7th centuries and went to help the Kōśar against Mōhūr, the general of the Pāṇḍya king Neḍunjeḷiyan.[*] Almost all the dynasties of rulers in the Dekhan and the South, such as the Ganga, the Kadamba, the Chāḷukya, the Rāshṭrakūṭa, the Hoysaḷa, the Sēvuṇa, the Kaḷachurya, the Raṭṭa, the Śilāhāra, the Kongāḷva, the Changāḷva, the Vaidumba, the Sinda, the Bāṇa, the Noḷamba, the Sāḷuva, the Sāntara, the Sēnavāra, the Punnāḍ and those of Vijayanagar, Mysore and Coorg, have been Karṇāṭa, as also the lines of Pāḷegārs or minor chiefs, such as those of Keḷadi, Ummattūr, Nuggehaḷḷi, Bēlūr, Sugaṭūr, Hadināḍu, Mudigere, Chitaldrug, Niḍugal, Chennapaṭṭaṇa, Māgaḍi, Elahanka, Sante-Bennūr, Piriyapaṭṭaṇa, Chikkanāyakanahaḷḷi, Maddagiri, Bijjavara, Kōṭe and Kaḷale. There were, moreover, Karṇāṭaka dynasties of rulers even in Gujarāt and Nēpāl.

The civilisation of the Kannaḍigas, as indicated by the indigenous words of their language, was by no means negligible, though not of a very high standard. The Kannaḍigas were well acquainted with agriculture[†] and possessed some knowledge of the ordinary arts of life, such as spinning, weaving, house building,[‡] etc. They knew some of the ordinary metals[§] such as gold, silver, iron and copper; and some of the planets[||] which were ordinarily known to the ancients such as the sun, the moon, the crescent, venus and the ascending node. They delighted in war and were armed with severa

---

* *Journal of the Royal Asiatic Society*, 1924, p. 666.

† ಉೞುವುದು, ಕುೞ, ಕುಂಟೆ, ಕೂರಿಗೆ, ಏರು, ಎತ್ತು, ಏತ, ಪಯಿರು, ಕಳೆ, ಕದಿರು, ತೆನೆ, ಬಯಲು, ಕೊೞ, ಕಾಲುವೆ, ಕೞಿ, ಏರಿ, ತೂಂಬು, ಅಱ, ಕೊಯಿಲು, ಕುಡುಗೋಲು, ಒಕ್ಕಣೆ.

‡ ನೂಲುವುದು, ಱಾಟೆ, ಪಟ್ಟೆ, ತುಬಟ; ನೇಯುವುದು, ಹಾಸು, ಹೊಕ್ಕು, ಪಟ; ಮನೆ, ಬಾಗಿಲು, ಸೂರು, ಹಿತ್ತಲು, ಓವರಿ, ಕಡೆ, ಕದ, ಜಗಲ, ಕೇರು, ಮಣ್ಣು, ಮರ, ಗಾರೆ, ಗಚ್ಚು, ಇತ್ಯಾದಿ.

§ ಪೊನ್, ಬೆಳ್ಳಿ, ಕರ್ಬೊನ್ (ಕಬ್ಬಿಣ), ಕಿಸು (ತಾಮ್ರ).

|| ನೇಸಱು, ತಿಂಗಳ್, ಪೆಱೆ, ಬೆಳ್ಳಿ, ಬಾಡ್ (ರಾಹು).

weapons* such as the bow, arrow, spear, shield and sword. They had marriage, medicines, hamlets, rafts, ships, festivals, numerals up to one thousand, measures of length, weight and capacity, and fractions.† They had all the necessary words for everyday use. The Tamilians acknowledged the existence of God and built temples to His honour. But the Kannaḍigas, like the Telugus, have no words expressive of the ideas of God and temple. Telugu has no indigenous words to denote even the sun and moon. The Kannaḍigas do not seem to have had alphabetical characters,‡ nor words to denote heaven and hell. The same was the case with the Telugus also. It may, however, be said that the Draviḍians as a whole did not know hell.

Phonology.

Of the Draviḍian alphabets, the Kannaḍa and the Telugu constitute but one alphabet, the differences between them being very few and unimportant. The same is the case with the Tamil and the Old Malayāḷam.

The alphabet.

The Kannaḍa and Telugu scripts, being adaptations of the Sanskrit alphabet, are tolerably perfect expressions of the sounds found in those languages. But the Tamil alphabet is a very imperfect system for expressing the Tamil sounds, and this is due, according to some scholars, to its not being adapted from a Sanskrit prototype. In old Telugu inscriptions the characters are almost identical with the Kannaḍa ones, and consequently this common script was known as the Kannaḍa-Telugu alphabet. Up to 1300 A.D., this alphabet presented scarcely any varieties or differences of form of the letters sufficient to justify a distinction being made; but from 1300 onwards, a

* ಪೋರ್, ಕೂಳುಗುಳ; ಬಿಲ್, ಕೋಲ್, ಇಟ್ಟಿ, ಅಡ್ಡಣ, ಕತ್ತಿ, ಕಡಿತಲೆ.

† ಮದುವೆ, ಮದ್ದು, ಬಾಡ, ತೆಪ್ಪ, ಹಡಗು, ಬೆಜಪ್ಪು, ಒಂದರಿಂದ ಒಂಬಯ್ನೂರ ತೊಂಬತ್ತೊಂಬತ್ತು; ಚೋಟು, ಗೇಣು, ಅಡಿ, ಮೊಳ, ಮಾರು; ಮಣ, ವೀಸ, ಕೊಳಗ, ಬಳ್ಳ; ಅರೆ, ಕಾಲು, ಬೇಳೆ, ವೀಸ.

‡ The words ಬರ, ಬರೆಹ, however, show that they were acquainted with writing.

marked divergence has arisen between the alphabets used by the Telugus of the coast and the Kannaḍigas, and this divergence has been much increased since the introduction of printing. The Tamil and Malayāḷam characters closely resemble the Grantha script which is used for writing Sanskrit in Southern India. It is generally agreed that all the Draviḍian alphabets, as also the Dēvanāgari, are derived, through the Cave characters, from the Brāhmi variety of the Aśōka alphabet. Another South Indian script, known as Vaṭṭeḻuttu on account of the round or cursive character of its letters, which was once used in the Madura and Tinnevelly Districts and also on the Malabar Coast, is supposed by some scholars to be the original of the Tamil alphabet. The earliest known records written in this script are those of the early Pāṇḍya king Jaṭilavarman Parāntaka I who reigned at the close of the 8th century. It was gradually supplanted by the modern Tamil character after the conquest of the Pāṇḍya kingdom by the Chōḷas in the 11th century; and it appears to have gone entirely out of use in the Tamil country by the 15th century, though it dragged on its existence till the end of the 18th century on the West Coast, giving way eventually to Malayāḷam. Some of the peculiarities of Vaṭṭeḻuttu are the writing of consonants which follow one another without the intervention of a vowel on the same line, not perpendicularly as is done in the other Indian alphabets, and the system of marking the secondary vowels. The first peculiarity has been adopted by the Tamil alphabet also. The Kannaḍa and Telugu alphabets have no such peculiarities in them. According to Burnell, the Tamil alphabet is a Brāhmanical adaptation of the Grantha letters corresponding to the old Vaṭṭeḻuttu, from which, however, the last four signs, namely ḻ (ழ), ḷ (ள), ṟ (ற) and ṉ (ன), have been retained, the Grantha not possessing their equivalents. Unlike the other Draviḍian alphabets, the Tamil uses ṉ (ன) as a distinct letter as was done in the Vaṭṭeḻuttu. Some scholars are of opinion that the Vaṭṭeḻuttu script is independent of the South Aśōka or Cave character, that both of them are independent adaptations of some foreign character, the first to a Draviḍian, the second to a Sanskritic language, and that the resemblances between the two point to a common Semitic origin. But there are others who think that the Vaṭṭeḻuttu is derived from the Brāhmi variety of the Aśōka alphabet, through the Cave character, just like all other alphabets of India—the Dēvanāgari, the Tamil-Grantha and the Kannaḍa-Telugu groups—though it had had a separate line of evolution. The Draviḍian numerals, too, are more or less cursive modifications of the Cave numerals.

Derivation from the Aśōka alphabet.

Some instances may now be given to illustrate the derivation of the letters of the various alphabets mentioned above from the Aśōka and Cave characters. The Aśōka *k* was a simple Latin cross 𑀓. From its modified Cave form are derived the Vaṭṭeḻuttu, the Tamil க, the Dēvanāgari क, the Grantha and the Kannaḍa and Telugu forms ಕ and క. The Aśōka symbol for *ch* was 𑀘. It was modified into in the Cave character. From this arose the Tamil ச, the Vaṭṭeḻuttu, the Dēvanāgari च, the Kannaḍa and Telugu forms, and the Grantha forms. *P* was represented by 𑀧 in the Aśōka alphabet. We can easily see how the Tamil ப, the Grantha, the Vaṭṭeḻuttu and the Dēvanāgari प are derived from it. The Kannaḍa and Telugu forms were derived thus. The Aśōka *y* was written 𑀬 The Cave symbol was. There can scarcely be any difficulty in deriving from these the Tamil and Grantha , the Vaṭṭeḻuttu , the Dēvanāgari य, and the Kannaḍa and Telugu ಯ, య.

The Aśōka *a* was . The Tamil அ, the Vaṭṭeḻuttu , the Dēvanāgari अ and the Grantha 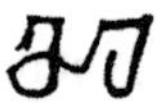 can be easily derived from it. The Kannaḍa-Telugu ಅ was got through the modified forms 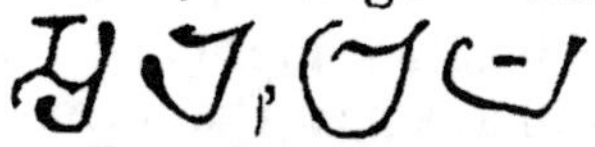. The Aśōka symbol for *i* was . The Tamil இ is got by welding all the three parts of the letter together. The same is more or less the case with the Dēvanāgari इ. The Grantha  and the Kannada-Telugu ఇ are derived through the intermediate forms 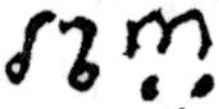 ఇ. *U* was represented in the Aśōka alphabet by the sign . From this the Tamil, the Vaṭṭeḻuttu and the Grantha உ are easily got. So also the Dēvanāgari उ. The Kannaḍa ಉ and the Telugu ఉ are got through the forms 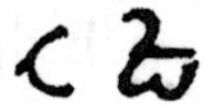.

With regard to the secondary vowels, the long *ā* sound of a consonant was denoted in the Aśōka alphabet by a short horizontal line added to the right of the letter thus—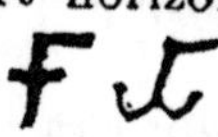. In the Cave character the line was curved down thus—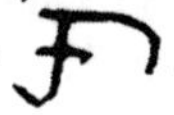. This form occurs in Kannaḍa, Telugu and Dēvanāgari. The bent symbol became a separate part of the letter in Tamil and Grantha thus—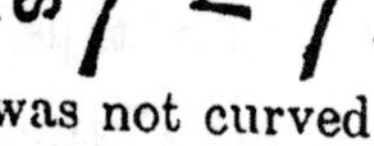. In the Vaṭṭeḻuttu the horizontal line was not curved but remained straight as in the Aśōka script, *e.g.*, .

The secondary *ē* was formed in the Aśōka alphabet by the addition of a similar line to the left of the letter at the top thus—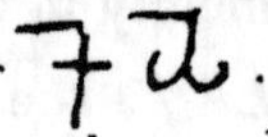. Later on, the line assumed a curved form thus—. This is the form found in Vaṭṭeḻuttu. In Tamil and Grantha the sign was detached from the letter and placed immediately to the left thus—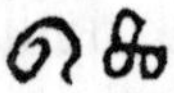; and in Dēvanāgari over the letter thus—के. But in Kannaḍa and Telugu the sign shifted its position more and more to the right of the letter and we have now the forms ಕೆ, కె.

To represent the secondary *ai* the Aśōka alphabet added two horizontal strokes to the left of the letter thus—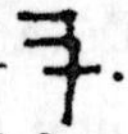. As in the case of *ē*, these strokes assumed a curved form, were detached from the letter and placed to the left in old Tamil and Grantha thus—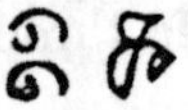; and in Dēvanāgari over the letter thus—कै. In modern Tamil and Vaṭṭeḻuttu the two strokes are welded into one by being placed side by side thus—ை : only in Tamil it is detached from the letter—கை, and in Vaṭṭeḻuttu attached to it—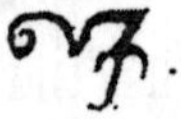. But in Kannaḍa and Telugu the lower curved sign which was added to the lower part of the letter was separated from it and placed below it thus—ಕೈ, కై.

The secondary *o* was formed in the Aśōka script by adding the symbol for the secondary *ā* to the symbol for the secondary *e* thus—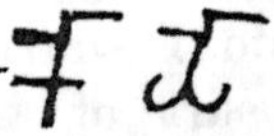. Later on, as stated before, the symbols assumed a curved form and were detached in Tamil and Grantha thus—கொ, and in Dēvanāgari thus—को. The form in Vaṭṭeḻuttu was 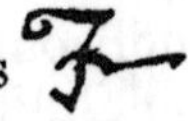 where, as stated before, the stroke representing *ā* has not assumed a curved form. The Kannaḍa and Telugu ಕೊ, కొ were got through forms like 

We have thus traced the evolution of some letters of various alphabets including Kannaḍa from the Aśōka character. The marked difference that is now observed in the formation of the Dēvanāgari characters and those of the Draviḍian languages is attributed to local influences and to the custom, universal in the Dekhan and the South, of writing on the palmira leaf with an iron style. Again, though the differences between the Tamil and Kannaḍa characters, as they now exist, are so great as to lead one to doubt their common derivation from the Aśōka script, still the evidence of old inscriptions written in the two characters is quite conclusive as regards, at any rate, the close resemblance, if not perfect identity, of the two alphabets at one time. The two alphabets which resembled each other so closely at one time have now become very much altered and disguised by natural and local influences.

Points of agreement and difference between the Kannaḍa and Tamil alphabets.

Both Kannaḍa and Tamil alphabets agree (1) in having a short *e* and *o*; (2) in not using the liquid semi-vowels *ṛi* and *lṛi*: Tamil has no letters corresponding to these, while Kannaḍa does not use them; (3) in having the three peculiar consonants *ṟ* (ಱ), *ḻ* (ೞ) and *ḷ* (ಳ); (4) in rarely using aspirated letters and sibilants, except in pronouncing and writing Sanskrit derivatives: even in pure Kannaḍa *s* occurs as *ś* does in Tamil; and (5) in not having the letter *h*: in Old Kannaḍa *h* is very rarely used, though it occurs very frequently in Modern Kannaḍa. The Tamil alphabet differs from the Kannaḍa (1) in not having aspirated letters: Kannaḍa, though possessing these letters, makes a sparing use of them, which is due, to some extent, to Sanskrit influence; (2) in using the same symbol for representing both surds and sonants; (3) in having two letters ந and ன to represent the *n* sound: the difference in the use of these letters is— (i) that ன mostly occurs as a final, and ந very rarely; (ii) that ன is always used in combination with ற (ṟ) to represent the peculiar Tamil sound *nṟa*; and (iii) that ண is invariably used as the nasal of *ṭ*; and (4) in having a peculiar symbol ஃ (similar to the Aśōka *i*) formed of three cyphers in the form of a triangle, called *āydam*, which occurs in the middle of only a few words and corresponds in a manner to the Sanskrit *visarga*: this letter is very seldom used in Modern Tamil and Kannaḍa does not use the *visarga* except in some indeclinables. The chief reason for the differences between the Tamil and Kannaḍa alphabets is to be found in the fact that the grammar of the Tamil language was, to a great extent, systematised independently of Sanskrit influences, and that Sanskrit modes of pronunciation being almost unknown to the Tamilians, their alphabet, though originally derived from the same source, was greatly altered so as to suit their peculiar phonetic system. The same independence of Sanskrit influences cannot be claimed for the alphabet of the Kannaḍa language, which has mostly adhered to the alphabetical system of Sanskrit. The same is the case with its grammar. Two of the three standard works on Kannaḍa grammar, namely, the *Bhāshābhūshaṇa* and the *Śabdānuśāsana* are composed not in the Kannaḍa language, but in Sanskrit. It may further be added that in the whole terminology of Kannaḍa grammar there does not occur a single term of purely Kannaḍa origin, all the terms without any exception having been borrowed from Sanskrit, whereas in Tamil the case is exactly the reverse.* Nevertheless, when due allowance is made for this and other causes which gradually made each of them an individual language, the grammatical structure of the two languages will be found to be essentially similar. The same remarks apply more or less to the Telugu language also.

* To give one or two instances: "Tamil grammarians designate vowels by a beautiful metaphor, as *uyir* or the *life* of a word; consonants as *mey* or the *body*; and the junction of a vowel and consonant as *uyir-mey* or *an animated body*".

Phonetic system.

As stated before, the Kannaḍa alphabet, as well as the Telugu, is a tolerably perfect expression of the sounds found in the respective languages. In Telugu the palatals *ch* and *j* are pronounced *ts* and *dz* respectively before all vowels except *i*, *ī*, *e*, *ē*, *ai*. This peculiarity is not found in Kannaḍa, nor in any other Draviḍian language. In Tamil only one sign stands for either a surd or a sonant according to its position. Kannaḍa has separate signs for surds and sonants, as also Telugu. Again, in Tamil nasals combine with sonants only, but in Kannaḍa and Telugu they combine with surds also. In Kannaḍa and Telugu *bindu* or *anusvāra* is optionally used for the nasal; but in Tamil the nasal is invariably used as there is no *bindu*. In Tamil the letters *r*, *l*, do not begin a word unless one of the vowels *a*, *i* or *u* is prefixed to them, *e.g.*, ಅರಶನ್, ಇರಾಮನ್, ಉಲೋಕಂ. Such is not the case in Kannaḍa and Telugu. Tamil has the peculiar sound ற்ற (*ṭṭra*) formed by the doubling of ற (*ṟ*) and this is represented by *tta* in Kannaḍa and *ta* in Telugu: ಮಾಟ್ಟಂ, ಮಾತು, ಮಾಟ. Another peculiar Tamil sound ன்ற (*ṇḍra*) formed by the combination of ன (*n*) and ற (*ṟ*) becomes *nda* in Kannaḍa and Telugu and *ñja* in Tuḷu: ಕನ್ಱು, ಕಂದು, ಕಂಜಿ. *Ś* is not used in literary Kannaḍa and Telugu, though very common in Tamil. In Tamil and Kannaḍa, as also sometimes in Telugu, initial *ai* and *au* are optionally changed into *ay* and *av* respectively: ಐಯರ್, ಅಯ್ಯರ್; ಕೈವಾರಂ, ಕಯ್ವಾರಂ; ಕೌವರ್, ಕವ್ವರ್; ಕೌಂಗು, ಕವುಂಗು; The letters ಱ (*ṟ*) and ೞ (*ḻ*), now obsolete in Kannaḍa, are in use in Tamil, Malayāḷam and Baḍaga, and ಱ (*ṟ*) in Telugu. ೞ (*ḻ*) however occurs in Telugu inscriptions of the 9th and 10th centuries.

Help of Tamil in determining words containing ಱ and ೞ.

The letters ಱ and ೞ are of intrinsic value for Draviḍian philology. The Old Kannaḍa alphabet had four letters, namely, ರ (*r*), ಳ (*ḷ*), ಱ (*ṟ*) and ೞ (*ḻ*) corresponding to the four letters of the Tamil alphabet ர, ள, ற and ழ respectively. Of these four letters of the Kannaḍa alphabet, the two letters, ಱ

and ೞ, corresponding to ற and ழ of Tamil, have, as stated above, become obsolete, and ರ and ಳ are substituted for them in Modern Kannaḍa. This is no doubt a matter for regret from a philological point of view. But the peculiarly close relationship of Tamil to Kannaḍa comes to our help in this matter, inasmuch as even if ಱ and ೞ are banished from the Kannaḍa alphabet a tolerably good knowledge of Tamil will enable us, in the majority of cases, to determine the words which contain these letters. A number of words containing ರ, ಳ, ಱ and ೞ corresponding to ர, ள, ற and ழ respectively of Tamil is given below. To find out which words ought to contain ರ and which ಱ, we have simply to examine the words in Tamil; and similarly with ಳ and ೞ. Kannaḍa words which have no corresponding words in Tamil, in this particular, are very few indeed.

Examples.

Tamil	*Kannaḍa.*	*Tamil*	*Kannaḍa.*
r	*ṟ*	*ḷ*	*ḻ*
ಅಮರ್	ಅಱು	ಅಳವು	ಅಗೞ್
ಅಲರ್	ಆಱು	ಉರುಳ್	ಅೞರ್
ಇರು	ಏಱು	ಕಳ್	ಅೞಿ
ಇರುಳ್	ಕಾಱು	ಕುಳಿರ್	ಕೞು
ಉದಿರ್	ತಱು	ಕೊಳ್	ಆೞ್
ಕದಿರ್	ನಾಱು	ತಳಿರ್	ಇೞಿ
ಕರಡಿ	ನೂಱು	ತಾಳ್	ಉೞು
ತೇರ್	ಪಾಱು	ನಳ್ಳಿ	ಕೋೞಿ
ನರ	ಮುಱು	ನೀಳ್	ಪೞಿ
ಪೋರ್	ಮೀಱು	ಪುಳಿ	ಪುೞು

The examples given above consist of words which are exactly the same in both the languages; they do not include any words that have undergone dialectic change. Words of the latter class are very numerous and the following are a few examples of them :—

Tamil	*Kannaḍa*	*Tamil*	*Kannaḍa*
r		*ṟ*	
ಅರುವಿ	ಅರ್ಬಿ	ಉಱುಂಗು	ಒಱಗು

Tamil	*Kannaḍa*	*Tamil*	*Kannaḍa*
r		*ṟ*	
ಇರರೈ	ಎರರೆ	ಕಱೈ	ಕಱೆ
ಕರೈ	ಕರೆ	ಶಿಱು	ಕಿಱು
ಪೆರಿದು	ಪಿರಿದು	ತುಱೈ	ತೊಱೆ
ವರೈ	ಬರೆ	ಪಿಱ	ಪೆಱ
ವಾರ್	ಬಾರ್	ಪಿಱೈ	ಪೆಱೆ
ḷ		*ḻ*	
ಇಳ	ಎಳ	ಶುೞಿ	ಸುೞಿ
ಉಳದು	ಒಳದು	ನಿೞಲ್	ನೆೞಲ್
[illegible]	ಕಳೆ	ಮೞೈ	ಮೞೆ
ವಳೈ	ಬಳೆ	ಮುೞಂಗು	ಮೊೞಗು
ವಾಳ್	ಬಾಳ್	ವೞಿ	ಬೞಿ
ವೆಳ್ಳಿ	ಬೆಳ್ಳಿ	ವೀೞ್	ಬೀೞ್

In Kannaḍa, as in Tamil, words convey different meanings according as ರ or ಱ and ಳ or ೞ occur in them. Both the pairs of letters being in use in Tamil, there is not the slightest difficulty in determining the meaning of words. Unfortunately, such is not the case in Kannaḍa. The letters ಱ and ೞ having disappeared, their places have been taken by the other letters ರ and ಳ, so that we are now deprived of the invaluable help which the difference in spelling would otherwise have afforded us in the determination of the meaning of words. Even a good knowledge of Kannaḍa by itself will not be of much use in finding out the meaning of the words in question, in consequence of the deceptive similarity in the spelling. A knowledge of Tamil, however, will afford immense help in the matter, inasmuch as it will give a clue to the meaning of the word by giving its proper spelling. The following examples will illustrate what is meant:—

Tamil	*Kannaḍa*	*Meaning*	*Tamil*	*Kannaḍa*	*Meaning*
ಕರೈ	ಕರೆ	shore	ಇರೈ	ಎರೆ	food
ಕಱೈ	ಕಱೆ	stain	ಇಱೈ	ಎಱೆ	master
ಅರಿ	ಅರಿ	to cut	ಅರೈ	ಅರೆ	half
ಅಱಿ	ಅಱಿ	to know	ಅಱೈ	ಅಱೆ	rock

Tamil	Kannaḍa	Meaning	Tamil	Kannaḍa	Meaning
ತಳೈ	ತಳೆ	tie	ವಾಳೈ	ಬಾಳೆ	a kind of fish
ತೞೈ	ತೞೆ	umbrella	ವಾೞೈ	ಬಾೞೆ	plantain
ವಾಳ್	ಬಾಳ್	sword	ಆಳ್	ಆಳ್	servant
ವಾೞ್	ಬಾೞ್	to prosper	ಆೞ್	ಆೞ್	to sink

Each pair of words given here is now spelt exactly alike in Kannaḍa. It is the corresponding Tamil words that give the proper spelling.

Baḍaga and Telugu may naturally be expected to give us some help in determining words with ೞ and ಱ respectively. But these languages cannot be taken as a safe guide in this matter since they show ೞ and ಱ respectively in several cases where we would expect ಳ and ರ, *e.g.*, ಅೞ್ಟ for ಅವಳು, ಇೞ್ಟು for ಇರುಳು, ಗೞಾಯಿ for ಗಾಳಿ, ಬೞಾಗು for ಬೆಳಕು; ವಱಕು for ವರೆಗೆ, ತೀಱು for ತೀರ್, ಅಕ್ಕಱ for ಅಬ್ಬಱು, ಅರುವು for ಅಱುವು. Still the help of these languages may be availed of to a limited extent as indicated by the following examples:—ಬೞೂ for ಬೇೞು, ಮೞುಗು for ಮುೞುಗು, ಸೞುಯಿ for ಸುೞಿ, ಕೞಾ for ಕಾೞು, ಆರು to become full, ಆಱು to dry; ತೇರು chariot, ತೇಱು to settle, to clarify; ಕರ shore, ಕಱ stain; ಏರು a plough with draught oxen, ಏಱು river.

Euphonic combination.

In Kannada, as also in Tamil and Telugu, as a general rule, hiatus between contiguous vowels is prevented by the insertion of *y* or *v*.

ಮನೆ + ಒಳ್ = ಮನೆಯೊಳ್; ಮನ್ನೈ + ಉಳ್ = ಮನ್ನೈಯುಳ್; ಪೂ + ಇಲ್ಲ = ಪೂವಿಲ್ಲ; ಪೂ + ಇಲ್ಲೈ = ಪೂವಿಲ್ಲೈ; ವಾರಿ + ಇಲ್ಲು = ವಾರಿಯಿಲ್ಲು; ತರು + ಉ = ತರುವು.

Final vowels of words are generally elided before vowels.

ಬೇಡು + ಇಲ್ಲ = ಬೇಡಿಲ್ಲ; ವೀಡು + ಇಲ್ಲೈ = ವೀಡಿಲ್ಲೈ; ರಾಮುಁಡು + ಏಗೆನು = ರಾಮುಁಡೇಗೆನು.

In combination, initial surds of the second word are generally changed into sonants.

ಕೆಂ + ತಳಿರ್ = ಕೆಂದಳಿರ್; ಶೆಂ + ತಳಿರ್ = ಶೆಂದಳಿರ್; ಕೆಂಪು + ತಾಮರ = ಕೆಂದಾಮರ.

In *tatpurusha* compounds Tamil doubles the surd and hardens it.

ಪುಲತ್ತೋರ್, ಪುಲದೋರ್; ಮರಕ್ಕೊಂಬು, ಮರಗೊಂಬು.

In Teḷugu the change of a surd into a sonant takes place even in *dvandva* compounds.

ಅನ್ನದಮ್ಮುಲು, ತಲ್ಲಿದಂಡ್ರುಲು.

Such is not the case in Kannaḍa and Tamil.

The final consonants of monosyllabic nominal and verbal themes with a short initial are doubled before vowels.

ಕಣ್ + ಇಲ್ಲ = ಕಣ್ಣಿಲ್ಲ ; ಕಣ್ + ಇರ್ಲೆ = ಕಣ್ಣಿರ್ಲೆ.

When *n* follows such themes ending in *ṇ*, it is changed into *ṇ*.

ತಣ್ + ನೆೞಲ್ = ತಣ್ಣೆೞಲ್; ತಣ್ + ನಿೞಲ್ = ತಣ್ಣಿೞಲ್. ಕಣ್ + ನೀರ್ = ಕಣ್ಣೀರ್ ; ಜಾಣ್ + ನುಡಿ = ಜಾಣ್ಣುಡಿ.

When the words ಕುಱು and ಚಿಱು are followed by words with an initial vowel, *ṟ* becomes double *t* in Kannaḍa; double *ṭ* in Telugu and is doubled in Tamil.

ಕುಱು + ಎಸಱ್ = ಕುತ್ತೆಸಱ್ ; ಕಿಱು + ಅಡಿ = ಕಿತ್ತಡಿ. ಕುಱು + ಉಸುರು = ಕುಟ್ಟುಸುರು ; ಚಿಱು + ಎಲುಕ = ಚಿಟ್ಟೆಲುಕ. ಕುಱು + ಉಯಿರ್ = ಕುಟ್ಟುಯಿರ್ (kuṭṭruyir); ಶಿಱು + ಎಲಿ = ಶಿಟ್ಟೆಲಿ (śiṭṭreli). The *ḍ* of ನಡು, ಕಡು and ಎಡು is changed into double *ṭ* in all the three languages.

ನಡು + ಆಱು = ನಟ್ಟಾಱು ; ನಡು + ಆೞು = ನಟ್ಟಾೞು ; ನಡು + ಏಱು = ನಟ್ಟೇಱು.

There are some changes in combination which are peculiar to Tamil and Telugu.

Vocalic harmony.

According to the law of Vocalic Harmony or Harmonic Sequence of vowels, as stated before (p. 17), a given vowel, in one syllable of a word, or in the root, requires an analogous vowel in the following syllables of the same word, or in the particles appended to it, which therefore alter their vowels accordingly. The prevalence of this law in Telugu has already been exemplified. Traces of this law appear to occur in Kannaḍa also in such forms as ಮಾಡುತ್ತೇನೆ, ಮಾಡುತ್ತೇವೆ, ಮಾಡುತ್ತೀರಿ, ಮಾಡಿದಿರಿ, etc. They are clearly seen in words such as ಬರುಕು, ಮುಱುಕು, ಕೞುಹು, ತಿೞುಹು, ಉಸುರು, ಉದುರು, ಬಿದುರು, ಬಸುಱು, ಅದುರು,

where the *i* of the second syllable has been altered into *u* so as to harmonise with the vowel of the suffix or last syllable.

Dialectic interchange.

A consideration of the dialectic interchange of letters is very important as it enables us to identify many words which, though appearing unconnected at first sight, are in reality the same. This interchange may be classed under two heads: interchange of vowels and interchange of consonants.

INTERCHANGE OF VOWELS.

(1) Initial *i*, either by itself or in combination with a consonant, of Tamil words, is generally changed into *e* in Kannaḍa and Telugu.

ಇಳ ಎಳ ಎಲ; ಶಿದಱು ಕೆದಱು ಚೆದಱು; ವಿಳಂಗು ಬೆಳಗು ವೆಲುಂಗು; ಶಿದರ್ ಗೆದರ್ ಚೆದಲು; ಶಿಱೈ ಸೆಱೆ ಚೆಱ; ಪಿಱ ಪೆಱ; ನಿಬಿರ್ ನೆಬಿರ್; ಇಡಱು ಎಡಱು; ಕಿೞವನ್ ಕೆೞವಂ; ಪಿಣಂ ಪೆಣಂ; ನಿಣಂ ನೆಣಂ; ಶಿಱಪ್ಪು ಚೆಱಪು. For further examples see under the next rule.

Exceptions: ಇಡು, ಇರುಳ್, ಇನಿದು, ಇಲಿ, ತಿಂಗಳ್, ಇಱು, ಇಡಿ, etc.

In ಕಡು ಚೆಡು ಕಿಡು; ಎದಿರ್ ಎದುರು ಇದಿರ್; ತೆಳಿವು ತೆಲವಿ ತಿಳಿವು; ಶೆವಿ ಚೆವಿ ಕಿವಿ; ನೆಡು ನಿಡು; ಎಱು ಇಱು; ಎಲ ಇಲ, etc., we see a converse change. But in Modern Kannaḍa in some cases the same forms—ಕಡು, ಎದಿರ್ occur.

(2) Final *ai* of Tamil words is changed into *e* in Kannaḍa and *a* in Telugu and Malayāḷam.

ಇರೈ ಎರೆ ಎರ; ತಲೈ ತಲೆ ತಲ; ಕೋರಿಕ್ಕೈ ಕೋರಿಕೆ ಕೋರಿಕ; ನಡತ್ತೈ ನಡತೆ ನಡತ; ಅಣೈ ಅಣೆ ಅನ; ಪಿಳ್ಳೈ ಪಿಳ್ಳೆ ಪಿಲ್ಲ; ಕೊಳ್ಳೈ ಕೊಳ್ಳೆ ಕೊಲ್ಲ; ಅರೈ ಅರೆ ಅರ; ತಂದೈ ತಂದೆ ತಂದ; ತಂಗೈ ತಂಗೆ ತಂಗ; ನಡತ್ತೈ ನಡತೆ ನಡತ್ತ; ಇಣೈ ಎಣೆ; ಇಡೈ ಎಡೆ; ಇರಲೈ ಎರಲೆ; ಪಿೞೈ ಪೆೞೆ; ಇಱೈ ಎಱೆ; ಇದೈ ಎದೆ; ತಿರೈ ತೆರೆ; ನಿನೈ ನೆನೆ; ನನೈ ನನೆ; ತೊಡೈ ತೊಡೆ; ಮೞೈ ಮೞೆ; ಕಡಲೈ ಕಡಲೆ; ಕುಡೈ ಕೊಡೆ; ಮಣೈ ಮಣೆ; ಪಡೈ ಪಡೆ; ಅಟ್ಟೈ ಅಟ್ಟೆ; ಅಟ್ಟೆ ಅಟ್ಟ.

(3) Initial *u*, either by itself or in combination with a consonant, of Tamil words, is generally changed into *o* in Kannaḍa and Telugu.

ಕುೞಿದು ಕೊೞಿದು ಕೊೞಿದು; ತುರೈ ದೊರೆ ದೊರ; ಮುಳೈ ಮೊಳೆ

ಮೊಲ; ಪುಗೞ್ ಪೊಗೞ್ ಪೊಗಡು; ಕುಳಂ ಕೊಳಂ ಕೊಲನು; ಉರರ್ ಒರರ್ ರೋಲು; ಕಾರರ್ ಕೊಱರ್; ಮುದರ್ ಮೊದರ್; ಉದವು ಒದವು; ಉದೈ ಒದೆ; ಉರೈ ಒರೆ; ಉಳದು ಒಳದು; ಪುನರ್ ಪೊನರ್; ಮುೞೈ ಮೊೞೆ; ತುೞೈ ತೊೞೆ; ಪುಡೈ ಪೊಡೆ; ನುಡೈ ನೊಡೆ; ಕುಡಂ ಕೊಡಂ.

Exceptions: ಉಡು, ಉಪ್ಪು, ಉಣ್, ಉದಿರ್, ಉೞು; ಶುಡು ಸುಡು; ಉಯಿರ್ ಉಸಿರ್; ಪುಗೈ ಪುಗೆ, etc.

In ಕೊಟ್ಟು ಕೊಟ್ಟು ಕುಟ್ಟು; ಕೊಡು ಕುಡು; ತೊಡು ತುಡು, etc., there is a converse change. But in Modern Kannaḍa the same forms—ಕೊಡು, ತೊಡು often occur.

(4) Final *a* of Tamil roots is changed into *e* in Kannaḍa.

ಇರ ಎರೆ; ಕಿಡ ಕೆಡೆ; ನಡ ನಡೆ; ಕೞ ಕೞೆ; ಮೞ ಮೞೆ; ಪುರ ಪೊರೆ; ಅಳ ಅಳೆ; ತಿೞ ತೇೞೆ; ಪರ ಪರೆ; ತುೞ ತೊೞೆ; ಮುಗ ಮೊಗೆ; ಕರ ಕರೆ.

(5) *Â* of some Tamil words is changed into *ē* in Kannaḍa and Telugu.

ನಾಣ್ ನೇಣ್; ನಾಯಿಱು ನೇಸಱು; ಶಾಣ್ ಗೇಣ್; ಮಾಡಂ ಮೇಡ; ಆರ್ ಏರು; ಆಱು ಏಱು; ನಾೞ್ ನೇನು; ಆಳ್ ಏಲು; ಯಾನೈ ಏನುಗು; ಆಂಡು ಏಂಡು; ಶಾಣ್ ಜೇನ.

In ಅಱು ಏಡು a short *a*, too, is changed into *ē*.

(6) A long vowel in Tamil is sometimes shortened in Kannaḍa and Telugu.

ಮೂಪ್ಪು ಮುಪ್ಪು ಮುಪ್ಪು; ಆರಾಯ್ ಆರಯ್ ಅರಯು; ತಪ್ಪಾದೇ ತಪ್ಪದೆ ತಪ್ಪಕ; ಆರ್ವಂ ಅರ್ವಂ ಅರುವಮು; ಅಱಿಯಾಮೈ ಅಱಿಯಮೆ; ಇಲ್ಲಾಮೈ ಇಲ್ಲಮೆ.

INTERCHANGE OF CONSONANTS.

(1) Uncombined medial and final *k* of Tamil words is changed into *g* in Kannaḍa and Telugu.

ಪುಕೞ್ ಪೊಗೞ್ ಪೊಗಡು; ಪುಕೈ ಪೊಗೆ ಪುಗ; ಪಕೈ ಪಗೆ ಪಗ; ಮುೞುಂಕು ಮುೞುಗು ಮುಣುಂಗು. ಅಕಲ್ ಅಗಲ್; ಅಕೞ್ ಅಗೞ್; ನಿಕೞ್ ನೆಗೞ್; ನಕೈ ನಗೆ; ಮುಕೈ ಮೊಗೆ; ಅರುಕು ಅರುಗು.

It has, however, to be stated that *k* in the above Tamil words is pronounced somewhat like *g*.

Initial *k*, too, is sometimes changed into *g*.

ಕೂನ್ ಗೂನ್ ಗೂನು; ಕುಂಡು ಗುಂಡು ಗುಂಡು; ಕೂಡೈ ಗೂಡೆ ಗೂಡ; ಕಿಳಿ ಗಿಳಿ; ಕೂಂಡು ಗೂಡು.

In some cases final double *k*, too, is changed into *g*.

ನೀಕ್ಕು ನೀಗು ನೀಁಗು ; ತೂಕ್ಕು ತೂಗು ತೂಁಗು ; ಮೂಕ್ಕು ಮೂಗು ; ವಡಕ್ಕು ಬಡಗು; ತೇಕ್ಕು ತೇಗು; ಅರಕ್ಕು ಅರಗು ; ತಾಕ್ಕು ತಾಗು; ಕಾಕ್ಕೈ ಕಾಗೆ.

(2) Uncombined *ś* of Tamil is generally changed into *s* in Kannaḍa and *ch* in Telugu.

ಶೆಂಡು ಸೆಂಡು ಚೆಂಡು (ಚೆಂಡು also in Modern Kannaḍa) ; ಶೀರೈ ಸೇರೆ ಚೇಲ ; ಶಿಱೈ ಸೆಱೆ ಚೆಱ ; ಶಾ ಸಾ ಚಚ್ಚು ; ಶೂರ್ ಸೂರ್ ; ಶುಡರ್ ಸೊಡರ್ ; ಶುಡು ಸುಡು ; ಶುಂಡು ಸುಂಡು ; ಶಿಲಂದಿ ಸಲಂದಿ ; ಪಶಲೈ ಪಸಲೆ ; ಕುಡಿಶೈ ಗುಡಿಸೆ ; ಅರಶು ಅರಸು.

In some cases initial *ś* is also changed into *ch* and *j* in Kannaḍa.

ಶೇಗು ಚೇಗು ; ಶೆಂಬು ಚೆಂಬುː ; ಶೆಪ್ಪೇಡು ಚೆಪ್ಪೇಡು ; ಶೆಕ್ಕೈ ಸೆಕ್ಕು (Old Kannaḍa), ಚಕ್ಕೆ (Modern Kannaḍa) ; ಶೋಱಂ ಜೋಱಂ ; ಶಲ್ಲಡೈ ಜಲ್ಲಡೆ ; ಶೋಡು ಜೋಡು ; ಶಿಣುಂಗು ಜಿನುಂಗು.

Besides the changes mentioned above, the letter *ś*, when an initial, followed by the vowels *i*, *ī*, *e*, *ē*, undergoes a further change into *k* in Kannaḍa, and *ch* in Telugu as before.

ಶಿಱು ಕಿಱು ಚಿಱು ; ಶಿದಱು ಕೆದಱು ಚೆದಱು ; ಶೆವಿ ಕಿವಿ ಚೆವಿ ; ಶೆಯ್ ಕೆಯ್ ಚೇನು ; ಶಿದಱ್ ಗೆದಱ್ ಚೆದಲು (here *ś* is changed into *g*). ಶಿಱಿ ಕಿಱಿ ; ಶಿಱೈ ಕೆಱೆ ; ಶಿಲದಿ ಕೞದಿ ; ಶಿಲರ್ ಕೆಲರ್ ; ಶಿಱೈ ಕೆಱೆ ; ಶಿೞಿಯರ್ ಕಿೞಿಯರ್ ; ಶೀ ಕೀ ; ಶೆಂ ಕೆಂ ; ಶೆರುಪ್ಪು ಕೆರ್ಪು ; ಶೆವಿಡು ಕಿವಿಡು ; ಶೇಱಿ ಕೇಱಿ ; ಶೇಁಱು ಕೆಸಱು ; ಶೇಁಬುː ಕೆಸವು ; ಶಿನಂ ಕಿನಿಸು.

Exceptions: ಶಿಲಂದಿ ಸಲಂದಿ ; ಶೇಗು ಚೇಗು ; ಶೇರ್ ಸೇರ್ ; ಶರ್ ಸರ್ ; ಶಿಱಪ್ಪು ಚೆಱಪು, etc.

In ಶಾಣ್ ಗೇಣ್ ಜೇನ, *ś* though followed by the vowel *ā* is changed into *g* in Kannaḍa and *j* in Telugu instead of into *k* and *ch* respectively as usual.

(3) Uncombined medial and final *t* of Tamil is generally changed into *d* in Kannaḍa and Telugu.

ಮುತರ್ ಮೊದರ್ ಮೊದಲು ; ಅತು ಅದು ಅದಿ ; ಇತು ಇದು ಇದಿ ; ಕತಿರ್ ಕದಿರ್ ಕದುರು ; ಕಾತಲ್ ಕಾದಲಂ ; ಅತಿರ್ ಅದಿರ್ ; ಉತೈ ಒದೆ ; ಓತು ಓದು.

It has, however, to be stated that *t* in the above Tamil words is pronounced somewhat like *d*.

Medial *t* is sometimes changed into *s* also:

ನುತರ್ ನೊಸರ್ ನೊಸಲು ; ಇತಟ್ ಎಸಟ್ ; ಮುತರೈ ಮೊಸರೆ.

In some cases initial *t*, too, is changed into *d*, and rarely into *s* and *j*.

ತಂದು ದಂಡು ದಂಡು ; ತಾಂತು ದಾಂಟು ದಾಟು ; ತುಡಿ ದುಡಿ ; ತಡಿ ದಡಿ ; ತುಯಿರ್ ಸುಸಿರ್ ; ತೋೞ್ ಸೋೞ್ ; ತೇಱ್ ಜೇಱ್.

(4) Medial *y* of Tamil is sometimes changed into *s* in Kannaḍa and Telugu.

ಉಯಿರ್ ಉಸಿರ್ ಉಸುರು ; ಪಯಱು ಪೆಸಱು ಪೆಸರು ; ಪೆಯರ್ ಪೆಸರ್ ; ಮಯಿರ್ ಮಸಿರ್ ; ತುಯಿಲ್ ಸುಸಿರ್ ; ನಾಯಿಱು ನೇಸಱು ; ವಯಿಱು ಬಸಿಱು ; ವೆಯಿಲ್ ಬಿಸಿಲ್ ; ಪೊಯ್ ಪುಸಿ. In ಪಯಱು ಪೆಸಱು ಪೆಸರು initial *a* is changed into *e*.

Y is rarely changed into *k* and *g* in Telugu and Kannaḍa. ವಾಯಿಲ್ ವಾಕಿಲಿ ಬಾಗಿಲ್.

(5) Initial *v* of Tamil is generally changed into *b* in Kannaḍa.

ವಾಯ್ ಬಾಯ್ ; ವಟ್ಟಿ ಬಟ್ಟೆ ; ವಟಿ ಬಟಿ ; ವಕೈ ಬಗೆ ; ವಾಳ್ ಬಾಳ್ ; ವಾಡ್ ಬಾಡ್ ; ವಿತಿರ್ ಬಿದಿರ್ ; ವರೈ ಬರೆ ; ವೆಯಿಲ್ ಬಿಸಿಲ್ ; ವೆತಿರ್ ಬಿದಿರ್ ; ವೀಶು ಬೀಸು.

It is sometimes changed into *m* also. ವತುವೈ ಮದುವೆ ; ವಿಂಜು ಮಿಂಚು.

(6) *Ṇ*, *ḻ* and *ḷ* of Tamil and Kannaḍa are respectively changed into *n*, *ḍ* and *l* in Telugu.

ಅಣ್ಣನ್ ಅಣ್ಣಂ ಅನ್ನ ; ಕಣ್ ಕಣ್ ಕನ್ನು ; ವೆಣ್ಣೆಯ್ ಬೆಣ್ಣೆ ವೆನ್ನ ; ಮಾಣ್ ಮಾಣ್ ಮಾನು ; ಪೂಣ್ ಪೂಣ್ ಪೂನು ; ಅಣೈ ಅಣೆ ಅನೆ ; ಅಣುಗು ಅನುಗು ; ಅಡ್ಡಣ ಅಡ್ಡನ ; ಅಣತಿ ಅನತಿ.

ಪುಕೞ್ ಪೊಗೞ್ ಪೊಗಡು ; ಏೞ್ ಏೞ್ ಏಡು ; ಪಾೞ್ ಪಾೞ್ ಪಾಡು ; ಅೞು ಅೞ್ ಏಡು ; ಕೋೞಿ ಕೋೞಿ ಕೋಡಿ ; ಅೞರ್ ಅೞರ್ ಅಡಲು ; ಊೞಿಯಂ ಊೞಿಗಂ ಊಡಿಗಮು ; ಕೞುವು ಕಡುಗು ; ಮೋೞಿ ಮೋಡಿ ; ತೆಗೞ್ ತೆಗಡು ; ಅೞಿಯಾಸೆ ಅಡಿಯಾಸ ; ಬೞರ್ ಬಡಲು.

ಕುಳಂ ಕೊಳಂ ಕೊಲನು ; ಮುಳೈ ಮೊಳೆ ಮೊಲ ; ಅಳ್ ಅಳ್ ಏಲು ; ಅಳವು ಅಳವು ಅಲವು ; ವಿಳಂಗು ಬೆಳಗು ವೆಲುಂಗು ; ಪಿಳ್ಳೈ ಪಿಳ್ಳೆ ಪಿಲ್ಲ ; ಇಳ ಎಳ ಎಲ ; ಕೊಳ್ಳೈ ಕೊಳ್ಳೆ ಕೊಲ್ಲ ; ಕಳ್ ಕಳ್ ಕಲ್ಲು ; ಅಗ್ಗಳಿಕೆ ಅಗ್ಗಲಿಕ ; ಅಳವಡು ಅಲವಡು.

Ḻ of Kannaḍa and Tamil is also changed into *r* and *ṇ* in Telugu. *R* occurs as the subscript of the first syllable in place of *ḻ* of the second syllable.

ಪೊೞಿಲ್ ಪೊೞಲ್ ಪ್ರೋಲು ; ಪೞೈಯತು ಪೞದು ಪ್ರಾತ ; ಕೀೞೇ ಕೆೞಗೆ ಕ್ರಿಂದ ; ಮುೞಂಗು ಮೊೞಗು ಮ್ರೋಗು ; ಪೊೞುತು ಪೊೞ್ತು ಪ್ರೊದ್ದು ; ಕೊೞುಪ್ಪು ಕ್ರೊವ್ವು ; ವಿೞುಂಗು ವ್ರಿಂಗು ; ಮುೞುಕು ಮುೞುಗು ಮ್ರುಣುಗು.

(7) Medial nasals of Tamil words generally disappear in Kannaḍa and sometimes in Telugu.

ಉಱಂಗು ಒಱಗು ಒಱಗು ; ಐಂದು ಐದು ಐದು ; ವಿೞುಂದು ಬಿೞ್ದು ; ಅೞುಂದು ಅೞ್ದು ; ಪರುಂದು ಪರ್ದು ; ತುಲಂಗು ತೊಳಗು ; ನೀಂಗು ನೀಗು ; ತಾಂಗು ತಾಗು ; ತೋಂಡು ತೋಡು ; ಪೊರುಂದು ಪೊರ್ದು ; ಇರುಂದು ಇರ್ದು ; ಕರುಂಬು ಕರ್ಬು ; ಪರಂಬು ಪರ್ಬು ; ಎಲುಂಬು ಎಲ್ವು ; ಉಣಂಗು ಒಣಗು ; ಕುರುಂದೈ ಕುರುದೆ ; ಕೂಂದು ಗೂಡು ; ವೀಂಗು ಬೀಗು ; ಕೂಂದರ್ ಕೂದರ್ ; ಮೂನ್ಱು ಮೂಱು.

But Telugu retains the nasal in a good number of words.

ಮರುಂದು ಮರ್ದು ಮಂದು ; ವಿರುಂದು ಬಿರ್ದು ವಿಂದು ; ಇರಂಡು ಎರಡು ರೆಂಡು ; ವೇಂಡು ಬೇಡು ವೇಂಡು ; ವಿಳಂಗು ಬೆಳಗು ವೆಲುಂಗು ; ಮುೞಂಗು ಮೊೞಗು ಮ್ರೋಂಗು.

In ಅಡಂಗು ಅಡಂಗು, ತಾಂಡು ದಾಂಟು, ತೂಂಬು ತೂಂಬು, ಎೞುಂಬು ಇೞುಂಪೆ, ಶಿಣುಂಗು ಜಿನುಂಗು, etc., the nasal is retained in Old Kannaḍa but disappears in Modern Kannaḍa. Telugu also retains the nasal in the first three words, but in the third *b* disappears (ತೂಮು).

In ವೇಂಬು ಬೇವು, ಪಾಂಬು ಪಾವು, ಕಾಂಬು ಕಾವು there is the change of *b* into *v* along with the disappearance of the nasal. Telugu, however, retains the nasal in the first two words but omits *b* as in ತೂಂಬು. The words become ವೇಮು and ಪಾಮು in it.

It has to be noted that rule 7 does not apply to the penultimate nasals of dissyllabic words with short initials.

ಅಂಜು ಅಂಜು ; ಪೊಂಗು ಪೊಂಗು ; ತಂಡು ದಂಡು ; ಅಂಬು ಅಂಬು ; ಶುಂಡು ಸುಂಡು ; ತೆಂಗು ತೆಂಗು ; ತಂಗು ತಂಗು ; etc. The first four are the same in Telugu also.

Exception : ಕನ್ಱು ಕಱು.

(8) Medial *ru* and *ḻu* of Tamil words generally lose *u* in Kannaḍa.

ಒರುಮೈ ಒರ್ಮೆ ; ಇರುಮೈ ಇರ್ಮೆ ; ಕೞುತ್ತೈ ಕೞ್ತೆ ; ಪೊೞುತು ಪೊೞ್ತು ; ಅೞುಕ್ಕೈ ಅೞ್ಕೆ ; ಉೞುತು ಉೞ್ತು.

U disappears along with the nasal (rule 7) in words such as the following :—

ಮರುಂದು ಮರ್ದು ; ತಿರುಂದು ತಿರ್ದು ; ಒರುಂಗು ಒರ್ಗು ; ಶುರುಂಗು

ಸುಕರ್ಱ್ ; ಪೊರುಂದು ಪೊರ್ದ್ಱ್ ; ಕರುಂಬು ಕರ್ಬ್ಱ್ ; ಪರುಂದು ಪರ್ದ್ಱ್ ; ಪುೞುಂಗು ಪುೞ್ಗು ; ಮೞುಂಗು ಮೞ್ಗು.

Exceptions : ಅರುಕು ಅರುಗು ; ಮುೞುಕು ಮುೞುಗು.

In some cases *r* and *ḻ* change their places.

ಎರುತು ಎೞ್ತು ; ಅರುತ್ತಿ ಅೞ್ತಿ ; ಪರುತ್ತಿ ಪೞ್ತಿ ; ಉೞುಂದು ಉರ್ದ್ಱ್ ; ಕೊೞುಪ್ಪು ಕೊಬ್ಱ್.

(9) Final double consonants, and sometimes medial ones, too, of Tamil words become single in Kaṅnaḍa and Telugu.

ಪೇಟ್ಟೈ ಪೇಟೆ ಪೇಟ ; ಶರಕ್ಕು ಸರಕು ಸರಕು ; ತೋಪ್ಪು ತೋಪು ತೋಪು ; ಕೋಟ್ಟೈ ಕೋಂಟೆ or ಕೋಟೆ ಕೋಟ ; ವೇಟ್ಟೈ ಬೇಂಟೆ or ಬೇಟೆ ವೇಟ ; ಆಟ್ಟಂ ಆಟಂ ಆಟ ; ಕೂಟ್ಟಂ ಕೂಟಂ ಕೂಟಮು ; ತೋಟ್ಟಂ ತೋಂಟಂ or ತೋಟಂ ತೋಟ ; ಓಟ್ಟಂ ಓಟಂ ; ಊಟ್ಟಂ ಊಟಂ.

This rule does not apply to double consonants which are the finals of dissyllabic words with short initials.

ಶಕ್ಕೈ ಸೆಕ್ಕೆ or ಚೆಕ್ಕೆ ; ಪತ್ತು ಪತ್ತು ; ಮೆಚ್ಚು ಮೆಚ್ಚು ಮೆಚ್ಚು ; ಪಚ್ಚೈ ಪಚ್ಚೆ ಪಚ್ಚ ; ಕಟ್ಟು ಕಟ್ಟು ಕಟ್ಟು ; ಉಪ್ಪು ಉಪ್ಪು ಉಪ್ಪು.

(10) *Nṟ* of Tamil words is generally changed into *nd*, and sometimes into *ṇṭ* and *ṇḍ*, in Kannaḍa and Teḷugu, and into *nn* in Malayāḷam.

ಪನ್ಱಿ ಪಂದಿ ಪಂದಿ ; ಒನ್ಱು ಒಂದು ಒಂದು ; ಕುನ್ಱು ಕುಂದು ಕುಂದು ; ಕನ್ಱು ಕಂದು ಕಂದು ; ಪೊನ್ಱು ಪೊಂದು ; ಅನ್ಱು ಅಂದು ; ಇನ್ಱು ಇಂದು ; ಎನ್ಱು ಎಂದು ; ಒನ್ಱು ಒಂದು (1) ; ಕನ್ಱು ಕಂದು (young plantain tree) ; ನಿನ್ಱು ನಿಂದು ; ಕೊನ್ಱು ಕೊಂದು ; ಕುನ್ಱಂ ಕುಂದಂ (ಮಣ್ ಕುನ್ಱಂ ಮಂಕುಂದ ; ಪೊಱ್ಕುನ್ಱಂ ಹೊಂಕುಂದ.)

ಒನ್ಱಿ ಒಂಟಿ ಒಂಟಿ ; ತಿನ್ಱಿ ತಿಂಡಿ ತಿಂಡಿ ; ಕುನ್ಱಂ ಕೊಂಡ.

ಮೂನ್ಱು ಮೂನ್ನು ; ಕನ್ಱು ಕನ್ನು ; ಶಯ್‌ಕಿನ್ಱ ಚೆಯ್ಯುನ್ನ.

(11) *Ṭṭr* (ற்ற) of Tamil words is generally changed into *t* and *ṭ* and sometimes into *ṭ* and *t* also in Kannaḍa and Telugu.

ಶುಱ್ಱು ಸುತ್ತು ಚುಟ್ಟು ; ಪಱ್ಱು ಪತ್ತು ಪಟ್ಟು ; ಮಾಱ್ಱಂ ಮಾತು ಮಾಟ ; ಕುಱ್ಱುಯಿರ್ ಕುಸ್ತುಸಿರ್ ಕುಟ್ಟುಸುರು ; ಶಿಱ್ಱಿಲ ಕಿತ್ತಿಲ ಚಿಟ್ಟೆಲುಕ ; ವಱ್ಱು ಬತ್ತು ; ತುಱ್ಱು ತುತ್ತು ; ಒಱ್ಱಿ ಒತ್ತೆ ; ಕುಱ್ಱಂ ಕುತ್ತಂ ; ಪುಱ್ಱು ಪುತ್ತು ; ಮಱ್ಱೈ ಮತ್ತೆ ; ಮುಱ್ಱಿರ್ ಮುತ್ತರ್ ; ಪೆಱ್ಱು ಪೆತ್ತು ; ಉಱ್ಱು ಉತ್ತು. ಶುಱ್ಱಂ ಚುಟ್ಟಮು ; ಊಱ್ಱು ಊಟೆ ಊಟ ; ನಾಱ್ಱು ನಾಟ ; ನೆಱ್ಱಿ ನೆತ್ತಿ ; ಏಱ್ಱಂ ಏತಂ ಏತಮು.

(12) *Ṟ* of Tamil and Kannaḍa words is generally changed into *d* and *j* in Tuḷu and sometimes into *t*.

ನೂಱು ನೂಱು ನೂದು ; ಪೊಱ್ತ್ತು ಪೋಱೆ ಪುದೆ ; ಉಱ್ತ್ತು ಒಱೆ ಉದೆ ; ಮುಱಿ ಮುಱಿ ಮುದಿ ; ಮಱೆ ಮಱೆ ಮದೆ ; ಶಿಱ್ತ್ತು ಕೆಱೆ ಕೆದು.

ಮೂನ್ರು ಮೂಱು ಮೂಜಿ ; ಅಱು ಅಱು ಆಜಿ ; ಕನ್ರು ಕಱು ಕಂಜಿ ; ವೆಱುಂ ಬಱು ಬಜಿ ; ವೇಱೆ ಬೇಱೆ ಬೇತೆ.

Ḻ is generally changed into *r* and sometimes into *ṇ*, and *ḷ* into *ṇ*.

ಕೋೞಿ ಕೋೞಿ ಕೋರಿ ; ಕುೞಿ ಕುೞಿ ಗುರಿ ; ಪೞೈಯದು ಪೞದು ಪರತ್ ; ಪುಕೞ್ ಪೊಗೞ್ ಪುಗರ್. ಕೞಲೆ ಕಣಲೆ ; ಗೞ ಗಣೆ. ಕೊಳ್ ಕೊಳ್ ಕೊಣ್ ; ಕೇಳ್ ಕೇಳ್ ಕೇಣ್.

Ṟ and *ḻ* are also changed into *r* and *ḷ* respectively, as in Modern Kannaḍa.

ಕೊಱು ಕುಱು ಕುರಿ ; ಶಿಱ್ತ್ತು ಸೆಱೆ ಸೆರೆ ; ಮೀಱು ಮೀಱು ಮೀರ್ ; ಉಱಂಗು ಒಱಗು ಒರಗ್ ; ಏೞ್ ಏೞ್ ಏಳ್ ; ಶುೞಿ ಸುೞಿ ಸುಳಿ ; ಪಾೞ್ ಪಾೞ್ ಪಾಳ್ ; ವಾೞ್ ಬಾೞ್ ಬಾಳ್.

(13) Many words in Tamil and Kannaḍa become altered in Telugu by displacement of their letters, especially by the first and second letters changing their places.*

ಅವರ್ ಅವರ್ ವಾರು ; ಉಕಿರ್ ಉಗುರ್ ಗೋರು ; ಉರಲ್ ಒರಲ್ ರೋಲು ; ಇಲ್ಲಾಮೈ ಇಲ್ಲಮೆ ಲೇಮಿ ; ಉಳ್ ಒಳ್ ಲೋ ; ಇೞೈಯದು ಎೞದು ಲೇತ ; ಅಕಾತು ಅಗದು ಕಾದು ; ಇವಕ್ಕು ಇವಗ್ಗೆ ವೀರಿಕಿ ; ಇರಂಡು ಎರಡು ರೆಂಡು ; ಇರ್ ಇರ್ ರೇ ; ಇರಾ ರೇಯಿ ; ಇಱ್ತ್ತು ಱೇಡು.

The examples given under the rules mentioned above are sufficient to give one some idea of the number of common words that occur somewhat disguised in these languages. They also show the closer similarity of the Tamil and Kannaḍa words than those of other languages.

---

* This displacement sometimes occurs in Modern Kannaḍa also, especially when the second letter is *h* : ಅಹಗೆ ಹಾಗೆ ; ಇಹಗೆ ಹೀಗೆ ; ಎಹಗೆ ಹೇಗೆ ; ಅಹುದು ಹವುದು ; ಅಹನು ಹೇನು, ಅಹನು ಹಾನು, etc.

CHAPTER III.

GRAMMAR.

Inflexion of nouns. Gender and number. Case. The nominative. Inflexional increments. The second case. The third and fifth cases. The fourth case. The sixth case. The seventh case. The vocative case. Adjectives. Numerals. Pronouns. Inclusive and exclusive. Verbs. Roots. Pronominal terminations. The past and future tenses. The present tense. The negative mood. Causative verbs. Appellative verbs. The imperative. The infinitive. The relative participle. The verbal participle. The passive voice. Indeclinables. Formation of words. Verbal nouns. Participial nouns. Abstract nouns. Derivative nouns. Com-pound nouns.

INFLEXION OF NOUNS.

IN the Dravidian languages the particles employed in nominal inflexions and in the declension of nouns are, generally speaking, nouns, *e.g.*, ಚೆಲ, ಚೆಲತ, ಉಳ್, etc. But the dative ಕು, ಕಿ, ಗೆ, ಕೆ seems to have lost its original meaning. Kannaḍa, like Tamil and Telugu, possesses not only proper, common and abstract nouns, but also appellative, verbal and participial nouns.

Gender and number.

In Tamil, nouns are divided into ಉಯರ್ ತಿಣೈ high caste, rational, and ಅಃಱಿಣೈ casteless, irrational. Similarly, there is a division of nouns into *mahat* (majors) and *amahat* (minors) in Telugu. The first term in both languages denotes masculine and feminine nouns and the second neuter nouns. Kannaḍa agrees with Tamil in distinguishing between rational and irrational objects in its gender, and in possessing, unlike Telugu which is destitute of the feminine singular, all the three genders of the third person singular. Telugu, as stated before, uses the neuter for the feminine singular, but it has a rational plural. The Tamil terminations for the masculine singular are ಅನ್ (*an*), ಆನ್ (*ān*); in Kannaḍa the termination is ಅನ್ (ಅಂ), *an* (*am*); and in Telugu the terminations are ಡು (*ḍu*),' ಉಡು (*uḍu*), ಅಡು, (*aḍu*). Though *an* is not seen in the Telugu terminations, we find it clearly in the words ವಾನಿಕಿ, ವೀನಿಕಿ. ಪೊನ್ನನ್, ಪಾವಾರ್ನನ್; ಪೊನ್ನನ್, ಪಾರ್ವನ್; ಅತಂಡು, ರಾಮುಂಡು. According to a phonetic rule in Kannaḍa, final *n* is changed into *m*, so that the above examples become ಪೊನ್ನಂ, ಪಾರ್ವಂ. In Modern Kannaḍa the suffix is *anu*, where the final *u* is merely a euphonic addition. It will thus be seen that the suffix in both Tamil and Kannaḍa is the same, namely, *an*, the longer form *ān* being only a euphonic variation retained in Tamil. The suffixes for the feminine singular in Tamil are ಅಳ್ (*aḷ*), ಆಳ್ (*āḷ*); and in Kannaḍa ಅಳ್ (*aḷ*). ಪೆರಿಯಾಳ್, ಇಲ್ಲಾಳ್; ಪಿರಿಯಳ್, ನಲ್ಲಳ್. There are besides three other suffixes which are the same in both Tamil and Kannaḍa—ಇತಿ (*iti*), ತಿ (*ti*) and ಇ (*i*). ಪಿರಾಮಣತ್ತಿ, ವಣ್ಣಾತ್ತಿ, ಮನ್ನೈವಿ; ಚಾಮರಿಗಿತಿ, ಪೊಲತಿ, ಸುಬ್ಬಿ. The only difference is the doubling of *t* in Tamil which is likewise the case in Modern Kannaḍa, *e.g.*, ಅಗಸಗಿತ್ತಿ. The corresponding suffix in Telugu is ಕತ್ತೆ (*katte*): ಚೆಲಕತ್ತೆ, ಪನಿಕತ್ತೆ. The suffixes ಅಲು (*alu*) and ಆಲು (*ālu*) also occur in Telugu corresponding to *aḷ* and *āḷ* of Tamil: ಮರದಲು, ಪೇದರಾಲು. In ಪೇದರಾಲು, ಗುಣವಂತುರಾಲು, etc., *r* is used to prevent hiatus, the termination being *ālu*. Further, the suffix ಅದಿ (*adi*) occurs in Telugu in place of *iti* of Kannaḍa: ಗೊಲ್ಲದಿ, ಗೊಲ್ಲತಿ. Another termination occurring in Tamil is ಐ (*ai*), the phonetic equivalent of which in Kannaḍa is, as stated before, *e*: ಮಡಂದೈ, ಮಂಗೈ, ತೆರಿವೈ; ಜೋಡೆ, ಪಾಣ್ಬೆ, ಸಿತಗೆ. *Âḷ* of Tamil and *ālu* of Telugu have no corresponding suffix in Kannaḍa, which has only *aḷ*. The neuter singular suffixes in Tamil and Kannaḍa are ಅಂ (*am*) and ಅದು (*adu*)—sometimes only *du*: ಮರಂ, ನಿಲಂ, ಪೆರಿಯದು, ಪೆರಿದು; ಮರಂ, ನೆಲಂ, ಪಿರಿಯದು, ಪಿರಿದು. The Telugu suffixes are ಮು (*mu*) or ವು (*vu*) and ಅದಿ (*adi*): ಪಲಮು, ಗೋವು, ಚಿನ್ನದಿ. *Du* sometimes appears as *tu* in Kannaḍa, *e.g.*, ಒಳ್ಳಿತು, ಮೆಲ್ಲಿತು. In Tamil and Telugu verbal nouns are formed by the suffixes *adu* and *adi* respectively; *adu* is likewise used in Modern Kannaḍa in some parts of the Kannaḍa country for this purpose, though in other parts the intermediate demonstrative *udu* is made use of instead of the remote demonstrative *adu* as is uniformly the case in Old Kannaḍa. ವರುವದು is ಬರುವದು in some parts of the Kannaḍa country, but ಬರುವುದು elsewhere and ಬರ್ಪುದು in Old Kannaḍa. ಶೆಯ್ವದು ಕೆಯ್ವುದು; ಕಾಣ್ಬದು, ಕಾಣ್ಬುದು; ವಂದದು, ಬಂದುದು; ಕೊಂಡದು, ಕೊಂಡುದು. The singular neuter noun is often used in a plural sense in these languages: ಕುದಿರೈ ವಂದದು, ಕುದಿರೈ ವಂದನ; ಕುದುರೆ ಬಂದುದು, ಕುದುರೆ ಬಂದುವು. Neuter nouns are rarely pluralised, and in Koḍagu they have no plural at all.

The suffixes of the epicene plural, which are common to Tamil and Kannaḍa, are *ar*, *kaḷ* or *gaḷ* and *var*: ಅವರ್ ಅವರ್; ಇವರ್ ಇವರ್; ಅರಶರ್ ಅರಸರ್; ಮಕ್ಕಳ್ ಮಕ್ಕಳ್; ಗುರುಕ್ಕಳ್ ಗುರುಗಳ್; ವೀರರ್ಕಳ್ ವೀರರ್ಗಳ್; ಅವರ್ಕಳ್ ಅವರ್ಗಳ್; ಮೂವರ್ ಮೂವರ್; ನಾಲ್ವರ್ ನಾಲ್ವರ್. In Tamil there are also the suffixes *mar* and *mār* which are represented by *bar* and sometimes by *vir* in Kannaḍa. *Mar* and *bar* are merely euphonic variations of *var*: ಎಣ್ಮರ್ ಎಣ್ಬರ್, ಪದಿನ್ಮರ್ ಪದಿಂಬರ್; ತಂದೆಮಾರ್ ತಂದೆವಿರ್; ತಾಯ್ಮಾರ್ ತಾಯ್ವರ್; ದೇವಿಮಾರ್ ತಂಬಿಮಾರ್. Another rational plural suffix common to Tamil and Kannaḍa is *ir*, though the lengthened form *īr* is also used in Tamil. ಪೆಂಡಿರ್ ಪೆಂಡಿರ್; ಮಕಳಿರ್, ತೊಟ್ಟಿರ್; ನೀವಿರ್. Kannaḍa has another rational plural suffix *dir* with nothing corresponding to it in Tamil. ಅವಂದಿರ್ ಅವಳ್ದಿರ್; ಮಗಂದಿರ್ ಮಗಳ್ದಿರ್; ಅಣ್ಣಂದಿರ್ ಅಕ್ಕಂದಿರ್. The plural suffix corresponding to the Tamil-Kannaḍa *kaḷ* or *gaḷ* is *lu* in Telugu and *kuḷu* in Tuḷu. ರಾಮುಲು, ಕವುಲು, ಪೆದ್ದಲು; ಗುರುಕುಳು, ನೀಕುಳು (compare ನೀಂಗಳ್ in Tamil and Kannaḍa). The Tamil-Kannaḍa *var* is generally represented by *vuru* or *guru* in Telugu. ಇರುವರ್ ಇರ್ವರ್ ಇರುವುರು or ಇರುಗುರು (also ಇದ್ದರು); ನಾಲ್ವರ್ ನಾಲ್ವರ್ ನಲುವುರು or ನಲುಗುರು. The double plural *ar-gaḷ* occurs in all these languages : ಅವರ್ಕಳ್ ಅವರ್ಗಳ್ ವಾರಲು. The termination of the neuter plural in Tamil and Kannaḍa is *gaḷ* and in Telugu *lu*. ಮರಂಗಳ್ ಮರಂಗಳ್ ವೃಕ್ಷಮುಲು ; ಉಕಿರ್ಕಳ್ ಉಗುರ್ಗಳ್ ಗೋರುಲು ; ಕೊಂಡಲು, ಅವುಲು. *Avai*, another suffix in Tamil, appears as *avu* and *uvu* in Kannaḍa, as *avi* in Telugu and as *ava* in Malayāḷam. ಪೆರಿಯವೈ ಪಿರಿಯವು ಪೆದ್ದವಿ ಪೆರಿಯವ ; ವಂದವೈ ಬಂದುವು ವಚ್ಚಿನವಿ ವಂದವ. The suffixes *an*, *aḷ* and *ar* are no doubt shortened forms of the pronouns *avan*, *avaḷ* and *avar*. In Kūi *āñu* means a man and *ālu* a woman. In Telugu, too, *ālu* means a woman. Compare *āñu* with *āṇ*, a male, and *āḷ* with *ālu*, a woman. We may thus explain perhaps the longer forms *ān* and *āḷ*.

Case.

As stated before, unlike the Indo-European languages which use two different sets of terminations for the singular and the plural, the Draviḍian languages use the same set of case signs for both numbers, the case ending being added to the base in the singular and to the sign of plurality in the plural.

The nominative.

In Tamil and Kannaḍa the crude base itself, without any addition or alteration, becomes, in very many cases, the nominative singular : ಪುಲ್ ಪುಲ್ ; ಮನೈ ಮನೆ ; ಪುಲ ಪುಲ ; ಆಳ್ ಆಳ್ ; ಪೆಣ್ ಪೆಣ್. The same is the case, to some extent, in Telugu also, though words of this language do not, as a rule, end in consonants : ಚೆವಿ, ಮಾಟ, ನಿಪ್ಪು, ತಿನ್ನು. But, masculine bases ending in *a* take *an* as their nominative termination in Tamil and Kannaḍa, and *ḍu* in Telugu. As stated before, *an* becomes *am* in Kannaḍa : ದೇವನ್ ದೇವಂ ದೇವುಡು ; ಶುಬ್ಬನ್ ಸುಬ್ಬಂ ಸುಬ್ಬುಡು. Neuter bases in *a* take *am* or *an* as their termination in both Tamiḷ and Kannaḍa, the remark about the masculine suffix *an* in Kannaḍa applying to the neuter suffix also. ಕುಳಂ ಕುಳನ್, ಕೊಳಂ. Though *n* of the Kannaḍa masculine suffix is changed into *bindu* when final, it resumes its former shape when followed by a vowel, but this is optional with the neuter suffix : ದೇವಂ ; but ದೇವಂ + ಅಂ = ದೇವನಂ ; ಕೊಳಂ ; but ಕೊಳಂ + ಅಂ = ಕೊಳಮಂ or ಕೊಳನಂ. In Telugu neuter bases in *a* generally take *mu* as their nominative termination : ಗುಣಮು, ಅನ್ನಮು.

Inflexional increments.

The inflexional increments used in Tamil and Kannaḍa are almost the same, as is also the mode of forming the oblique bases. The following table shows the similarity in the formation of the inflexional base of the oblique cases in the two languages :—

		Base.	*Inflexional increment.*	*Oblique base.*	*Examples.*
(1)	Tamil	ಮರಂ	ಅತ್ತು attu	ಮರತ್ತು	ಮರತ್ತುಳ್
	Kannaḍa	ಮರಂ	ಅದ್ ad	ಮರದ್	ಮರದೊಳ್
(2)	Tamil	ಗುರು	ಇನ್ in	ಗುರುವಿನ್	ಗುರುವಿನುಳ್
	Kannaḍa	ಗುರು	ಇನ್ in	ಗುರುವಿನ್	ಗುರುವಿನೊಳ್
(3)	Tamil	ಪಲ	ಅಱ್ಱು aṭṭru	ಪಲವಱ್ಱು	ಪಲವಱ್ಱುಳ್
	Kannaḍa	ಪಲ	ಅಱ್ aṟ	ಪಲವಱ್	ಪಲವಱೊಳ್

In (1) and (3) the Tamil inflexional increment is nothing but the Kannaḍa increment with its final doubled and *u* added. In (2) the increment is the same in both the languages, and its use is likewise optional in both. There are some inflexional increments in Telugu also which are known as *aupavibhaktịkas.* These are *ṭi, ti, i.* ಅನ್ನಟಿನಿ, ನಾಂಗಟಿಚೇ from ನಾಂಗಲಿ; ಪೇತಿಚೇ from ಪೇಯಿ, ಚೇತಿರೊಬೇ from ಚೇಯಿ; ಮ್ರಾನಿನಿ from ಮ್ರಾನು, ಚೋಟಿನಿ from ಚೋಟು. It will be seen that these do not exactly correspond to the ones in Tamil and Kannaḍa. *I* has to be looked upon rather as a change of vowel due to vocalic harmony than as an inflexional increment. The Telugu increment corresponding to *in* of the other languages is *ni* or *na* : ದಿನಕಿ, ಗುರುವುನಕು. In Tamil and Telugu oblique bases formed by the addition of inflexional increments are capable of being used alone without case suffixes and bear the signification of genitives : ಮರತ್ತು, ಚೇತಿ, ವಾಕಿಟಿ. This is not, however, the case with Kannaḍa.

The second case.

The termination for the second case is *ai* in Tamil, *e* in Malayāḷam, *am* in Kannaḍa and *nu* or *ni* in Telugu : ಎನ್ನೈ, ಎನ್ನೆ,

ಎನ್ನಂ, ನನ್ನು ದರಿದ್ರುನಿ. *An* also occurs in Telugu as the suffix for the second case: ದೊರಣ, ದೊರಲಣ. In Modern Kannaḍa *am* is shortened into *a* by the omission of the *bindu*. Kannaḍa uses no inflexional increment in the second case after neuter bases in *a*, while Modern Tamil invariably uses *attu*: ದೇವನ್ನೈ, ದೇವನಂ ದೇವನ ; ಮರತ್ತೈ, ಮರನಂ ಮರವುಂ. If we take *a* as the Kannaḍa suffix, we may connect it with the *ai* of Tamil, since *ai* in Tamil is sometimes changed into *a* in Kannaḍa, *e.g.*, ಇಲ್ಲೈ ಇಲ್ಲ, ಪೈಂ ಪಂ.

The third and fifth cases.

In Kannaḍa the same suffix *im* is used for both the instrumental and oblative cases. There is, however, a so-called oblative suffix *attaṇim* which is merely the *im* of the instrumental with a demonstrative *attaṇ* prefixed to it. The same is the case in Tamil also, in Old Tamil at any rate. Though the present instrumental terminations in Tamil are *āl* and *ān* to which there is no suffix answering in Kannaḍa, still in Old Tamil occurs the suffix *in*, *e.g.*, ನಿನ್ನಿಱಂದ *ninniṟ-ṟanda* (given by you), which is the same as the Kannaḍa suffix. And the oblative suffix in Tamil is also *in* or *il*. The Telugu suffixes for the third case are *chēta* and its contraction *chē*, and for the fifth case *valana* and *kaṇṭe*. The suffix for the social or conjunctive case in Tamil is *ōḍu* or *uḍan*, in Kannaḍa *oḍane* and in Telugu *tōḍa*, or *tō*. Some scholars connect the Telugu *tōḍa* with the Tamil word *tōḻa* which means a companion or friend and believe that the radical *t* has been lost in the Tamil and Kannaḍa suffixes. Other suffixes for the third case in Kannaḍa are *indam* and *inde*. In Baḍaga the suffix is *end* and in Toda *edd*.

The fourth case.

The suffix for the fourth case is *ku* in Tamil, *ke* or *ge* in Kannaḍa and *ki* or *ku* in Telugu. ಮನ್ನೈಕ್ಕು ಕುಳಕ್ಕು ; ಮನೆಗೆ ಕೊಳಕ್ಕೆ ; ತಲ್ಲಿಕಿ ತಲಕು. The forms ಕುಳಕ್ಕು, ಕಯುಕ್ಕು are found only in Old Tamil poetry, Modern Tamil invariably inserting the inflexional increment *attu* between the base and the suffix: ಕುಳತ್ತುಕ್ಕು, ಕಯುತ್ತುಕ್ಕು. In Kannaḍa no inflexional increment is used. In Telugu grammars *ki* and *ku* are mentioned as genitive suffixes and *kai* as the dative suffix : ಧರ್ಮಮುಕ್ಕೈ. *Ku* is also the suffix in Malayāḷam and *ikka* or *ikki* in the Behistun tablets. ನಿನಕ್ಕು, ನೀ ಇಕ್ಕ, ನೀ ಇಕ್ಕಿ (to thee).

The sixth case.

The only suffix for the sixth case in Kannaḍa is *a* : ಪುಲಿಯ, ಮನೆಯ, ಅವನ, ಎನ್ನ, ತನ್ನ, ನಿನ್ನ, ಮರದ. This suffix also occurs as the genitive of personal and reflexive pronouns in Tamil, Telugu and Tuḷu : ಎನ, ನಿನ, ತನ; ತನ, ತಮ, ಮನ ; ಯಾನ, ನಿನ. As stated before, oblique bases are used as genitives in Tamil and Telugu, but not in Kannaḍa : ಮರತ್ತು, ಚೇತಿ. Another suffix common to Tamil and Kannaḍa is *adu* : ಅವನದು ಅವನದು, ಎನದು ಎನ್ನದು, ನಿನದು, ನಿನ್ನದು, Kannaḍa has besides the forms *atu* and *attu* to express the genitive : ಎನತು ಎನತ್ತು, ನಿನತು ನಿನತ್ತು, ತನತು ತನತ್ತು. Other suffixes given are *uḍaiya* in Tamil and *yokka*, *lō* and *lōpala* in Telugu : ಇರಾಮನುಡ್ಡೈಯ, ಚೆಟ್ಟುಯೊಕ್ಕ, ಏಟಿರೋ, ಕೊಂಡಲರೋಪಲ. *Lō* is, properly speaking, a locative suffix corresponding to the Tamil *uḷ* and the Kannaḍa *oḷ*.

The seventh case.

The suffixes for the seventh case in Kannaḍa are *oḷ* and *alli* which correspond to *uḷ* and *il* of Tamil and *lō* and *andu* of Telugu : ಮನೆಯೊಳ್ ಮನೈಯುಳ್ ಇಂಟಿರೋ ; ಮರದೊಳ್ ಮರತ್ತಿಳ್ ಮ್ರಾನಿರೋ ; ವಚನದಲ್ಲಿ ವಚನತ್ತಿಲ್ ವಚನಮುನಂದು. Another suffix in Telugu is *na* : ತೂರ್ಪುನ.

The vocative case.

The changes that nouns undergo in the vocative case are more or less the same in Kannaḍa, Tamil and Telugu. ರಾಮ ರಾಮಾ ರಾಮನೇ, ದೇವ ದೇವಾ ದೇವನೇ, ರಾಮುಡ ರಾಮುಡಾ. In the plural *ira* is the suffix in Kannaḍa, *ir* or *īr* in Tamil and *āra* in Telugu : ದೇವರ್ಕಳಿರ ನಂಬಿರಿರ, ಶೆಟ್ಟಿರ್ ಶಾಸ್ತ್ರೀರ್, ರಾಮುರಾರ.

ADJECTIVES.

In the Draviḍian languages adjectives are not compared. They are prefixed to substantives without any declensional change. Dr. Caldwell's statement that Draviḍian adjectives, properly so called, are nouns of quality or relation, which acquire the signification of adjectives merely by being prefixed to substantive nouns, does not appear to be quite correct. Tamil and Kannaḍa, as well as Telugu to some extent, possess words which are as much entitled to be called adjectives as good, long, short, etc., are in English. ನನ್ಮೈ ನಲ್ಮೆ (goodness) may properly be called a noun of quality; but as soon as the suffix *mai* or *me* (ness) is removed we have only an adjective of quality ನಲ್ ನಲ್ (good). left. The word that is prefixed to a substantive is not ನನ್ಮೈ ನಲ್ಮೆ, which is supposed to acquire an adjectival meaning as soon as it is put before the noun, but the primitive ನಲ್ ನಲ್ from which ನನ್ಮೈ ನಲ್ಮೆ is derived. Exception may indeed be taken to the so-called adjectives such as ಶುಧಮಾನ ಪೆರುನ್ಮೈಯಾನ, ಪಣಮುಳ್ಳ ; ಶುಧವಾದ, ಪಿರಿದಾದ, ಪಣಮುಳ್ಳ ; ಶುಧಮಯಿನ, which are merely nouns with the relative participles *āna* (Kannaḍa *āda* and Telugu *ayina*) and *uḷḷa* affixed to them. These languages form a large number of adjectives in this way owing to the paucity of adjectives properly so called in them. But no manner of exception can be taken to the following list of adjectives of quality which, I think, have every right to be so called. It is noteworthy that all of them are common to both Tamil and Kannaḍa.

Tamil	*Kannaḍa*	*Tamil*	*Kannaḍa*
ವೆಳ್	ಬೆಳ್	ಇೞ	ಎೞ
ತಣ್	ತಣ್	ಪುದು	ಪೊಸ
ಪಶು	ಪಸು	ಅರು	ಅರು
ನೇರ್	ನೇರ್	ನಱು	ನಱು
ಪೆರು	ಪೆರ್	ಶಿಱು	ಕಿಱು
ಕಡು	ಕಡು	ನೆಡು	ನಿಡು
ವಲ್	ಬಲ್	ಮೆಲ್	ಮೆಲ್
ಕುಱು	ಕುಱು	ಕೂರ್	ಕೂರ್
ಶೆಂ	ಕೆಂ	ಕರು	ಕರ್
ತೆೞ್	ತೆೞ್	ಇೞ	ಇೞ

Tamil	*Kannaḍa*	*Tamil*	*Kannaḍa*
ನರ್	ನಲ್	ಪೞ	ಪೞ
ನುಣ್	ನುಣ್	ಕೊಡು	ಕುಡು
ವೆಂ	ಬೆಂ	ನಡು	ನಡು
ವಟ್ಟಂ	ಬಟ್ಟೆ	ನಳಿ	ನಳಿ

Among Telugu adjectives may be mentioned ನಲ್ಲ, ಎಱ್ಱ, ಪುಲ್ಲ, ಮಂಚಿ, ಪೆದ್ದ, ಚಿನ್ನ.

It is worthy of notice that the changes which many of these adjectives undergo in combination are almost the same in Tamil and Kannaḍa.

(1) Some adjectives lengthen their initial letter before vowels, sometimes before consonants also:
ಕರು + ಉಡಲ್ = ಕಾರುಡಲ್, ಕರ್ + ಒಡಲ್ = ಕಾರೊಡಲ್ ; ಪೆರು + ಅಡವಿ = ಪೇರಡವಿ, ಪೆರ್ + ಅಡವಿ = ಪೇರಡವಿ. ಕರು + ಮುಗಿಲ್ = ಕಾರ್ಮುಗಿಲ್, ಕರ್ + ಮುಗಿಲ್ = ಕಾರ್ಮುಗಿಲ್.

(2) Some double their final letter before vowels:
ನೆಡು + ಇದೞ್ = ನೆಟ್ಟಿದೞ್, ನಿಡು + ಎಸೞ್ = ನಿಟ್ಟೆಸೞ್ ; ನಡು + ಅಡವಿ = ನಟ್ಟಡವಿ ; ಶಿಱು + ಇದೞ್ = ಶಿಱ್ಱಿದೞ್ ; ಕಿಱು + ಎಸೞ್ = ಕಿತ್ತೆಸೞ್. Compare Telugu ನಟ್ಟೇಱು, ನಿಟ್ಟೂರ್ಪು.

(3) The adjective ಪಶು ಪಸು is sometimes altered into ಪೈಂ in Tamil; the same occurs in Kannaḍa also, the phonetic equivalent of ಪೈಂ being ಪಂ. ಪಶುಂದೊೞ ಪಸುಂದೊೞ ; ಪೈಂದೊೞ ಪಂದರೆ. This adjective also doubles its final letter before vowels: ಪಶು + ಇಲೈ = ಪಚ್ಚಿಲೈ, ಪಸು + ಎಲೆ = ಪಚ್ಚೆಲೆ.

(4) Besides being used exactly as they stand in the above list, some of the adjectives take the suffix *iya* : ಪೆರಿಯ ಪಿರಿಯ, ಕರಿಯ ಕರಿಯ, ನೆಡಿಯ ನಿಡಿಯ, ಶಿಱಿಯ ಕಿಱಿಯ, ಇನಿಯ ಇನಿಯ, ಪಶಿಯ ಪಸಿಯ.

It was stated before that oblique bases in Tamil and Telugu bear the signification of genitives, and these are frequently used as adjectives. ನಾಟ್ಟು, ನಾಟಿ. In Kannaḍa, on the other hand, oblique bases are not used independently, and only genitives are used as adjectives: ನಾಡಿನ.

Numerals.

1 and 2.—The numerals corresponding to these in Tamil, Kannaḍa and Telugu are respectively ಒನ್ಱು ಒಂದು ಒಕಟಿ, ಇರಂಡು

ಎರಡು ರೆಂಡು. The *u* of the Tamil ಒರು and ಇರು in combination is dropped in Kannaḍa. ಒರು ಒರ್, ಒರುವನ್ ಒರ್ವಂ, ಒರುವಳ್ ಒರ್ವಳ್, ಒರುಮೈ ಒರ್ಮೆ ; ಇರು ಇರ್, ಇರುವರ್ ಇರ್ವರ್, ಇರುಮೈ ಇರ್ಮೆ. The corresponding Telugu forms for ಒರ್ ಒರ್ವಂ ಒರ್ವಳ್ are ಒಕ ಒಕಡು ಒಕತೆ; and for ಇರ್ವರ್, ಇರುವುರು ಇರುಗುರು or ಇದ್ದಱು. In both Tamil and Kannaḍa the initial of ಒರು ಒರ್, ಇರು ಇರ್, is lengthened before vowels : ಒರು + ಉಡಲ್ = ಓರುಡಲ್, ಒರ್ + ಒಡಲ್ = ಓರೊಡಲ್ ; ಇರು + ಐಂದು = ಈರೈಂದು, ಇರ್ + ಐದು = ಈರೈದು. But in Tamil it is lengthened even before consonants. ಓರ್ನಾೞಿ ಓರ್ಯಾನೈ ; ಈರ್ನಾೞಿ ಈರ್ಯಾನೈ. The form ಎರಟ್ for ಎರಡು occurring in combination, is peculiar to Kannaḍa : ಎರಟ್ಟಾತು. Though ಒರು and ಒರ್ have *r*, the word ಒಱ್ಱೈ single, derived from the same root, has *ṟ*.

3 and 5.—The words for these in the three languages mentioned above are respectively ಮೂನ್ಱು ಮೂಱು ಮೂಡು ; ಐಂದು, ಅಯ್ದು or ಐದು, ಅಯಿದು or ಏನು. They become ಮೂ or ಮು and ಐ or ಅಯ್ or ಏ in combination. ಮೂವುಲಕು ಮೂಲೋಕಂ, ಮುಪ್ಪಟಂ ಮುಪ್ಪೊೞಿಲ್ ಮುಪ್ಪಾತಿಕ, ಮೂವರ್ ಮೂವರ್ ಮುಗ್ಗುರು, ಮುಪ್ಪದು ಮೂವತ್ತು ಮುಪ್ಪದಿ ; ಐಮುಗನ್ ಐವೊಗಂ, ಐವಗ್ಗೈ ಐವಡಿ ಏನಾಳ್ಳು (5 days), ಐವರ್ ಐ (or ಅಯ್) ವರ್ ಅಯಿದುಗುರು or ಏಗುರು, ಐಂಬದು ಐ (or ಅಯ್) ವತ್ತು ಏಬದಿ.

The Kannaḍa forms ಎರಡು and ಮೂಱು without nasals are supposed to be older than the Tamil ಇರಂಡು and ಮೂನ್ಱು. Compare ಇರಟ್ಟೈ with ಎರಡು. But in the Telugu ರೆಂಡು the nasal occurs.

4.—The words for this numeral in the three languages are ನಾನ್ಗು ನಾಲ್ಕು ನಾಲುಗು. Though the present form of the Tamil numeral does not show the radical *l* as those of the other languages, the form ನಾಲ್ಕು exactly like the Kannaḍa one occurs in Old Tamil poetry : ಪಾರ್ ಪುರ್ಕ್ಕೆ ಪುರವಿ ನಾಲ್ಕುಡನ್ ಪೂಟ್ಟಿ (Porunarāṭṭruppaḍai). ನಾನ್ಮುಗನ್ ನಾಲ್ಮೊಗಂ ನಲುವಂಕಲು ; ನಾಲ್ವರ್ ನಾಲ್ವರ್ ನಲುಗುರು ; ನಾಱ್ಪದು ನಾಲ್ವತ್ತು ನಲುವದಿ. In Tamil *l* is changed into *n* before *m* and into *ṟ* before *p*.

6 and 7.—These numerals are the same in the three languages except for the substitution of *ḍ* for *ḻ* in the Telugu numeral for 7: ಆಱು ಆಱು ಆಱು; ಏೞು ಏೞು ಏಡು. The initials of these numerals are generally shortened in combination and their *u* is sometimes dropped. ಅಱುತಿಂಗಳ್ ಅಱುದಿಂಗಳ್, ಅಱುವರ್ ಅಱ್ವರ್ ಆಱುಗುರು, ಅಱುಪದು ಅಱುವತ್ತು ಅಱುವದಿ; ಏೞ್ಕಡಲ್ ಏೞ್ಕಡಲ್, ಎೞುವರ್ ಏೞ್ವರ್ ಏಡುಗುರು, ಎೞುಪದು ಏೞ್ಪತ್ತು ಡೆಬ್ಬದಿ. *Ḍe* of the last word is derived from *ēḍu* by the consonant and initial vowel changing their places as is usual in Telugu.

8 and 9.—The numerals corresponding to these in the three languages are ಎಟ್ಟು ಎಣ್ಟು ಎನಿಮಿದಿ; ಒನ್ಬದು ಒಂಬತ್ತು ತೊಮ್ಮಿದಿ. The Kannaḍa form clearly shows the radical *ṇ*. The numeral nine is a compound word in all the Dravidian languages—ಒಂಬದು (Malayāḷam), ಒಯಿಂಬದು (Koḍagu), ಒರ್ವ್ಬ (Tuḷu). It will be seen that the Telugu form ತೊಮ್ಮಿದಿ differs from all the others. Its first part is the same as that of the Kannaḍa ತೊಂಬತ್ತು (90); but *tom* of ತೊಮ್ಮಿದಿ is supposed to be connected with *tol* (before) and *tom* of ತೊಂಬತ್ತು with *toṇḍu* (nine). ತೊಮ್ಮಿದಿ is thus explained as the number before ten and ತೊಂಬತ್ತು as nine times ten. The Tamil word for 90 is ತೊಣ್ಣೂಱು and for 900 ತೊಳ್ಳಾಯಿರಂ. The first part of these words, *toḷ*, is also supposed to mean before, and the words are explained as the last ten before a hundred and the last hundred before a thousand. This is indeed ingenious, but not convincing. The Telugu numeral ಎನಿಮಿದಿ also looks like a compound word. It has to be stated here that instead of the usual suffix *guru*, the Telugu words denoting eight and nine persons have the new suffix *aṇḍru*. This suffix also occurs in words denoting 18, 19, 20, 30, 40, 50, 60, 70, 80 and 90 persons: ಎಣ್ಡ್ರಶ್ಕೈ ಎಣ್ಟ್ಸೆ, ಎಣ್ಮರ್ ಎಣ್ಬರ್ ಎನಮಂಡ್ರು, ಎಣ್ಬದು ಎಣ್ಪತ್ತು ಎನುಬದಿ. In Tamil *t* following *ṇ* is changed into *ḍ*. ಒನ್ಬದಿನ್ಮರ್ ಒಂಬದಿಂಬರ್ ತೊಮ್ಮಂಡ್ರು, ತೊಣ್ಣೂಱು ತೊಂಬತ್ತು ತೊಂಬದಿ.

10.—This numeral in the three languages is ಪತ್ತು

ಪತ್ತು ಪದಿ. ಪದಿನ್ಮರ್ ಪದಿಂಬರ್ ಪದುಗುರು or ಪದುಗುಂಡ್ರು. In combination the Tamil numeral becomes ಪದು at the end of words: ಇರುಪದು ಇರ್ಪತ್ತು ಇರುವದಿ, ನಾಱ್ಪದು ನಾಲ್ಪತ್ತು ನಲುವದಿ, ಎಣ್ಬದು ಎಣ್ಪತ್ತು ಎನುಬದಿ. The numeral becomes ಪದಿನ್ ಪದಿನ್ ಪದುನ್ in the three languages before the numbers 3 to 8, but the final *n* is dropped in Kannaḍa and Telugu before 3 and 4. It is dropped before 3 even in Modern Tamil: ಪದಿನ್ಮೂನ್ಱು ಪದಿಮೂಱು ಪದುಮೂಁಡು, ಪದಿನಾನ್ಗು ಪದಿನಾಲ್ಕು ಪದುನಾಲುಗು, ಪದಿನ್ಮೈಂದು ಪದಿನ್ಮೈದು ಪದುನಯಿದು or ಪದುನೇನು, ಪದಿನಾಱು ಪದಿನಾಱು ಪದುನಾಱು, ಪದಿನೇೞು ಪದಿನೇೞು ಪದುನೇಡು, ಪದಿನೆಟ್ಟು ಪದಿನೆಣ್ಟು ಪದುನೆನಿಮಿದಿ. In Tamil final *n* not preceded by a single short vowel is elided when followed by another *n*. Accordingly ಪದಿನ್ + ನಾನ್ಗು becomes ಪದಿನಾನ್ಗು. The same is the case with the corresponding Kannaḍa and Telugu words, though the Tamil rule is not known to Kannaḍa and Telugu grammarians. This Tamil rule clearly explains the word ಜೇನೆಯ್ which is another form of the Tamil ತೇನೆಯ್. The numeral undergoes no change in Kannaḍa and Tamil before 9 but becomes *pan* or *pam* in Telugu. ಪತ್ತೊನ್ಬದು ಪತ್ತೊಂಬತ್ತು ಪಂದೊಮ್ಮಿದಿ. It becomes *pan* before 2 in the three languages, but before 1 it becomes *padin* in Tamil, *pan* in Kannaḍa and *padun* in Telugu: ಪನ್ನಿರಂಡು ಪನ್ನೆರಡು ಪಂಡ್ರೆಂಡು; ಪದಿನೊನ್ಱು ಪನ್ನೊಂದು ಪದುನೊಕಟಿ.

The three languages have the word *nūṛu* for a hundred, Telugu having also an additional word ವಂದ. There is further an indigenous word ವೇಯು in Telugu for a thousand, the other languages having to borrow a word from Sanskrit. The word in Tamil is ಆಯಿರಂ and in Kannaḍa ಸಾಸಿರಂ, both derived from the Sanskrit ಸಹಸ್ರ. The Tamil numerals for 90 and 900 greatly differ from the corresponding ones of the other two languages: ತೊಣ್ಣೂಱು ತೊಂಬತ್ತು ತೊಂಬದಿ; ತೊಳ್ಳಾಯಿರಂ ಒಂಬಯ್ನೂಱು ತೊಮ್ಮಿನೂಱು. The suffixes for ordinals in the three languages are respectively ಆಂ ಅನೆಯ ಅವ: ಇರಂಡಾಂ ಎರಡನೆಯ ರೆಂಡವ,

ಐಂದಾಂ ಐದನೆಯ ಅಯುದವ. ಅಂ stands for ಅಗುಂ from ಅಗು to become. Similarly *ava* stands for ಅಗ from ಅಗು to become. The origin of the Kannaḍa suffix ಅನೆಯ is not, however, clear. I venture to think that it is identical with the Tamil particle of similarity ಅನ್ನೈಯ and means *like* or *of the measure of*.

PRONOUNS.

Philologists are of opinion that pronouns afford the most conclusive evidence of the relationship between languages, as, of all words in a language, they appear to possess the greatest amount of tenacity and permanence. In the Indo-European languages the base of the oblique cases of pronouns is different from the base of the nominative. Such is not the case in the Draviḍian languages. The table in the next page exhibits the general similarity of the personal and reflexive pronouns in Tamil, Kannaḍa and Telugu.

	Nominative	Oblique base	Dative	Genitive with *a*	Genitive with *adu* or *adi*
First Person Singular—					
Tamil ...	ಯಾನ್ ನಾನ್	ಎನ್	ಎನಕ್ಕು	ಎನ	ಎನದು
Kannaḍa ...	ಆನ್ ನಾನ್	ಎನ್ ನನ್	ಎನಗೆ ನನಗೆ	ಎನ್ನ ನನ್ನ	ಎನ್ನದು ಎನತು ನನ್ನದು
Telugu ...	ಏನು ನೇನು	ನಾ	ನಾಕು	(ನಾ)	ನಾದಿ
First Person Plural—					
Tamil ...	ಯಾಂ ನಾಂ	ಎಂ ನಂ	ಎಮಕ್ಕು ನಮಕ್ಕು	ಎಮ ನಮ	ಎಮದು ನಮದು
Kannaḍa ...	ಆಂ ನಾಂ	ಎಂ ನಂ	ಎಮಗೆ ನಮಗೆ	ಎಮ್ಮ ನಮ್ಮ	ಎಮ್ಮದು ಎಮತು ನಮ್ಮದು
Telugu ...	ಏಮು ಮೇಮು ನೇಮು	ಮಾ	ಮಾಕು	(ಮಾ)	ಮಾದಿ
Second Person Singular—					
Tamil ...	ನೀ	ನಿನ್ ಉನ್	ನಿನಕ್ಕು ಉನಕ್ಕು	ನಿನ ಉನ	ನಿನದು ಉನದು
Kannaḍa ...	ನೀನ್	ನಿನ್	ನಿನಗೆ	ನಿನ್ನ	ನಿನ್ನದು ನಿನತು
Telugu ...	ನೀವು ಈವು	ನೀ	ನೀಕು	(ನೀ)	ನೀದಿ
Second Person Plural—					
Tamil ...	ನೀಯಿರ್ ನೀವಿರ್ ನೀರ್	ನುಂ ಉಂ	ನುಮಕ್ಕು ಉಮಕ್ಕು	ನುಮ ಉಮ	ನುಮದು ಉಮದು
Kannaḍa ...	ನೀಂ	ನಿಂ	ನಿಮಗೆ	ನಿಮ್ಮ	ನಿಮ್ಮದು ನಿಮತು
Telugu ...	ಮೀರು ಈರು	ಮೀ	ಮೀಕು	(ಮೀ)	ಮೀದಿ
Reflexive Singular—					
Tamil ...	ತಾನ್	ತನ್	ತನಕ್ಕು	ತನ	ತನದು
Kannaḍa ...	ತಾನ್	ತನ್	ತನಗೆ	ತನ್ನ	ತನ್ನದು ತನತು
Telugu ...	ತಾನು	ತನ	ತನಕು	ತನ	ತನದಿ
Reflexive Plural—					
Tamil ...	ತಾಂ	ತಂ	ತಮಕ್ಕು	ತಮ	ತಮದು
Kannaḍa ...	ತಾಂ	ತಂ	ತಮಗೆ	ತಮ್ಮ	ತಮ್ಮದು ತಮತು
Telugu ...	ತಾಮು ತಮರು	ತಮ	ತಮಕು	ತಮ	ತಮದಿ

The forms of the reflexive pronoun are nearly the same in all the three languages. But there are some points of difference with regard to the personal pronouns of the first and second persons which have to be noticed. The initial *y* of the Tamil pronoun of the first person does not occur in Kannaḍa and Telugu. There are, besides, several words in Tamil which are supposed to be more correct with an intitial *y* than without it, *e.g.*, ಯಾನೈ, ಯಾಕ್ಕೈ, ಯಾಂಡು, ಯಾರ್. The Kannaḍa pronoun of the second person singular has retained the radical *n* which the Tamil pronoun has lost. Although the plurals of the Tamil pronoun of the second person end in *r*, in the Modern Tamil plural ನೀಂಗಳ್, we clearly see the form *nīm* which is identical with the Kannaḍa plural. Tamil shares with Brāhūī the peculiarity of using *num* for the second person plural, though Kannaḍa and Malayāḷam use *nim*. The doubling of *n* and *m* seen in some of the Kannaḍa genitives also occurs in Modern Tamil. The form *ninna* occurs in Old Tamil poetry, *e.g.*, ನಿನ್ನ ತನ್ಮೈಯಿನ್ನದೆನ್ನ (*Tiruchchandaviruttam*, verse 5). The change of *ā* into *ē* in the Telugu pronouns of the first person has to be regarded as dialectic. Another peculiarity in Telugu is that while the other languages shorten the vowel of the nominative in the oblique cases of the pronouns of the first and second persons, it retains the long vowel of the nominative in all oblique cases except the second, *e.g.*, ನಾಕು, ಮಾಚೇತ, ನೀಕು, ಮೀವಲನ; ನಿನ್ನು, ಮಿಮ್ಮು, ನನ್ನು, ಮಮ್ಮು. A third peculiarity is the substitution of *m* for the initial *n* of the pronouns in the plural. A fourth is the absence of genitive pronouns ending in *a* except ತನ, ತಮ and ಮನ, and the substitution for them of the oblique bases of the pronouns.

In all the languages *tan* is used as an honorific pronoun of the second person. The double plurals ನೀಂಗಳ್ ನೀಂಗಳ್ ಮೀರಲು also occur in them.

In most of the Dravidian languages, are used, as stated before, two different forms of the plural of the

6*

personal pronoun of the first person, the one inclusive and the other exclusive of the person addressed—

		Tamil	*Malayāḷam*	*Telugu*
Inclusive	....	ಯಾಂ, ನಾಂ	ನಾಂ	ಮನಮು
Exclusive	....	ನಾಂಗಳ್	ಞಾಙ್ಙಳ್	ಏಮು, ಮೇಮು.

Some scholars doubt whether this peculiarity is an originally Draviḍian feature, not only because it is not found in Gōṇḍi, Brāhūī and several minor dialects of the Draviḍian group, but also because it is found in languages outside that group such as Mahrāṭhi, Gujarāti, etc.: Gujarāti—*ame* (we), *āpaṇe* (we and you); Mahrāṭhi—*āmhī* (we), *āpaṇ* (we and you). It is believed that Kannaḍa, too, does not possess this feature. I think Kannaḍa does possess two forms of the plural of the personal pronoun of the first person just like its sister languages of Southern India. And this not only in the Old language but also in the Modern.

		Old Kannaḍa	*Modern Kannaḍa*
Inclusive	....	ಅಂ	ನಾವು
Exclusive	....	ನಾಂ	ನಾವುಗಳು

In the instance ಇನಿಬರುಮೊಂದಾಗಿ ಕಾದುವಂ ಫಲ್ಗುಣನೊಳ್, given under sūtra 229 of the *Śabdamaṇidarpaṇa*, the subject ಅಂ, which is understood, is clearly inclusive. It is very rarely that ನಾಂ is used in Old Kannaḍa.

Another table showing the similarity of the demonstrative and interrogative pronouns and adjectives in the three languages is given in the following pages.

	Remote Demonstrative			Proximate Demonstrative		
	Tamil	Kannaḍa	Telugu	Tamil	Kannaḍa	Telugu
Masculine singular	ಅವನ್	ಅವನ್	ವಾಂಡು	ಇವನ್	ಇವನ್	ವೀಂಡು
Feminine singular	ಅವಳ್	ಅವಳ್	ಅದಿ	ಇವಳ್	ಇವಳ್	ಇದಿ
Neuter singular	ಅದು	ಅದು	ಅದಿ	ಇದು	ಇದು	ಇದಿ
Epicene plural	ಅವರ್	ಅವರ್	ವಾರು	ಇವರ್	ಇವರ್	ವೀರು
Neuter plural	ಅವೈ	ಅವು	ಅವಿ	ಇವೈ	ಇವು	ಇವಿ
Adjectives	ಅ	ಆ	ಆ	ಇ	ಈ	ಈ
Adverbs	ಅನ್ಱು	ಅಂದು	(ಅಪ್ಪುಡು)	ಇನ್ಱು	ಇಂದು	(ಇಪ್ಪುಡು)

	Intermediate Demonstrative			Interrogative			
	Tamil	Kannaḍa	Telugu	Tamil	Old Kannada	Modern Kannada	Telugu
Masculine singular ...	ಉವೞ	ಉವೞ		ಯಾವೞ ಎವೞ	ಆವೞ	ಯಾವಂ	ಎವ್ಁಡು ಏಁಡು
Feminine singular ...	ಉವಳ್	ಉವಳ್		ಯಾವಳ್ ಎವಳ್	ಆವಳ್	ಯಾವಳ್	ಎವತೆ ಎವರಿತೆ
Neuter singular ...	ಉದು	ಉದು		ಯಾದು ಎದು	ಆವುದು	ಯಾವುದು	ಎದಿ ಏದಿ
Epicene plural ...	ಉವರ್	ಉವರ್		ಯಾವರ್ ಯಾರ್ ಎವರ್	ಆರ್	ಯಾರ್	ಎವರು
Neuter plural ...	ಉವೈ	ಉವು		ಯಾವೈ ಎವೈ	ಆವುವು	ಯಾವುವು	ಎವಿ
Adjectives ...	ಉ	ಊ		ಯಾ ಎ	ಆವ	ಯಾವ	ಏ
Adverbs ...	ಉಙ್ಗು	ಉಂದು		ಎಙ್ಗು	ಎಂದು	ಎಂದು ಯಾವಾಗ	(ಎಪ್ಪುಡು)

The Tamil and Kannaḍa forms are almost indentical. The initial *y* of the Tamil interrogatives is dropped in Old Kannaḍa but retained in Modern Kannaḍa. We thus see that the Tamil forms with *yā* are colloquial in Kannaḍa and the Kannaḍa *ār* is colloquial in Tamil. The Kannaḍa and Telugu demonstrative adjectives are merely lengthened forms of the Tamil ones. The forms వారు, వీండ్రు, etc., in Telugu are, as stated before, the result of the peculiar dialectic changes in that language. Another peculiarity, also mentioned before, is the absence of the feminine singular in Telugu and the use of the neuter singular instead. Telugu does not possess intermediate demonstratives. Its interrogatives closely resemble the Tamil ones beginning with *e*. The Telugu adverbs ಅಂದು, ಇಂದು, ಎಂದು, though identical in form with the Kannaḍa ones given in the table, do not convey the same meaning: they are adverbs of place, and not of time as in Kannaḍa. The adverbs in Telugu corresponding to the Kannaḍa ones are *appuḍu* (*appoḻuḍu*, *āpoḻtu*), *ippuḍu* and *eppuḍu*. One more set of words may be added which is similar in the three languages, only there is an interchange of *t* and *n* in the Tamil words:

		Remote Demonstrative.	*Proximate Demonstrative.*	*Interrogative.*
Tamil	....	ಅತ್ತನೈ	ಇತ್ತನೈ	ಎತ್ತನೈ
Kannaḍa	....	ಅನಿತು	ಇನಿತು	ಎನಿತು
Telugu	....	ಅಂತ	ಇಂತ	ಎಂತ

Kannaḍa and Telugu have also honorific demonstrative pronouns, both masculine and feminine, which are not found in Tamil:

		Remote.	*Proximate.*
Kannaḍa—			
Masculine	....	ಆತಂ	ಈತಂ
Feminine	....	ಆಕೆ	ಈಕೆ
Telugu—			
Masculine	....	ಆತನು ಅತಂಡು ಆತಂಡು	ಈತನು ಇತಂಡು ಈತಂಡು
Feminine	....	ಆಕೆ ಆಮೆ ಆಪೆ	ಈಕೆ ಈಮೆ ಈಪೆ

Kannaḍa has no forms corresponding to the Telugu *āme*, *āpe*, *īme*, *īpe*, nor has Telugu any forms corresponding to the Kannaḍa intermediate ಉತಂ and ಉಕೆ. Telugu has, however, the interrogative honorific forms ಎತಁಡು ಏತಁಡು, ಏಕೆ ಏಮೆ ಏಪೆ which are not found in Kannaḍa. The honorific pronouns in Kannaḍa have plurals ಅತಂಗಳ್, ಅಕೆಯರ್, but not those in Telugu. The Kannaḍa forms corresponding to the Telugu ಅಂದಱು, ಇಂದಱು, ಎಂದಱು and ಕೊಂದಱು are respectively ಅನಿಬರ್, ಇನಿಬರ್, ಎನಿಬರ್ and ಕೆಲಬರ್. It may be added here that *udu* the intermediate demonstrative in Kannaḍa and Tamil, is the proximate demonstrative in Tuḷu.

VERBS.

Roots.

A comparison of Tamil and Kannaḍa under this head reveals remarkable coincidences, as will appear in the sequel, amounting, in most cases, to perfect identity, in the roots, personal terminations and the formation of the different tenses, moods and participles. The same cannot be said of the Telugu language. Of the four cultivated languages of the South, the farthest removed from each other are Tamil and Telugu. It is true that many of the verbal roots and forms in both these languages are similar, but they are often so disguised by inflexional and dialectic changes peculiar to Telugu that the similarity does not easily reveal itself. Unlike the roots in Tamil and Kannaḍa, many of which end in consonants, the roots in Telugu always end in vowels. The number of Telugu roots which are identical with those in Tamil are far fewer in number than those in Kannaḍa. The same remark applies to roots in Telugu whose identity is disguised by dialectic and other changes. I give in the following pages lists of roots which are common either to all the three languages some or to only any two of them, as well as of those which have undergone change in one or two languages :—

Roots common to Tamil, Kannaḍa and Telugu.

ಕಟ್ಟು, ಒಟ್ಟು, ಕಿಟ್ಟು, ಮೆಚ್ಚು, ಆಡು, ಕೂಡು, ಕೊಂಡಾಡು, ಒಪ್ಪು, ತಪ್ಪು, ಅಱು, ನಚ್ಚು, ಮೀಱು, ಅಂಜು, ತಗು, ತಟ್ಟು, ತುಮ್ಮು, ನಗು, ಪೊಂಗು, ಪಾಡು, ಮಾಱು, ಪಡು.

Tamil roots and those corresponding to them in Kannaḍa and Telugu that have undergone change.

ನಡ	ನಡೆ	ನಡಚು	ತುಡೈ	ತೊಡೆ	ತೊಡಯು
ವರೈ	ಬರೆ	ವ್ರಾಯು	ಅಲೈ	ಅಱೆ	ಅಲಯು
ನಡುಂಗು	ನಡುಗು	ನಡುಂಕು	ಇೞು	ಎೞೆ	ಈಡುಚು
ಶೇರ್	ಸೇರ್	ಚೇರು	ಮುೞೈ	ಮೊಳೆ	ಮೊಲಚು
ತರು	ತರ್	ತೆಚ್ಚು	ತೆಳಿ	ತಿಳಿ	ತೆಲಯು
ಎೞು	ಏೞ್	ಲೇಚು	ತಿಱ	ತೆಱೆ	ತೆಱಚು
ಆರಾಯ್	ಆರಯ್	ಅರಯು	ಎಣ್	ಎಣಿಸು	ಎಂಚು
ಶೆಯ್	ಕೆಯ್	ಚೇಯು	ಅೞು	ಅೞ್	ಏಡು
ಅೞುಂದು	ಅೞ್ದು	ಅದ್ದು	ಪುಗೞ್	ಪೊಗೞ್	ಪೊಗಡು
ಶಿದಱು	ಕೆದಱು	ಚೆದಱು	ಶಾ	ಸಾ	ಚಚ್ಚು
ಮಱ	ಮಱೆ	ಮಱಚು			

Roots common to Tamil and Telugu.

ತಡವು	ತಡವು	ತಿನ್	ತಿನು
ತೂಱು	ತೂರು	ಅಲರ್	ಅಲರು
ಅನುಪ್ಪು	ಅನುಪು	ಈನ್	ಈನು
ಶೆಪ್ಪು	ಚೆಪ್ಪು	ತೇಯ್	ಕೇಯು
ತೋಂಡು	ತೋಂಡು	ಪೋರ್	ಪೋಲು
ಅಲಮರು	ಅಲಮುಗು	ಮಡಿ	ಮಡಿಯು
ಮೇಯ್	ಮೇಯು*	ಪಾೞು	ಪಾೞು

Tamil roots and those corresponding to them in Telugu that have undergone change.

ನಂಬು	ನಮ್ಮು	ಆಗು	ಅಗು
ಅಮೈ	ಅಮಯು	ಕೊಳ್	ಕೊನು
ತಿರುಪ್ಪು	ತ್ರಿಪ್ಪು	ತುಳ್ಳು	ತ್ರುಳ್ಳು
ಈ	ಇಚ್ಚು	ಅೞಲ್	ಅಡಲು
ಕಾಣ್	ಕನು	ಪಱ್ಱು	ಪಟ್ಟು
ನಿಱೈವೇಱು	ನೆಱವೇಱು	ತಣಿ	ತನಿಯು
ಮುೞುಗು	ಮುನುಂಗು		

Roots common to Kannaḍa and Telugu.

ಪುಟ್ಟು, ತಿರುಗು, ದೂಱು, ಪಿಂಡು, ನೆಱಪು, ಅಡುಕು, ಅಲ್ಲಾಡು, ಮಾದ್ದಾಡು,

* In this and the succeeding Telugu roots the final *u* is merely enunciative. As stated before, Telugu roots invariably end in a vowel.

ದಾಂಟು, ಅಂಟು, ಕಡಂಗು, ತೂಱು, ತೊಲಂಗು, ಅಱಚು, ತೊಡಂಗು, ನಂಜು,* ನಾನು, ದಕ್ಕು, ದುಮುಕು, ದೊರಕು, ಅದುಮು, ತೇರಾಡು, ನುಱುಚು, ತಗುಲು, ದೋಂಚು, ತೋಂಡು, ಮಾರಲು, ಕರಂಗು.

Kannaḍa roots and those corresponding to them in Telugu that have undergone change.

ಎೞ್	ಅನು	ಅಳ್ಕು	ಅಲುಕು
ಮಾಣ್	ಮಾನು	ತಿರ್ದು	ದಿದ್ದು
ಕೊಯ್	ಕೋಯು	ನೆಗೞ್	ನೆಗಡು
ತೆರಳ್	ತೆರಲು	ಅಱಿ	ಎಱುಗು
ತೆಪ್ಪಱು	ತಪ್ಪಿಱು	ಝುಳಪಿಸು	ಝುಳಿಪಿಂಚು
ನಿಳ್ಕು	ನೀಲುಗು	ಈಸು	ಈದು
ದಬ್ಬು	ದೊಬ್ಬು	ನುಡಿ	ನುಡುಗು
ಬಡರ್	ಬಡಲು	ಅಪ್ಪಳಿಸು	ಅಪ್ಪಳಿಂಚು
ಅದಿರ್	ಅದರು	ನೂಂಕು	ನೂಕು
ಪೂಣ್	ಪೂನು	ತಱುಂಬು	ತಱುಮು
ಅಳವಡು	ಅಲವಡು	ತಳರ್	ತಲರು
ನಿರ್	ನಿಲುಚು	ತಿಣುಕು	ತಿನುಕು

Roots common to Tamil and Kannaḍa.

ಈ, ಕಾ, ಕೋ, ನೋ, ಪೂ, ಕಾಣ್, ಕಾಯ್, ಉಣ್, ನಿಲ್, ಕಲ್, ಪೊರ್, ಕೊಲ್, ಕನಲ್, ಕಟರ್, ಕೊಳ್, ತಾಳ್, ಆಳ್, ಅಟ್, ಪೆಱು, ಉಱು, ಏಱು, ನಾಱು, ಕಾಱು, ಪೊಱು, ಅಱು, ಕುಱು, ಪಱಿ, ತಱಿ, ಅಟಲ್, ಆಗು, ಪುಗು, ಏಗು, ಅಡಂಗು, ತಾಂಗು, ಪಿಡಿ, ಕುಡಿ, ಮುಡಿ, ಕಡಿ, ಮಡಿ, ಇಡಿ, ಅಡು, ಉಡು, ನಡು, ಇಡು, ಓಡು, ಕುಂಬಿಡು, ಮಾಡು, ಕುತ್ತು, ಊದು, ಮೋದು, ಓದು, ನಂದು, ಮುತ್ತು, ಮುನಿ, ಕುನಿ, ಮುಳಿ, ತಿೞ್, ಎೞ್, ಈೞ್, ತಳಿ, ತಣಿ, ನಂಬು, ಅರಿ, ಅಮರ್, ನಿಮಿರ್, ಅಡರ್, ತೊಡರ್, ಅದಿರ್, ಉದಿರ್, ಅಲರ್, ಮಲರ್, ತಳಿರ್, ಕುಳಿರ್, ನೂಲ್, ನಯ್, ಕೊಯ್, ಪಾಯ್, ನೀಳ್, ಕಟಿ, ಪಟಿ, ಇಟಿ, ಅಟಿ, ಮುಱುಗು, ಪೋೞ್, ಉಳ್, ಕಳ್, ಉರುಳ್, ಪೋರ್, ಆರ್, ಪಾರ್, ಪೋರ್, ನಕ್ಕು, ಮುಕ್ಕು, ತಾಟ್, ಮುಱುಗು, ಮುಱಿ, ತೂಱು, ತೇಱು, ಪಿಟಿ, ತುತ್ತು, ತಗು, ಪುನಿ, ಉಗು, ಎಟ್ಟು, ಪತ್ತು, ಕರಿ, ಮಾಣ್, ಪೂಣ್, ಅಲಂಬು, ಮುಂದು, ಕುಟಿ, ಕವಿ, ನುಂಗು, ಕೇಳ್, ಅಗೞ್.

Tamil roots and those corresponding to them in Kannaḍa that have undergone change.

ವರಿ	ಬರಿ	ವೀೞ್	ಬೀೞ್
ವೀ	ಬೀ	ಪೇೞ್	ಬೇೞ್
ವೇ	ಬೇ	ವಿಡು	ಬಿಡು
ವದಿರ್	ಬದಿರ್	ವಾಡು	ಬಾಡು
ವರು	ಬರ್	ವಿಕ್ಕು	ಬಿಕ್ಕು
ವಿತ್ತು	ಬಿತ್ತು	ತೋಯ್	ತೋ
ಪೈ	ಬಯ್	ಪುಟುಂಗು	ಪುಟ್ಗು
ವೀಶು	ಬೀಸು	ಅರೈ	ಅರೆ
ವಿಱೈ	ಬೆಱೆ	ಊಳೈಯುಡು	ಊಳಿಡು
ವಟಿ	ಬಟಿ	ಪಿಣೈ	ಪೆಣೆ
ವಾೞ್	ಬಾೞ್	ನಿರಪ್ಪು	ನೆರಪು

* This and the following in Modern Kannada.

ನಶಿ	ನನಿ
ಕಜಿ	ಸಜಿ
ಕೆಡು	ಕಿಡು
ಕೊಡು	ಕುಡು
ಶುಡು	ಸುಡು
ಶುಷ್ಟು	ಸುತ್ತು
ಶೊರಿ	ಸುರಿ
ಪೊರಿ	ಪುರಿ
ಕೊದಿ	ಕುದಿ
ಶುರುಳ್	ಸುರುಳ್
ವಷ್ಟಿ	ಬತ್ತು
ವಿಳ್ಕೈ	ಬೆಳೆ
ವೇಂಡು	ಬೇಡು
ತೋಂಡು	ತೋಡು
ಉಣಂಗು	ಒಣಗು
ನಿರ	ನೆರೆ
ಪದುಂಗು	ಪದುಗು
ಪೊರುಂದು	ಪೊದರ್ು
ಒಟುಗು	ಒಟ್ಟು
ಮೇಯ್	ಮೇ
ಪರಂಬು	ಪಬರ್ು
ಪೆರುಗು	ಪೆಚರ್ು
ಪುಱಪ್ಪಡು	ಪೊಱಮಡು
ಪಡ್ಕೈ	ಪಡೆ
ನಾರ್	ನೇರ್
ಉರ್ಕೈ	ಒರೆ
ನನ್ಕೈ	ನನೆ
ನಿನ್ಕೈ	ನೆನೆ
ಮರ್ಕೈ	ಮರೆ
ಪದ್ಕೈ	ಪದೆ
ನಿಱ್ಕೈ	ನೆಱೆ
ಕಳ್ಕೈ	ಕಳೆ
ನುಡ್ಕೈ	ನೊಡೆ
ಶಮ್ಕೈ	ಸಮೆ
ಕಡ್ಕೈ	ಕಡೆ
ತಡ್ಕೈ	ತಡೆ
ಪುಡ್ಕೈ	ಪೊಡೆ
ಉದ್ಕೈ	ಒದೆ
ಇರ	ಎರೆ
ಕಿಡ	ಕೆಡೆ
ಪುರ	ಪೊರೆ
ತುಱ	ತೊಱೆ
ಅಳ	ಅಳೆ
ಮುಗ	ಮೊಗೆ
ಕರ	ಕರೆ
ವಿಳಂಗು	ಬೆಳಗು
ಶುರ	ತೊರೆ

ಮುಱಂಗು	ಪೊಱಗು
ಮಾಟುಂಗು	ಮಟ್ಗು
ವೇಂಗು	ಬೇಗು
ಒನ್ಡು	ಒಂದು
ಕುನ್ಡು	ಕುಂದು
ಉಱಂಗು	ಒಱಗು
ಮಿನುಂಗು	ಮಿನುಗು
ಕೀ	ಕೀ
ತಿರುತ್ತು	ತಿದರ್ು
ನೀಕ್ಕು	ನೀಗು
ಪುರಳ್	ಪೊರಳ್
ಶೂಡು	ಸೂಡು
ಪೂಶು	ಪೂಸು
ಅಲಶು	ಅಲಸು
ಶುಟ್ಟು	ಸುಟ್ಟು
ಶಾರ್	ಸಾರ್
ಶೋರ್	ಸೋರ್
ಶೆರ್	ಸರ್
ವಿರ್	ಬರ್
ತ್ರೋರ್	ಸೋಲ್
ಶುಪ್ಕೈ	ಸವಿ
ತುಳಂಗು	ತೊಳಗು
ಪರ	ಪರೆ
ತುಡಂಗು	ತೊಡಗು
ಶುರುಂಗು	ಸುಕರ್ು
ತಗ್ಕೈ	ತಗೆ
ತೇಯ್	ತೇ
ನಾಟ್ಟು	ನಾಟು
ತಪು	ತವು
ತಡುಮಾಱು	ತಡಮಾಡು
ತದ್ಕೈ	ನಡೆ
ಪರಪ್ಪು	ಪರಪು
ಪಶಿ	ಪಸಿ
ಎಱಿ	ಇಱಿ
ಎರಿ	ಉರಿ
ಇಡಱು	ಎಡಱು
ಕದಱು	ಗದಱು
ಉದಱು	ಒದಱು
ಉಳಱು	ಒಳಱು
ಕುಱ್ಕು	ಕೊಱೆ
ತೋನ್ಱು	ತೋಱು
ಉದವು	ಒದವು
ಕಿಱುಕ್ಕು	ಕಿಱುಕು
ತಾಕ್ಕು	ತಾಗು
ತೂಕ್ಕು	ತೂಗು
ಉಟು	ಉಟ್

ಎಯಿರ್	ಬೆಮರ್	ಕರುಗು	ಕಱ್ಗು
ಉಣರ್	ಒಣರ್	ತೂಳಾಬು	ನೂವುರ್
ಪೊನ್ದು	ಪೊಂದು	ತೊಡು	ತುಡು
ಕನ್ದು	ಕಂದು	ಸೋಲ	ಸೋಲ್
ಎಟುಪ್ಪು	ಎಟ್ಟು	ಕವ್ಮು	ಕೆವ್ಮು
		ಕಿರ್ರೆ	ಕರೆ

The same roots have in some cases acquired different meanings in one or other of the three languages. Thus, the root ಪಾರ್ once meant to see or study in all the languages as is indicated by the words for a Brāhman ಪಾರ್ಪಾನ್ in Tamil, ಪಾರ್ವಂ in Kannada and ಬಾಪಡು in Telugu, which mean "one who sees or studies (the Vedas)." In Tamil the original meaning of the root, to see, is still retained; in Kannaḍa it now means to look for, and in Telugu the root has lost the original meaning altogether, though the verbal noun ಪಾರುವ corresponding to the Tamil ಪಾರ್ವೈ means sight or glance. The Tamil root ತಿಗಳ್ means to shine, but the corresponding roots ತೆಗಳ್ in Kannaḍa and ತೆಗಡು in Telugu, mean to blame. Again, ನಿಗಳ್ in Tamil means to take place, but the corresponding ನೆಗಳ್ in Kannaḍa and ನೆಗಡು in Telugu mean to be famous. ಈನ್ in Kannaḍa and ಈನು in Telugu mean to bring forth, as cattle and other beasts, but in Tamil it is used in connection with human beings also. Further, Telugu possesses two roots, ಅಡಗು and ವಿನು, to express the senses of asking and listening, but Tamil and Kannaḍa have only one root ಕೇಳ್ to express both the senses. As an instance of specialisation may be given the distinction made in Tamil with regard to the meaning of the three synonymous roots, ಈ, ತಾ, ಕೊಡು (to give), which is not found in Kannaḍa. Sūtra 448* of the Tamil Grammar Nannūl says that of the three roots ಈ, ತಾ, ಕೊಡು, ಈ is to be used by an inferior to a superior when asking for something, ತಾ by an equal to an equal, and ಕೊಡು by a superior to an inferior.

* ಈ ತಾ ಕೊಡುವೆನು ಮೂನ್ರು ಮುಱೈಯೋ
ಇೞಿಂದೋನೊಪ್ಪೋನ್ ಮಿಕ್ಕೋನಿರಪ್ಪುರೈ.

Pronominal terminations.

The system of conjugation in these languages is remarkably simple. In fact, there is only one conjugation, as most of the trivial changes that are observed are merely euphonic, and not of sufficient importance to constitute different conjugations. There are only four moods, namely, the indicative, the imperative, the infinitive and the negative. The similarity of the pronominal terminations in the three languages is shown in the following table :—

	1st Person		2nd Person		3rd Person				
	Singular	Plural	Singular	Plural	Masculine Singular	Feminine Singular	Neuter Singular	Epicene Plural	Neuter Plural
Tamil	ಎನ್ ಏನ್	ಎಂ ಏಂ	ಆಯ್ ಐ ಇ	ಇರ್ ಈರ್	ಅನ್ ಆನ್	ಅಳ್ ಆಳ್	ಅದು ಱು ಟು ತು	ಅರ್ ಆರ್	ಅನ ಅ
Kannaḍa	ಎನ್	ಎಂ	ಅಯ್ ಐ	ಇರ್	ಅನ್	ಅಳ್	ಉದು ತ್ತು ತು	ಅರ್	ಉವು
Telugu	ನು	ಮು	ವು	ರು	ಁಡು	ಅದಿ	ಅದಿ	ರು	ಅವಿ

It will be seen that the Tamil and Kannaḍa terminations are nearly identical and that the Telugu terminations show only a slight similarity. Only the shorter forms of the Tamil suffixes are generally used in Old Kannaḍa, but both the forms occur in Modern Kannaḍa, the shorter in the past and future tenses, and the longer, in the present, the only exception being the suffix ಆಯ್. The longer suffix ಏನ್ also occurs rarely in Old Kannaḍa poetry, *e.g.*, ನಿನಗೀವೇನಂಟೆ ಕಂಪಂ (*Kabbigarakāva*, 317). But other longer forms such as ಆನ್ and ಆರ್ are very common in ancient Kannaḍa inscriptions, as also the forms ಒನ್ and ಒರ್ which also occur in Tamil. The shorter form ಒನ್ or ಒಂ for the usual ಅನ್ or ಅಂ of the third person masculine singular is also frequently used in Old Kannaḍa poetry. The termination for the first person singular in Kannaḍa is really ಎನ್, but, as stated before, the final *n* is changed into a *bindu,* so that the singular and plural suffixes assume the same form, and we have to find out from the context whether ಎಂ is singular or plural. The Tamil suffixes for the neuter singular and plural, as given in the table, are ಅದು and ಅ, ಅನ. ಅ is only a shortened form of ಅನ, and *n* of ಅನ may be looked upon as a euphanised form of *v*, so that ಅನ is identical with ಅವ (the Malayāḷam neuter plural) or ಅವೈ, the neuter plural. We thus see that Tamil and Telugu use for the neuter suffixes the remote forms ಅದು ಅವೈ and ಅದಿ ಅವಿ, while Kannaḍa uses the intermediate forms ಉದು ಉವು.

The past and future tenses.

The formation of the past and future tenses is mostly the same in Tamil and Kannaḍa. Not only are the temporal particles the same, namely, *t* or *d* for the preterite and *v*, *p* or *b* for the future, but also the changes that these particles undergo.

Preterite: ಶೆಯ್ದೇನ್, ಕೆಯ್ದಂ; ಪೆಱ್ಱೇನ್, ಪೆತ್ತಂ; ಕಂಡೇನ್, ಕಂಡಂ; ಮಿಕ್ಕೇನ್ ಮಿಕ್ಕಂ.

Future: ಶೆಯ್ವೇನ್ ಕೆಯ್ವಂ; ಇರುಪ್ಪೇನ್, ಇರ್ಪೆಂ; ಕಾಣ್ಬೇನ್ ಕಾಣ್ಬಂ.

A few of the peculiarities common to both the languages in the formation of the past tense may be noticed here:—

(1) Some verbs form their preterite by the reduplication of their final consonants.

ಕಟ್ಟಾನ್ ಕೆಟ್ಟಂ; ಪುಕ್ಕಾನ್ ಪೊಕ್ಕಂ; ಪೆಱ್ಱಾನ್ ಪೆತ್ತಂ. But ಕೊಟ್ಟಂ ಕೊಡುತ್ತಾನ್; ಪೊತ್ತಂ ಪೊಱುತ್ತಾನ್.

(2) Some shorten their initials when the sign of the past tense is affixed.

ವಾ, ವಂದಾನ್, ವಂದದು; ಬಾ, ಬಂದಂ, ಬಂದುದು. ಕಾಣ್,

ಕಂಡಾನ್; ಕಾಣ್ ಕಂಡಂ ; ನೋ, ನೊಂದದು ; ನೋ, ನೊಂದುಧು ; ವೇ, ವೆಂದದು; ಬೇ, ಬೆಂದುದು.

The roots ಬೀಡ್ ವೀಡ್ and ಅಡ್ ಅಟ್ shorten their initials in Kannaḍa but not in Tamil: ಬಿಟ್ಟಂ, ವೀಡ್ನಾನ್ ; ಅಟ್ಟಂ, ಆಡ್ನಾನ್.

(3) Some change the temporal particle *d* into *ḍ* and other letters.

ಉಂಡಾನ್, ಉಂಡಂ ; ಕಂಡಾನ್, ಕಂಡಂ ; ಕೊಂಡಾನ್, ಕೊಂಡಂ. ಶುಟ್ಟಾನ್, ಸುಟ್ಟಂ ; ಪುಕ್ಕಾನ್, ಪೊಕ್ಕಂ ; ಶೆತ್ತಾನ್, ಸತ್ತಂ.

In ಕೊನ್ಱಾನ್, ಕೊಂದಂ ; ನಿನ್ಱಾನ್, ನಿಂದಂ ; ಶೆನ್ಱಾನ್, ಸಂದಂ—*nd* of the Kannaḍa verbs is, as stated before, the phonetic equivalent of the Tamil *nṟ* ; in ವಾಡ್ನಾನ್, ಬಾಡ್ಡಂ ; ವಿಟ್ಟಂದಾನ್, ಬಿಟ್ಟಂ ; ಕಟಿಂದಾನ್, ಕಟಿದಂ—a nasal is inserted in the Tamil verbs ; and in ಕಱ್ಱಾನ್, ಕಲ್ತಂ ; ಪೋನ್ಱಾನ್, ಪೋಲ್ತಂ the concurrent consonants of the Tamil verbs are euphonically changed according to the phonetic rules of that language, while those of the Kannaḍa verbs undergo no change.

Another temporal particle used for forming the past tense in all the three languages is *i*, which is followed by *d* in Kannaḍa and *n* in Tamil and Telugu. ಪಾಡಿದಂ, ಪಾಡಿನಾನ್, ಪಾಡಿನಾಂಡು. This is the only particle in Telugu, while Tamil and Kannaḍa have the two particles *i* and *d*. In ಪಾಡಿದಂ *i* is the sign of the past tense and *d* which follows, though an old sign of the preterite, is supposed to be used here for preventing hiatus, just like *n* in Tamil. In classical Tamil occur the verbs ಶೆಯ್ದು and ಶೆಯ್ದುಂ (ಕೆಯ್ದು and ಕೆಯ್ದುಂ) as the singular and plural of the first person not only in the past tense but also in the future. There is likewise another form of the past tense ಪಾಡೆನು: in Telugu which does not show the temporal particle *i*, but the plural ಪಾಡಿರಿ shows it clearly. In Telugu grammars *e* also is given as a sign of the preterite.

As stated before, the future tense is mostly alike in Tamil and Kannaḍa. But one or two peculiarities in Tamil may be noted here. Classical Tamil has, as a sign of the future tense, ಕು or ಗು for the first person singular and ಕುಂ or ಗುಂ for the first person plural : ಶೆಯ್ಗು. ಶೆಯ್ಗುಂ. Kannaḍa, too, possesses the suffix ಕುಂ or ಗುಂ, which is, however, used not in the first person but in the third person singular and plural of all the three genders. ಅವಂ, ಅವಳ್, ಅದು, ಅವರ್, ಅವು—ಇರ್ಕುಂ, ನಡೆಗುಂ. It has further to be noted that Tamil does not form its third person neuter singular by affixing the temporal particles *v*, *p* or *b*, but has to borrow the aorist future in ಉಂ which also serves as the future relative participle. Thus, instead of ವರುವದು it uses the form ವರುಂ. In this respect Kannaḍa is more regular since it uses the form ಬರ್ಪುದು or ಬರುವುದು containing the temporal particle *p* or *v*. In Telugu the future tense is formed not by affixing any temporal particle but by the use of the auxiliary verb ಕಲುಗು : ಕೊಟ್ಟೆಗಲನು, I shall strike ; ಕೊಟ್ಟೆಗಲಮು, we shall strike. There is, however, a peculiar tense in Telugu known as ತದ್ಧರ್ಮಮು, corresponding to the present indefinite, which is used to express what is true at all times. This may be taken as another future tense. In this the third person neuter singular is formed by adding the suffix ನು to the root : ಚೇಯುನು, ಅವುನು. And this form corresponds to the Tamil neuter singular in *um*—ಶೆಯ್ಯುಂ, ಆಗುಂ.

The present tense. There does not appear to be a proper present tense in the Draviḍian dialects. Formerly Tamil had only the past and future tenses and no present tense. The oldest grammar of the Tamil language, *Tolkāppiyam*, does not mention it, and it is only the later grammar *Nannūl* of the 12th century, that gives the suffixes ಆನಿನ್ರು, ಕಿನ್ರು and ಕಿರು for the present tense. The suffix in Old Kannaḍa is ದಪ and in Modern Kannaḍa ಉತ or ಉತ್ತ. And the suffix in Telugu is ಉಚು. ಶೆಯ್ಗಿನ್ರೇನ್, ಶೆಯ್ಗಿನ್ರೇನ್ ಶೆಯ್ಗಿರೇನ್ ; ಗೆಯ್ದಪೆಂ ಗೆಯ್ಯುತ್ತೇನೆ ; ಚೇಯುಚುನ್ನಾನು. From the Telugu form we see that the present tense in that language is formed by adding the substantive verb ಉನ್ನಾನು to the present verbal participle ಚೇಯುಚು of the verb ಚೇಯು *to do*. The same is the case with the Aryan vernaculars of the North. The Bengāli present tense ಕರಿತೇಛ is made up of the present participle ಕರಿತೇ and the substantive verb ಆಛ. The Kannaḍa suffixes are quite different from those of Tamil, but the Modern Kannaḍa suffix ಉತ is similar to the Telugu suffix ಉಚು, the colloquial form of which is ಉತು. The form ಗೆಯ್ಯುತ್ತೇನೆ of Modern Kannaḍa is a corruption of ಗೆಯ್ಯುಥೇನು which is even now heard in some parts of the Kannaḍa country, and ಗೆಯ್ಯುಥೇನು is made up of the present verbal participle ಗೆಯ್ಯುತ or ಗೆಯ್ಯುತೆ and the substantive verb ಇಹೆನು, exactly like the Telugu form. Similarly the correct forms for the third person singular, masculine and feminine, are ಗೆಯ್ಯುಥಾನು and ಗೆಯ್ಯುಥಾಳು which stand for ಗೆಯ್ಯುತ + ಅಹನು and ಗೆಯ್ಯುತ + ಅಹಳು. In the same manner the Old Kannaḍa form ಇರ್ದಪೆಂ is corrupted into ಇದ್ದೇನು which is compounded of the past verbal participle ಇದ್ದು and the verb ಅಹೆನು. Similarly ಗೆಯ್ದಪೆಂ = ಗೆಯ್ದು + ಅಹೆಂ, so that the temporal particle has to be taken as ಅಪ or ಅಪ್ಪ and not as ದಪ as given in the grammars. We thus see that the present tense in Kannaḍa is formed by annexing the verbs ಇಹೆಂ or ಅಹೆಂ (ಅಪ್ಪೆಂ) to the present and past verbal participles: ಇರು·ಥೇನು (ಇರುತಿಹೆಂ or ಇರುತಹೆಂ), ಇದ್ದೇನು (ಇರ್ದಹೆಂ). In ಕೂಡಿದಪೆಂ *d* is used to prevent hiatus as is the case in the past tense ಕೂಡಿದಂ. The final *e* was subsequently added either as a mark of emphasis or as a help to enunciation. More probably it was used as a mark of distinction between the present and the contingent forms. This *e* is not found in Tamil and Telugu. In Tamil the present tense is very seldom seen in early poetical works and has never been found in old inscriptions, thus showing that it is of recent origin. This probably accounts for the unusual fact that Tamil and Kannaḍa which agree so closely in the formation of the past and future tenses differ so widely in the formation of the present tense. .The so-called present tense in these languages is really an imperfect tense. It may also be added here that unlike Tamil, Kannaḍa and Telugu possess a contingent future: ಅಡಿಯಾನು ಅಡಿಯಾಳು ಅಡೀತು ; ಅಡೇನ ಅಡಿಯಾರು ಅಡೇರು ; ಅಡೀಯೆ ಅಡೇವು ; ಅಡೀರಿ ಅಡೇರು ; ಅಡಿಯೇನು ಅಡೇನು ; ಅಡಿಯೇವು, ಅಡೇಮು.

The negative mood.

The negative mood or voice forms, as stated before, one of the distinctive features of the Dravidian family of languages. Tamil and Kannaḍa are in perfect agreement in the formation of this mood, both of them annexing the pronominal suffixes directly to the verbal theme: ಕೊಡೇನ್ ಕುಡೆಂ ; ಶೆಯ್ಯೇನ್ ಕೆಯ್ಯೆಂ ; ವಾರಾನ್ ಬಾರಂ ; ಶೆಯ್ಯಾದು ಕೆಯ್ಯದು. In Telugu, however, *a*, the negative particle, is inserted between the root and the termination. ಚೇಯನು ಚೇಯಮು ; ಚೇಯವು ಚೇಯರು ; ಚೇಯಂಡು ಚೇಯರು. The same is the case in the other languages also as is evidenced by the forms ಅಱಿಯಾದೇ ಅಱಿಯದೆ ; ಅಱಿಯಾದ ಅಱಿಯದ, corresponding to the Telugu forms ಚೇಯಕ ಚೇಯನಿ ; only the negative particle is *a* in Kannaḍa as in Telugu, and *ā* in Tamil. But, in very early Kannaḍa the particle *ā*, too, occurs as in Tamil, *e.g.*, ತಪ್ಪಾದೆ. The particles are also clearly seen in the negative abstract nouns ಶೆಯ್ಯಾಮೈ ಕೆಯ್ಯಮೆ ಚೇಯಮಿ. The negative particle *a* may probably be a contraction of *al* and in this form it occurs in the imperative mood in Old Tamil and Kannaḍa poetry: ಪಯನಿರ್ ಶೊಱ್ಬಾರಾಟ್ಟು ವಾನ್ಮೈ ಮಗನೆನರ್, ಶೆಯ್ಯಱ್ಕ, ಶೆಯ್ಯನ್ಮಿನ್ ; ಬನದಲ್ಲಿ ಪುಗರ್ ಪುಗರೆಂಬ ಗಂಡುಗೋಗಿರೆ, ಬಗೆಯರ್, ಬಗೆಯಲಂ. *Al* does not occur in Telugu: ಚೇಯಕುಮು. In poetical Tamil ಶೆಯ್ಯಾ is used for ಶೆಯ್ಯಾದು. Similarly ಅಗ or ಅಗಾ is used for ಅಗದು in Kannaḍa.

Causative verbs.

The causative particle used in Tamil is *v* which euphonically assumes the shapes of *p* and *b* also. *P* also occurs as a causative particle in Kannaḍa and Telugu: ಅಱಿವಿ ಕಿಡವಿ ಕಾಣ್ಬಿ ; ತೆಳಿವಿ ತಿಳಿಪು ತೆಲುಪು ; ತಿರುಪ್ಪು ತಿರುಪು ತ್ರಿಪ್ಪು ; ಅಱಿಪು ಕೆಡಪು ಕಾಣ್ಪು

ಮಡಿಪು ಇಟಿಪು; ಡೂಪು ಮೇಪು ರೇಪು ಉಡುಪು ನೇರುಪು. Besides *p*, Kannaḍa has in common with Telugu the suffix *chu*, and also *isu* the corresponding Telugu suffix being *inchu*: ಘೋಣರ್ಚ್, ಅಟಿಲ್ಚು, ಸಾರ್ಚ್; ತೇಲುಚು ಪೂನುಚು, ಕುದುರುಚು; ಕಟ್ಟಿಸು ಕಟ್ಟಿಂಚು; ಮಾಣಿಸು ಮಾನಿಂಚು; ಕರಗಿಸು ಕರಗಿಂಚು; ಗುಣಿಸು ಗುಣಿಯಿಸು ಗುಣಿಂಚು ಗುಣಿಯಿಂಚು. The suffix *chu* also occurs in Modern Tamil—ಪಾಯ್ಚ್ಚು.

I may add here that in Tamil intransitive verbs become transitive by the doubling and hardening of the consonant of the formative or tense sign: ಪೆರುಗು ಪೆರುಕ್ಕು; ಪೋಡು ಪಾಟ್ಟು; ತಿರುಂದು ತಿರುತ್ತು; ಶೇರ್ಗಿಱೇನ್ ಶೇರ್ಕ್ಕಿಱೇನ್.

Appellative verbs.

The formation of appellative verbs is similar in all the three languages, only Telugu has not a proper third person singular except the neuter singular: ಶೇವಗನೇನ್ ಸೇವಕನೇನ್ ಸೇವಕುಡನು; ಶೇವಗನಯ್ ಸೇವಕನಯ್ ಸೇವಕುಡವು. The plural forms are regular in Tamil, plurality being expressed by the personal termination alone; but in Kannaḍa and Telugu the noun, too, is pluralised. ಶೇವಗನೇಂ ಸೇವಕರೆವು ಸೇವಕುಲಮು. Kannaḍa has two plural forms when pronouns and adjectives are used as appellative verbs: ಪಿರಿಯೆವು ಪಿರಿಯರೆವು; ಪೆಱೆವು ಪೆಱರೆವು; ಪಿರಿಯಿರ್ ಪಿರಿಯರಿರ್.

The imperative.

All the three languages agree in using the verbal theme or root as the second person singular in the imperative mood: ಶೆಯ್ ಕೆಯ್ ಚೇಯು; ಕೊಳ್ ಕೊಳ್ ಕೊನು; ಪಾಡು ಪಾಡು ಪಾಡು. In Telugu, however, the suffix *mu* is generally added to the root: ಚೇಯುಮು ಪಾಡುಮು ಪಿಲುವುಮು ರಕ್ಷಿಂಪುಮು. In Tamil and Kaṇnaḍa the suffix *a* is added to the root when it is intended to express wish or entreaty rather than command: ನೀ ಪಿರಂಗ, ಪೊಲಯು; ನೀಂ ಕೇಳ, ನೋಡ. In Telugu the suffix *mu* becomes *ma*: ಚೇಯುಮ ಪೋಷಿಂಪುಮ. The second person plural suffix is ಮಿನ್ in Tamil, ಇಂ in Kannada and ಡು in Telugu: ಶೆಯ್ಮಿನ್ ಕೆಯ್ಯಿಂ ಚೇಯುಡು If, as some scholars suppose, the *m* of the Tamil suffix *min* is euphonic, then the identity of the Tamil and Kaṇnaḍa suffixes becomes clear. Modern Tamil uses *um* in place of *min*: ಪಾಡುಂ ವಾೞುಂ. Modern Kannaḍa either omits the *m* of the suffix *im*, or adds the suffix *iri* which corresponds to the Tamil suffix *īr*, the final *i* being merely enunciative: ಕೇಳಿ ನೋಡಿ; ಕೇಳಿರ್ ಕೇಳಿಂ. The forms used for the negative are also nearly identical in Tamil and Kannaḍa, but different in Telugu: ಶೆಯ್ಯನ್ಮೆನ್ ಕೆಯ್ಯಲಂ ಚೇಯಕುಂಡು. The first person plural suffix in Kannaḍa is *am* and in Telugu *dam*: ಕೆಯ್ವಂ ಚೇಯುದಿಮು. If *d* is considered euphonic, the suffixes become the same in both languages. The verbal noun with the suffix ಅದು and its equivalents is used as an imperative in all the three languages: ಪೋವದು ಪೋಪುದು ಪೋವುನದಿ. In Tamil *al* is both the affirmative and negative suffix in the second person singular, but in Kannaḍa only the negative suffix: ಪಯಱಿಲ್ ಶೊಱಿಪ್ಪರಾಟ್ಟುವಱನ್ಮೆ ಮಱಗನೆನಲ್। ಮಕ್ಕಟ್ಟ ದಡಿಯೆನಲ್; ಪುಗಲ್. The suffix for the third person singular and plural is *ke* or *ge* in Kannaḍa and *ka* in Tamil: ಕಿಡುಗೆ ಕೆಡುಗ; ಬಾೞ್ಗ ವಾೞ್ಗ; ರಕ್ಷಿಕ್ಕೆ ಇರಕ್ಷಿಕ್ಕ. Modern Kannaḍa has also the forms ಪೋಗ ಆಗ. The suffixes in Telugu are quite different: ಎದುನ್ and ತನ್. ಪೋಷಿಂಚೆದುನ್ ಪೋಷಿಂಚುತನ್; ವೆಲುಗಲಗೆದುನ್ ಮೇಲುಗಲುಗುತನ್.

The infinitive.

The infinitive suffix common to the three languages is *a*. ಶೆಯ್ಯ, ಕೆಯ್ಯ, ಚೇಯ. Sometimes datives of verbal nouns in ಅಲ್ in Tamil and Kannaḍa and in ಉಟ in Telugu are used as infinitives: ಕಾಣಱ್ಕು ಕಾಣಲ್ಕೆ ಕನುಟಕು; ಶೆಯ್ಯಱ್ಕು ಕೆಯ್ಯಲ್ಕೆ ಚೇಯುಟಕು. In Kannaḍa infinitives end in *al* also: ದೇದಲ್ ಕೊಲ್ಲಲ್ ಕೆಯ್ಯಲ್. These forms are identical with the Tamil verbal nouns ವೇಂಡಲ್ ಕೊಲ್ಲಲ್ ಶೆಯ್ಯಲ್. They are not, however, used as verbal nouns in Kannaḍa at present, though there seems to be a great probability of their having been so used at one time as the following examples seem to indicate: ಕೆಯ್ಯಲಾಯ್ತು ಶೆಯ್ಯಲಾಯಿಱ್ಱು; ಕೂಡಲರಿದು ಕೂಡಲರಿದು; ಕೆಯ್ಯಲ್ವೇಟ್ಕುಂ ಶೆಯ್ಯಲ್ವೇಂಡುಂ; ಕೆಯ್ಯಲ್ ತಕ್ಕುದು ಶೆಯ್ಯಲ್ತಕ್ಕದು. In the examples ಮಾಡವೇಟ್ಕುಂ, ಪೋಗ

ಕೂಡದು, ತರವೇಡ್ we have to suppose that *l* is omitted. Similarly in ಚೇಯಂಗೂಡದು, ಚೇಯರಾದು, ಚೇಯುವರೆನು the suffix ಉಟ may be supposed to be omitted. In ಮಾಡಲ್‌ಪೋದಂ, ಕೇಳರ್‌ಬಂದಂ the dative suffix *ke* is understood.

The relative participle.

As stated before, the use of the relative participle is a characteristic feature of the Draviḍian languages. The relative participle is a participial adjective invariably followed by a noun. It very well answers the purpose of the relative pronoun which the Draviḍian languages do not possess. The suffix most largely used in the three languages in the formation of this participle is *a*, which is invariably annexed to the temporal particles: ಶೆಯ್ದ ಕೆಯ್ದ ಚೇಸಿನ; ನಡಂದ ನಡೆದ ನಡಚಿನ; ಪಾಡಿನ ಪಾಡಿದ ಪಾಡಿನ; ಶೆಯ್ಯುನ್ಱ ಕೆಯ್ಯುತ್ತಿರ್ಪ ಚೇಯುಚುನ್ನ; ಓದುವ ಚದುವಗಲ.

In the formation of the preterite relative participle appear the same peculiarities as were noticed in the formation of the past tense In Kannaḍa and Telugu there is no proper present relative participle; what is used as such is formed by the addition of the substantive verb, *e.g.*, ಪಾಡುತ್ತಿರುವ (and not ಪಾಡಿದಪ), ಪಾಡುಚುನ್ನ. Tamil has the forms ಪಾಡಾನಿನ್ಱ, ಪಾಡುಗಿನ್ಱ, ಪಾಡುಗಿಱ. Tamil has now no future relative participle corresponding to the Kannaḍa one in *a*, ಬರ್ಪ ಬರುವ, though instances of such participles occur in Old Tamil poetry: ಕುನ್ಱಮೋರ್ ವರುವಪೋರ್ ಕಲುಟೆ ಮೇರ್ ವಂದು ತೋನ್ಱಿನಾನ್ (*Kamba-Rāmāyaṇam, Bālakāṇḍam*). The existence in Tamil of a future relative participle in *a* is also indicated by forms such as ಪೋವದು, ಕಾಣ್ಬವನ್, etc. The form now used instead is the aorist future in *um*, ಶೆಯ್ಯುಂ, ಪಾಡುಂ, ಕೊಲ್ಲುಂ, without any temporal suffix. Besides the regular form, Kannaḍa makes use of this form also: ಪಾಡುಂ ಕುಯಿರ್ ಪಾಡುಂಗೋಗಿರೆ. ಆಡುಂಬೊಲಂ, ಪಱುಂಜವ್ವನಂ, ತೂಗುಂದೊಟ್ಟಿರ್, ಕುತ್ತುಂಗಱು, ಇಟಿಯುಂಡೊಟ್ಟು. Again, both the languages omit the suffix *um* and use the root alone in combination: ಸುಡುಗಾಡು ಸುಡುಗಾಡು; ಅಡುಗೂಡ್ ಅಡುಗೂಡ್; ಕೊರ್ಯಾನೈ,

ಬಿಡುಗಣ್, ಬಿಡುವಾಯ್. In Telugu, too, there is no regular future relative participle, this participle being formed in that language by the addition of ಗಲ from the root ಕಲುಗು. ಚೇಯಂಗಲ ಕೊಟ್ಟಂಗಲ. There are also the suffixes ಎಡು and ಎಡಿ added to the root to express the same idea: ಚೇಯೆಡು ಚೇಯೆಡಿ; ಕೊಟ್ಟೆಡು ಕೊಟ್ಟೆಡಿ. Further, the root alone is also used in combination as in Tamil and Kannaḍa: ಚದುವು ಪಾಠಮು, ಚೇಯುಪನಿ. The negative relative participle in Telugu ends in *ni* unlike those of Tamil and Kannaḍa which end in *a*. The particle of negation is *ā* in Tamil and *a* in Kannaḍa and Telugu: ಶೆಯ್ಯಾದ ಕೆಯ್ಯದ ಚೇಯನಿ; ಪಾಡಾದ ಪಾಡದ ಪಾಡನಿ.

The verbal participle.

The formation of the preterite verbal participle is exactly the same in Tamil and Kannaḍa. The suffixes used are *u* and *i*, of which *u* is always annexed to the temporal particle, while *i* is annexed directly to the verbal theme: ವಾಟ್ನ್ದು ಬಾಟ್ದು; ಕಂಡು ಕಂಡು; ಕಱ್ಱು ಕಲ್ತು; ಶೆಯ್ದು ಕೆಯ್ದು; ಆಡಿ ಆಡಿ; ವೇಂಡಿ ಬೇಡಿ; ತಿರುಪ್ಪಿ ತಿರುಪಿ. Telugu uses only one suffix *i*: ಪಾಡಿ, ಕೊಟ್ಟಿ, ಮಱಚಿ, ಪೋಷಿಂಚಿ. Telugu agrees with Kannaḍa in having a present participle which is not found in Tamil, as also in not having a future participle which is found in Tamil. The present participle is formed in Kannaḍa by the addition of ಉತೆ or ಉತ್ತೆ and ಉತಂ or ಉತ್ತುಂ, and in Telugu by the addition of ಉಚು: ಪಾಡುತೆ ಪಾಡುತ್ತೆ; ಪಾಡುತುಂ ಪಾಡುತ್ತುಂ; ಪಾಡುಚು. ತಿನುತುಂ ತಿನುಚು. The negative verbal participle ends in ದು in Tamil, in ದೆ in Kannaḍa and in ಕ in Telugu, the particle of negation being, as in the negative relative participle, ಆ in Tamil and ಅ in Kannaḍa and Telugu: ತಪ್ಪಾದು ತಪ್ಪದೆ ತಪ್ಪಕ; ಶೆಯ್ಯಾದು ಕೆಯ್ಯದೆ ಚೇಯಕ. In ancient Kannaḍa the Tamil form ತಪ್ಪಾದೆ with a long *a* occurs.

The passive voice, etc.

The passive voice is rarely used in the Dravidian languages. It has no special suffix and the passive signification is expressed by auxiliary verbs such as ಪಡು signifying "to suffer": ಕಟ್ಟಪ್ಪಟ್ಟದು ಕಟ್ಟರ್ ಪಟ್ಟುದು ಕಟ್ಟಬಡೆನು. There are several ways in which an active verb is used to express a passive sense: ಉಡೈಂದದು ಒಡೆಯಿತು ವಿಱಿಗೆನು (it was broken); ಎೞುದಿನಪುತ್ತಗಂ ಬರೆದ ಪುಸ್ತಕಂ ವ್ರಾಸಿನ ಪುಸ್ತಕಮು (a written book); ಶೆಯ್ಯಲಾಯಿಱ್ಱು ಕೆಯ್ಯಲಾಯ್ತು ಚೇಯುಟ ಅಯಿನದಿ (it was done); ಅಡಿಯುಂಡಾನ್ ಏಟುತಿಂದನು ದೆಬ್ಬದಿನೆನು (he was beaten).

As stated before, Malayāḷam has dropped the personal terminations and uses the verbal participle as a finite verb: ಞಾನ್ ಅಡಿಚ್ಚು (ಅಡಿತ್ತು), I beat; ನೀ ಅಡಿಚ್ಚು, you beat; ಅವನ್ ಅಡಿಚ್ಚು, he beat.

Telugu does not possess, like Tamil and Kannaḍa, distinct suffixes for denoting different genders, numbers and persons. It uses, as has already been stated, the neuter suffix for the third person feminine singular. Again in the present, future and indefinite tenses the forms for the second and third person plurals are the same—ಕೊಟ್ಟುಚುನ್ನಾರು, ಕೊಟ್ಟಗಲರು, ಕೊಟ್ಟುದುರು, ಕೊಟ್ಟೆದರು; in the past and indefinite tenses the forms for the third person singular of the three genders and the third person neuter plural are the same—he, she, it, they ಕೊಟ್ಟೆನು, ಕೊಟ್ಟುನು, ಕೊಟ್ಟೆಡುನು, ಕೊಟ್ಟೆನಿ; and in the future tense the forms for the second person singular and the third person neuter plural are the same—ಕೊಟ್ಟಗಲವು.

INDECLINABLES.

Some of the indeclinables are either identical or similar in form in all the three languages or any two of them. The conjunctive *um*, the emphatic *ē*, the interrogative *ē* and *ō*, the particles of doubt *ā* and *ō*, and the particle of similarity *pōl* are the same in Tamil and Kannaḍa. The emphatic *ē*, the interrogative *ō* and the particle of doubt *ā* are also found in Telugu. The conjunctive particle in Telugu is *nu* or *yu*. ಅಯ್ಯೋ, ಆಹಾ,

ಓಹೋ, ಚೀ are common to the three languages. Some similar forms found in Tamil and Kannaḍa are:

ಮಱ್ಱು ಮತ್ತು, ಇನಿ ಇಂ, ಮುನ್ ಮುಂ, ಪಿನ್ ಪಿಂ, ಮಿಗ ಮಿಗೆ, ತವ ತವೆ, ಶಾಲ ಸಲೆ, ವೆಱುಮನ್ನೆ ಬಱಿದೆ, ಉಱು ಉಱೆ, ವೇಱು ಬೇಱೆ, ಶುಮ್ಮಾ ಸುಮ್ಮನೆ, ಉಡನ್ ಒಡನೆ, ಅನ್ಱು ಅಂದು, ಇನ್ಱು ಇಂದು, ಎನ್ಱು ಎಂದು, ನಾಳೈ ನಾಳೆ, ಎನ್ಱರೋಡುಂ ಎನಱೊಡಂ, ವರುವದುಂ ಬರ್ಪುದುಂ, ತನ್ನೈಯುಂ ತನಕ, ಪಡಪಡೆನ ಪಟಪಟನೆ.

A few found in Kannaḍa and Telugu are:

ಮೊನ್ನೆ ಮೊನ್ನ, ಅಕ್ಕಟ ಅಕ್ಕಟ, ತಟಕ್ಕನೆ ತಟುಕ್ಕುನ, ಕಟ್ಕನೆ ಗ್ರಕ್ಕುನ, ಇಗೋ ಇಗೋ, ಮಾತ್ತು ಮಱು.

A few similar forms found in the three languages are:

ನೆನ್ನರ್ ನಿನ್ನೆ ನಿನ್ನ; ನಾಳೈನಿನ್ಱು ನಾಳಿದ್ದು ಎಲ್ಲುಂಡಿ; ಯಾದಾನುಂ (ಯಾದಾಯಿನುಂ) ಏನಾನುಂ ಏಮಯಿನ.

Formation of Words.

Simple words are formed from verbal or nominal roots by the addition of suffixes.

Verbal nouns.

Verbal nouns are formed either by adding certain suffixes to the verbal theme or by some internal change in the root itself such as the lengthening of the root vowel, etc. In some cases, however, the verbal noun is identical with the root itself. Some suffixes are similar in the three languages and some in two, while others are peculiar to each language:

ತರ್ ತ ತ—ಶೆಯ್ದರ್ ಕೆಯ್ತ ಚೇತ; ಅಱೈದರ್ ಅಱೆತ ಅಱತ. ಕ್ಕೈ ಕೆ ಕ—ಪಡುಕ್ಕೈ ಪಡೆಕೆ ಪಡುಕ; ಅಮರಿಕ್ಕೈ ಅಮರ್ಕೆ ಅಮರಿಕ; ಅಂಜಿಕ್ಕೈ ಅಂಜಿಕೆ ಅಂಜಿಕ. ವಡಿಕ್ಕೈ ವಡಿಕೆ ವಡಿಕ—ನಡವಡಿಕ್ಕೈ ನಡವಡಿಕೆ ನಡವಡಿಕ. ವು ವು ವಿ—ತೆಳಿವು ತಿಳಿವು ತೆಲಿವಿ. ವು ವು ವು—ಶಾವು ಸಾವು ಚಾವು. ವಡಿ ವಳಿ ವಡಿ—ನಡವಡಿ ನಡೆವಳಿ ನಡವಡಿ. (Negative) ಆಮೈ ಅಮೆ ಅಮಿ—ಶೆಯ್ಯಾಮೈ ಕೆಯ್ಯಮೆ ಚೇಯುವಿ.

Suffixes which are similar in Tamil and Kannaḍa.

ಉಳ್—ವಿಕ್ಕುಳ್ ಬಿಕ್ಕುಳ್; ವು—ಅಟಿವು ಅಟಿವು, ಅಱಿವು ಅಱಿವು; ಅವು— ಕಳವು ಕಳವು, ವರವು ಬರವು, ಶೆಲವು ಸಲವು; ಅಂ—ಆಟಂ ಆಟಂ, ನಡುಕ್ಕಂ ನಡುಕಂ, ಆಟ್ಟಂ ಆಟಂ. ಕೂಟ್ಟಂ ಕೂಟಂ; ಐ ಎ—ಕೊರೈ ಕೊರೆ, ನಗೈ ನಗೆ, ಕೊಡೈ ಕೊಡೆ; ಪು ಪು or ಪಿ—ಕಾಪ್ಪು ಕಾಪು, ನಿನೈಪ್ಪು ನೆನಪು,

ನೋನ್ಬು ನೋಂಬಿ ; ವಿ ವೆ or ಬಿ—ಮಱವಿ ಮಱವೆ, ಕೇಳ್ವಿ ಕೇಳ್ವೆ, ಕಲ್ವಿ ಕಲ್ಪಿ ; ಟ ತೆ—ಪುಗಟ್ಚಿ ಪೊಗಡ್ತ, ನಿಗಟ್ಚಿ ನೆಗಡ್ತ.

Suffixes which are similar in Kannaḍa and Telugu.

ಮೆ ಮಿ—ತಾಳ್ಮೆ ತಾಲಮಿ ; ಗಡೆ ಗಡ—ತೇಱುಗಡೆ ತೇಱುಗಡ, ಬಿಡುಗಡೆ ವಿಡುಗಡ ; ವು—ತಡವು ತಡವು ; ವಳಿ ಬಡಿ—ಸಾಗುವಳಿ ಸಾಗುಬಡಿ ; ಪ— ತಿರಿಪಂ ತಿರಿಪಮು.

Suffixes peculiar to Tamil.

ವೈ—ಪಾರ್ವೈ ; ಕು—ಪೋಕ್ಕು ; ದಿ—ಮಱದಿ ; ಚಿ—ಪುಣರ್ಚ್ಚಿ ; ಕಾಡು —ಶಾಕ್ಕಾಡು.

Suffixes peculiar to Kannaḍa.

ಇಸು—ಉಣಿಸು ; ಗುಳ್—ಬಯ್ಗುಳ್ ; ಪ—ಬರೆಪಂ ; ವಿ—ಬಗವಿ ; ಹು—ಬಾಹು.

Suffixes peculiar to Telugu.

ಉಟ—ಚೇಯುಟ ; ಪು—ಐದುಪು ; ಕಿ—ಕೋರಿಕಿ ; ಅ—ಎಂಡ ; ಅಕ— ಅಮ್ಮಕಮು ; ಡು—ದಿಗುಡು ಅಮ್ಮುಡು.

In all the three languages a large number of verbal nouns is formed by internal change such as the lengthening of the root vowel, etc.

ಕೇಡು ಕೇಡು ಚೇಟು ; ಪಾಡು ಪಾಡು ಪಾಟು ; ಪಾಟ್ಟು ಹಾಡು ಪಾಟ ; ಮುಟುಕ್ಕು ಮುಟುಕು ಮುನುಕ ; ಕೋಳ್ ಕೋಳ್ ; ಶೂಡು ಸೂಡು ; ವೀಡು ಬೀಡು. ಎಟುತ್ತು, ಮಾರ್. ಕೋಡು, ಏಸು. ಅಟು (from ಅಡುಚು), ಪೋಟು (from ಪೊಡುಚು).

Some verbal nouns in these languages are, as stated before, of the same form as the verbal theme itself.

ಕಟ್ಟು, ತಪ್ಪು ; ದಾಂಡು ದಾಂಟು ದಾಟು ; ಶೊರ್, ಮುಱು ; ತಡೆ, ನುಡಿ ; ತಿಟ್ಟು ಮೆಟ್ಟು.

In Tamil and Kannaḍa participial nouns are formed by affixing either demonstrative pronouns or pronominal terminations to the relative participles ending in *a*.

Participial nouns.

ವಂದಾನ್ ವಂದೋನ್ ವಂದವನ್, ಬಂದಂ ಬಂದೊಂ ಬಂದವಂ ; ವಂದಾಳ್ ವಂದವಳ್, ಬಂದಳ್ ಬಂದವಳ್ ; ವಂದಾರ್ ವಂದವರ್, ಬಂದರ್ ಬಂದವರ್ ; ವಂದದು, ಬಂದುದು, ವಂದವೈ ಬಂದುವು ; ವರುವಾನ್ ವರುಬವನ್, ಬರ್ಪಂ ಬರ್ಪವಂ ; ವರುವಾಳ್ ವರುಬವಳ್, ಬರ್ಪಳ್ ಬರ್ಪವಳ್ ; ವರುವಾರ್ ವರುಬವರ್, ಬರ್ಪರ್ ಬರ್ಪವರ್ ; ವರುವದು ಬರ್ಪುದು, ವರುಬವೈ ಬರ್ಪುವು ; ವಾರಾದಾನ್ ವಾರಾದವನ್, ಬಾರದಂ ಬಾರದವಂ ; etc.

In Telugu demonstrative pronouns alone are added.

ಚೇಸಿನವಾಂಡು, ಚೇಯಂಗಲವಾಂಡು; ಚೇಸಿನದಿ, ಚೇಯಂಗಲದಿ, etc.

Tamil has participial nouns of the present tense also: ವರುಗಿನ್ರಾನ್ ವರುಗಿನ್ರವರ್, etc.

But in Old Kannaḍa there is no present participial noun according to Kēśirāja (*Śabdamaṇidarpaṇa*, sūtra 73), though Bhaṭṭākaḷanka allows it (*Śabdānuśāsana*, sūtra 447) ಬಂದಪನಂ, etc. In Modern Kannaḍa, however, as in Telugu, the present participial noun is formed from the substantive verb added to the present verbal participle: ಪಾಡುತ್ತಿರುವಂ, ಪಾಡುತ್ತಿರುವವಂ, ಪಾಡುಚುನ್ನವಾಂಡು, etc. The neuter participial noun is used in three senses—as the third person neuter of the verb, as a neuter relative participial noun and as a verbal participial noun. Thus ಮಾಡುವುದು or ಶೆಯ್ಗಿಱದು means 'it does,' or 'that which does,' or 'the doing' or 'to do.' The participial noun formed from the future is very common as a verbal noun in Kannada. Tamil possesses abstract relative participial nouns of the present and past tenses as well as participial nouns of the first and second persons, which are not found in Kannaḍa and Telugu · ವರುಗಿನ್ರವೈ, ವಂದವೈ; ವಂದೇನೈ, ವಂದಾಯೈ, etc.

Abstract nouns.

A few of the suffixes used in the formation of abstract nouns are common to all the three languages, while others are special to each or any two of them. The common suffixes are ಮೈ, ಪು and ತನಂ. They are generally added to the crude form of the adjectives of quality:

ಪೆರುಮೈ ಪೆರ್ಮೆ ಪೇರಿಮಿ; ಮೇನ್ಮೈ ಮೇರ್ಮೆ ಮೇಲಿಮಿ; ನನ್ಮೈ ನಲ್ಮೆ, ವನ್ಮೈ ಬಲ್ಮೆ, ಪಶುಮೈ ಪಸುಮೆ; ಶಿವಪ್ಪು ಕೆಂಪು ಕೆಂಪು; ವೆಳುಪ್ಪು ಬೆಳ್ಪು ತೆಲುಪು; ಇನಿಪ್ಪು ಇಂಪು; ಕಱುಪ್ಪು ಕರ್ಪು; ಪೆರಿಯತನಂ ಪಿರಿಯತನಂ ಗೊಪ್ಪತನಮು; ಕಲತನಂ ಕಲತನಮು; ಅಗ್ಗಳಿಕೆ ಅಗ್ಗಲಿಕ.

Of the special suffixes may be mentioned ಗು, ಅಂ in Tamil ನನ್ಗು, ನಲಂ; ಱಿಕ, ನ in Telugu ಚಿನ್ನಱಿಕಮು, ನಲ್ಲನ; and ಉ in Kannaḍa ಕಿವುಡು, ಗುಜ್ಜು.

Derivative nouns.

Derivative nouns are formed in these languages by adding what are known as *taddhita* suffixes to nominal themes. Very few suffixes are common to the three languages and even of these the meaning is not always quite the same:

ಗುಣವಾನ್ ಗುಣವಂತಂ ಗುಣವಂತುಁಡು ; ಗುಣಮುಳ್ಳಾನ್ ಗುಣಮುಳ್ಳಂ ; ಪೆರುಮೈಯುಡೈಯಾನ್ ಪೆರ್ಮೆಯೊಡೆಯಂ ; ಅಟಮಟಿಗ ಅಟಮಟ್ಟೀಁಡು, ಮಾವಟಿಗ ಮಾವಟೀಁಡು ; ಪಣಕ್ಕಾರನ್ ಹಣಗಾಱಂ ; ಆಟಗಾಱ ಆಟಕಾಁಡು ; ತಿಂಡಿಪೋತ ತಿಂಡಿಪೋತು ; ಮುಕ್ಕಿಁಡಿ ಮೂಕೊಱ ; ಕುಱ್ಱವಾಳಿ ; ಮಡಿವಳ, ಕಲ್ಲಾಯ್ತ್ತು, ಅಲರಿಚ, ಲಂಚಂಗುಳಿ ; ವಗಲಾಁಡು, ಕೊಂಡಕಾಁಡು, ಚಱುತುಕ ; ಪಾಂಬಾಟ್ಟಿ ಪಾವಡಿಗಂ ಪಾಮುಲವಾಁಡು.

Compound nouns.

Under the heading euphonic combination (p. 60) a few compound nouns which are similar in two or three of the Dravidian languages of Southern India have already been given. „ A few more may be added here:

ಶೆಂದಾಮರೈ ಕೆಂದಾವರೆ ಕೆಂದಾಮರ ; ಶೆಂಗಣ್ಣನ್ ಕೆಂಗಣ್ಣಂ ; ಶಾರೈಪ್ಪಾಂಬು ಕೇರೆಹಾವು ; ಪೆರಿಯಮಗನ್ ಪಿರಿಯಮಗಂ ; ಕರುಂಗುದಿರೈ ಕರ್ಗುದುರೆ ; ಅರಮನೈ ಅರಮನೆ ; ಮಲ್ಲಿಗೈನನೈ ಮಲ್ಲಿಗೆನನೆ ; ಇಱಯುಂಪೋಱು ಇಱಯುಂದೊಱ್ತು ; ಮಾಂಗಾಯ್ ಮಾಂಗಾಯ್ ; ಕೆಱುನೀರ್ ಚೆಱುವುನೀರು, ಮೇಂಗಾರ್ ಮೀಂಗಾಲು ; ಪೆಡದರ ಪೆಡತಲ ; ಮೂಜಗಂಗ್ಗಳ್ ಮುಜ್ಜಗಮುಲು ; ಪೆಳ್ಗುದುರೆ ತೆಲ್ಲಗುಱ್ಱಮು ; ಮುಕ್ಕಣ್ಣಂ ಮುಕ್ಕಂಟಿ ; ಸಾಸಿರಗಣ್ಣಂ ವೇಗಂಟಿ ; ಚಿಗುರುದುಟಿ ಚಿಗುರುಮೋವಿ ; ಕೈದಾವರೆ ಕೇಲುದಮ್ಮಿ ; ತೆಂಡೆರರ್ ತಮ್ಮೆರ.

In Tamil there is a peculiar class of elliptical compounds known as ಅನ್ಮೊಚಿತ್ತೊಗೈ in which certain words are to be understood which is not usual in the other languages. Compounds like ಪೆಲ್ಲಡಿ ಮೆಲ್ಲಡಿ, 'ಪವಳವಾಯ್ ಪವಳವಾಯ್, ಪಿಱೈನುದರ್ ಪೆಱೆನೊಸರ್, ಪೊಱೊಡಿ ಪೊಂಬಳೆ mean in Kannaḍa a soft foot, a coral-like lip, a crescent-like forehead and a gold bracelet, respectively, but in Tamil they convey the additional sense of a possessor of these things, especially a woman—possessor of soft or delicate feet, etc. Similar forms are rarely met with in Kannaḍa—ಕಿತ್ತಡಿ (an ascetic), ದೆಳ್ಗಡಿ (Śiva) and ಕಲ್ಲೆರ್ದೆ (a hard-hearted person) ಕರುಣಿಂ ಗೆಟ್ಟಾಕೆ ಕೈಕೆ ಕಲ್ಲೆರ್ದೆಯಕ್ಕುಂ (*Pampa-Rāmāyaṇa*, vi 164.)

CHAPTER IV

Vocabulary. Dēśya. Tatsama and Tadbhava. Tatbhava from Prākṛit and Tamil. Anyadēśya. Portuguese, Persian, Maharāṭhi, Arabic, Hindustāni, English. Sanskrit Avyayas. Northern and Southern Schools in Kannaḍa. R. Raghunatha Rao's Plea of Telugu influence. Controversy with him on three suggested points. Stages of the Kannaḍa Language. Primitive Old Kannaḍa. Haḷagannaḍa or Old Kannaḍa. Mediæval Kannaḍa. Modern Kannaḍa. Forms once condemned have become current. Explanation of Kēśirāja's 60th Sūtra.

VOCABULARY.

The vocabularies of Tamil, Kannaḍa and Telugu contain chiefly four classes of words, namely, *tatsama*, pure Sanskrit words; *tadbhava*, Sanskrit words changed to suit the languages; *dēśya*, indigenous words; and *anyadēśya*, foreign words. The dēśya class alone represents the pure essential part of these languages as distinguished from what has been imported from Sanskrit or other sources. A large number of words in the three languages is almost identical, but many are often so disguised by peculiarities of inflection and dialectic changes that not one entire sentence in one of the languages is intelligible to those who are acquainted with only one of the other two. If a Tamil, a Telugu, a Kannaḍiga and a Malayāḷi happen to travel together in a Railway train, the speech of one will not be understood by any of the other three. They will have to make gestures to make themselves mutually intelligible. To illustrate this, a funny sentence is given, namely, ಈ ಮೂಟ ಅಟ್ಟ ಪಡಿಯುಣ್ಣೀ, said to have been spoken by a Telugu man, a stranger, on entering into a Tamil man's house. The meaning of the sentence in Telugu is "Let this bundle lie over there." The Tamil man interpreted it thus: 'Flies, bugs, leeches and a measure of ticks'—and thinking that the bundle contained all this, threw it away at once to the surprise and consternation of the stranger. And yet the ancestors of these people speaking the four languages, most probably spoke one and the same language.

Dēśya. As we have already dealt in a way with verbal roots, adjectives and numerals which are either identical or similar in the three languages, we may now confine our attention to nouns only. It may be stated that the number of Kannaḍa nouns which are identical with those in Tamil are far greater than those in Telugu. The same remark also applies to Kannaḍa nouns whose identity is disguised by dialectic and other changes. Below are given some examples of nouns which are common either to all the three languages or to only any two of them; as well as of those which have undergone change in one or two languages:

Examples of nouns common to Tamil, Kannaḍa and Telugu:—

ಅಚ್ಚು, ಅಡ್ಡಿ, ಅಂಬು, ಅವಗಡಂ, ಅಪರಂಜಿ, ಉಪ್ಪು, ಕತ್ತಿ, ಕಪ್ಪಂ, ಕುಱುಚ್ಚು, ಗಂಜಿ, ಚಟ್ಟಂ, ತೆಪ್ಪಂ, ತುಂಡು, ತಗಡು, ತಗರು, ತೀರ್ಪು, ತೊಟ್ಟಿ, ದಂಡು, ದಿಡ್ಡಿ, ನೂಱು, ನಾಡು, ಪುರುಡು, ವಟ್ಟಂ, ಪಲ್ಲಿ, ದೊಟ್ಟು, ಮಟ್ಟಂ, ಮೂದೇವಿ.

Examples of Tamil nouns and those corresponding to them in Kannaḍa and Telugu that have undergone change:—

Tamil	*Kannaḍa*	*Telugu*
ಶಿಱೈ	ಸೆಱೆ	ಚೆಱ
ಯಾನೈ	ಆನೆ	ಏನಿಕ, ಏನುಂಗು
ಶೋನೈ	ಸೋನೆ	ಸೋನ
ಪಾಂಬು	ಪಾವು	ಪಾವು
ಅಟ್ಟೈ	ಅಟ್ಟೆ	ಅಟ್ಟ
ಇಣೈ	ಎಣೆ	ಎನ
ತಿರೈ	ತೆರೆ	ತೆರ
ನಿಟರ್	ನೆಟರ್	ನೀಡ
ಉರರ್	ಒರರ್	ರೋಲು

Tamil	*Kannaḍa*	*Telugu*
ಪುಗೈ	ಪೊಗೆ	ಪೊಗ
ಮುದಲ್	ಮೊದಲ್	ಮೊದಲು
ಮುಳೈ	ಮೊಳೆ	ಮೊಲಕ
ಕಿಳಿ	ಗಿಳಿ	ಚಿಲುಕ
ವಾಡಿಕ್ಕೈ	ವಾಡಿಕೆ	ವಾಡುಕ
ಅಱೈ	ಅಱೆ	ಅಱಯು
ವಾಯಿಲ್	ಬಾಗಿಲ್	ವಾಕಿಲ
ಕೈಯಿದು	ಕೈದು	ಕೈದುವು
ಪಿಳ್ಳೈ	ಪಿಳ್ಳೆ	ಪಿಲ್ಲ
ಕೂದೈ	ಗೂಡೆ	ಗೂಡ

Tamil	*Kannaḍa*	*Telugu*	*Tamil*	*Kannaḍa*	*Telugu*
ಮಡಂದೈ	ಮಡದಿ	ಮಡಁತಿ	ಮೂಕ್ಕು	ಮೂಗು	ಮುಕ್ಕು
ವೆದಿರ್	ಬಿದಿರ್	ವೆದುರು	ಶರಿ	ಸರಿ	ಸರಿ
ವರೈ	ಬರೆ	ವಲ	ಕೈ	ಕೆಯ್	ಚೇಯಿ
ತಂಬಿ	ತಮ್ಮಂ	ತಮ್ಮುಡು	ನೋನ್ಬು	ನೋಂಪಿ	ನೋಮು
ಪಾಟ್ಟು	ಹಾಡು	ಪಾಟ	ಎರುದು	ಎೞ್ತು	ಎದ್ದು
ಉಡೈಮೈ	ಒಡಮೆ	ಒಡಮಿ	ಕಾರ್	ಗಾಳಿ	ಗಾಲಿ
ಉಡರ್	ಒಡರ್	ಒಡಲು	ವೆಳ್ಳಿ	ಬೆಳ್ಳಿ	ವೆಂಡಿ
ಪೊೞುದು	ಪೊೞ್ತು	ಪ್ರೊದ್ದು	ಮರುಂದು	ಮರ್ದು	ಮಂದು
ಪೆಯರ್	ಪೆಸರ್	ಪೇರು	ಎಚ್ಚಿರ್	ಎಂಜರ್	ಎಂಗಿಲ

Examples of nouns common to Tamil and Telugu :—

Tamil	*Telugu*	*Tamil*	*Telugu*	*Tamil*	*Telugu*
ಪೆರುಗು	ಪೆರುಗು	ಅಪ್ಪಂ	ಅಪ್ಪಮು	ನೆಯ್	ನೆಯಿ
ಕೂಂಡು	ಗೂಁಡು	ಆ	ಆವು	ತಾಯ್	ತಾಯಿ
ನೀಱು	ನೀಱು	ಕೊಪ್ಪು	ಕೊಪ್ಪು	ತೆರು	ತೆರುವು
ವಿತ್ತು	ವಿತ್ತು	ಅಪ್ಪಳಂ	ಅಪ್ಪಳಮು	ತಲ್ಲಿ	ತಲ್ಲಿ

Examples of Tamil nouns and those corresponding to them in Telugu that have undergone change :—

Tamil	*Telugu*	*Tamil*	*Telugu*
ಪುೞು	ಪುರುಗು	ಪನ್ದಿ	ಪಂದಿ
ಕೂೞ್	ಕೂಡು	ಅಂಗಾಡಿ	ಅಂಗಡಿ
ವಿೞುಂಗು	ಮ್ರಿಂಗು	ಪಣಿ	ಪನಿ
ಇರುಂಬು	ಇನಮು	ಕಪ್ಪರ್	ಕಪ್ಪಲ
ಅಗಪ್ಪೈ	ಅಗಪ	ಅರ್ವಂ	ಅರುವಮು
ತಿತ್ತಿಪ್ಪು	ತೀಪು	ತುಣುಕ್ಕು	ತುನುಕ
ತೆಂಗು	ತೆಂಕಾಯ	ತಟ್ಟು	ತಟ್ಟ
ತಳಿರ್	ತಲಿರು	ಅಡೈಯಾಳಂ	ಅಡಿಯಾಲಮು
ನನೈ	ನನ	ನಂಜೈ	ನಂಜ
ನೆರುಪ್ಪು	ನಿಪ್ಪು	ಆಂಡು	ಏಡು
ತಿನ್ದಿ	ತಿಂಡಿ	ಕೊಂಬು	ಕೊಮ್ಮು
ತಮುಕ್ಕು	ಟಮುಕು	ತಿಣ್ಣೈ	ತಿನ್ನೆ
ತೆರಿವೈ	ತೆಱವ	ಅಕ್ಕರೈ	ಅಕ್ಕರ
ಅಡಿಮೈ	ಅಡಿಮೆ	ಏಂದೈ	ಏಂತ
		ಶೆಡಿ	ಚೆಟ್ಟು

Examples of nouns common to Kannaḍa and Telugu :—
ಪಂದಿ, ತೊಡವು, ದಾರಿ, ನಂಟು, ನುಡಿ, ಅಂಚು, ಅಂಬಲ, ಅದಟು,

ಕೊಂಡೆ, ಠವಳಿ, ಠೀವಿ, ಠಾವು, ಡೊಂಕು, ಡೋಲು, ತಟವಟ, ಡಾಲು, ಟಕ್ಕು, ಅಲಪು, ಒಂಟಿ, ತರವಾರಿ, ತವುಡು, ಕೋತಿ, ಅಡ್ಡ, ಅಪ್ಪಟ, ಅಪ್ಪಟ್ಟಿ, ಅನು, ಗುಡಿಸ, ಅಸ್ತಿಭಾರ, ದುಟ್ಟಿ, ದಾರ, ದಪ್ಪ, ದೊಡ್ಡ, ನಗ, ನಿಚ್ಚಲು, ಕತ್ತಳಂ,* ನಿಕ್ಕುವಂ, ನೆಮ್ಮದಿ, ಅಂದಂ, ಕತಂ, ತೇಮಂ, ಗಾಣಂ (singer).

Examples of Kannada nouns and those corresponding to them in Telugu that have undergone change :—

Kannada	*Telugu*	*Kannada*	*Telugu*
ದಾಟಿ	ದಾಡಿ	ಬಿದಿರ್	ವೆದುರು
ದೋಣಿ	ದೊನ	ತಕ್ಕಡಿ	ತಕ್ಕೆಡ
ನವಿರ್	ನಮಿಲ	ತೊಳೆ	ತೊಲ
ದುಬ್ಬಳ	ದುಬ್ಬನಮು	ಅಡ್ಡಣ	ಅಡ್ಡನ
ಡಿಂಗರಿಗಂ	ಡಿಂಗರೀಂಡು	ಅಳವಿ	ಅಲವಿ
ತೆವುಲು	ತೆಗುಲು	ತಡಿಕೆ	ತಡಕ
ಅಡ್ಡಾಯುಧ	ಅಡಿದಮು	ಅಂಗುಳ್	ಅಂಗಿಲ
ಅಟ್ಟುವೆ	ಅರಕಮು	ತಂಬಿಗೆ	ತಂಬುಗ
ನೆಲ	ನೇಲ	ತುದಿ	ತುದ
ಅಂಕೆ	ಅಂಕ	ಅಕಡೆ	ಅಕ್ಕಡ
ತವಕಂ	ತವಕಮು	ಅದವಟರ್	ಅದವದ
ಅಂದುಗೆ	ಅಂದಿಯ	ಕುತ್ತಿಗೆ	ಕುತ್ತಿಕ
ಅಗ್ಗ	ಅಗ್ಗುವ	ಗೂಬಿವಿ	ಕೊಬಿವಿ
ತೊಟ್ಟಿಲ್	ತೊಟ್ಟಿಲ	ಕಡವೆ	ಕಡಮ

Examples of nouns common to Tamil and Kannada :—

ಪುಟು, ಕೂಟ್, ಪಾಟ್, ತೆಂಗು, ತೊಟ್ಟಿಲ್, ಪರರ್, ತಳಿರ್, ನಾಣ್, ಪೀಲಿ, ಈಡು, ಕದಿರ್, ಪಡಗು, ಒಪ್ಪಂ, ಮುನ್ನೀರ್, ನಂಜು, ಪಳ್ಳಿ, ಅಣ್ಣ,

---

* This word is common in Telugu in the sense of an armour. It also occurs rarely in Kannada in the same sense. The following stanza found in Śravaṇa Beḷgoḷa inscription No. 117 of A. D. 1123 contains the word :—

ಬಳಯುತರಂ ಬಲುಸುವ ಲತಾಂತಶರಂಗವಿರಾಗಿ ತಾಗಿ ನಂ ।
ಚಳಿಸೆ ಪಳಂಚಿ ತೂಳ್ದು ವನನೋಡಿಸಿ ಮೆಯ್ಯುಗೆಯಾದದೂಸಱಂ ॥
ಕಳೆಯದೆ ನಿಂದ ಕರ್ಬುನದ ಕರ್ಗಿದ ಸಿಪ್ಪಿನಮುರ್ಕೆವೆತ್ತ ಕ ।
ತ್ತಳವೆನಿಸಿತ್ತು ಪುತ್ತಡರ್ದ ಮೆಯ್ಯ ಮಳಂ ಮಳಧಾರಿದೇವರಾ ॥

As he became the natural enemy of the flower-arrowed (cupid) who harasses (even) the strong, having engaged him in a terrific fight, vanquished and chased him away, the dirt on Maladhāridēva's body, which was overgrown with an anthill, looked as if it were a close-fitting *armour* of black iron that had not yet been doffed.

ಮೆಯ್, ಮಾಡಂ, ಮಣ್, ತಾಯ್, ತೇರ್, ಅಡಿ, ಮುಡಿ, ಕಾಡು, ಪನಿ, ಅರುಂಬು, ಕಣ್, ತೋರ್, ಪಾರ್, ಪುಳಿ, ಕೊಡಿ, ಆಡು, ಕೇಡು, ತೊಂಗರ್, ನೆಯ್, ಪೆಣ್, ಶುರ್, ಪೂ, ಮುಗಿಲ್, ಅರಿಶನಂ, ಎಳ್, ತಿಂಗಳ್, ಕಡೞ, ಕಡರ್, ಕಂಬು, ಕರಗಂ, ಕರ್, ಕಳಂ, ನೀರ್, ಕಣ್ಣಿ, ಕರಡಿ, ಕಲ, ಕಳವು, ಕತ್ತು, ಕಂದು, ಕಂಬಿ, ಕರಿ, ಕಳ್ಳಿ, ಅಗಲಂ, ನೀಳಂ, ಆಟಂ, ಅಲರ್, ಅಗಟ್, ಅಂಗೈ, ಪೋರ್, ಕಾರ್, ಅಚ್ಚುಕಟ್ಟು, ಅತ್ತಿ, ಅಪ್ಪೞ, ಅಂಬಾರಂ, ಅಂಬಾರಿ, ಅಮ್ಮೞ, ಮದಿರ್, ಕೊತ್ತಳಂ, ಅಳವು, ಅಱಂ, ಅನ್ನೞ, ತಗರಂ, ಪಗರ್, ಇರುಳ್, ಕಿಚ್ಚು, ನಚ್ಚು, ತೊಡರ್, ಪಡಿ, ಪಿಡಿ, ಪಣಂ, ಅಣಿ, ಪುಣ್, ಪಿಂಡಿ, ಚೆಂಡು, ಪದಂ, ಕದವು, ತಿಪ್ಪಿ, ಕಂಬು ಕೊಂಬು, ಚೆಂಬು, ತುಮ್ಮಲ್, ಪಯಿರ್, ಪಾಡು, ಅರುಗು, ಕರುಳ್, ಕುರುಳ್, ಮರುಳ್, ಅಲಗು, ಮಲರ್, ಪ್ರೊಲಂ, ಪುಲ, ನೆರ್, ಪರ್, ಪುರ್ ನವಿರ್, ಅಟರ್, ಕಟನಿ, ಕುಟಿ, ಪಟಿ, ಪಟುವಂ, ಪುಳಿ, ಮುಳ್, ಕಳ್, ಪಳ್ಳಂ, ಕಳ್ಳಿ, ಕೊಳ್ಳಿ, ನಳ್ಳಿ, ಮುಳ್ಳಿ, ಅಱಿವು, ಪ್ರೊೞ, ಮೋಟಿ, ಅಱು, ಮಾಡಂ, ಇತ್ಯಾದಿ.

Examples of Tamil nouns and those corresponding to them in Kannaḍa ṭhat have undergone change.—

Tamil	*Kannaḍa*	*Tamil*	*Kannaḍa*
ಕೊಕ್ಕು	ಕುಕ್ಕು	ಶಿಲ	ಕೆಲ
ಎಣ್ಣೆಯ್	ಎಣ್ಣೆ	ಉಡಂಬು	ಒಡಂಬಿ
ವಲಂ	ಬಲ	ಅರುವಿ	ಅರ್ಬಿ
ಶೂರ್	ಸೂರ್	ಕಣ್ಣಡಿ	ಕನ್ನಡಿ
ವಱಿದು	ಬಱಿದು	ಕಱಿವೈ	ಕಱಿವು
ಮುಱ್ಱುಗೈ	ಮುತ್ತುಗೆ	ಕಱೈ	ಕಱೆ
ಕುಱ್ಱಂ	ಕುತ್ತಂ	ಪೊಱೈ	ಪೊಱೆ
ನೆಱ್ಱಿ	ನೆತ್ತಿ	ಶಾಱು	ಸಾಱು
ಪುಱ್ಱು	ಪುತ್ತು	ಶೇಱು	ಕೆಸಱು
ಮಱ್ಱು	ಮತ್ತು	ಶೂಱೈ	ಸೂಱೆ
ಕಯುನಿ	ಕೈನೆ	ಮನೈ	ಮನೆ
ಎಲುಮಿಚ್ಚೈ	ಇಲಮಿಂಚಿ	ವಾೞ	ಬಾೞ
ಕೈಯಡೈ	ಕೆಯ್ಯಡೆ	ಮಡೈ	ಮಡೆ
ಕುಱಡು	ಕೊಱಡು	ವಾಡೈ	ಬಾಡೆ
ಪುಗರ್	ಪೊಗರ್	ವಟ್ಟಂ	ಬಟ್ಟೆ
ವಿಳಕ್ಕು	ಬೆಳಕು	ವಟ್ಟಿಲ್	ಬಟ್ಟಲ್
ಪರುತ್ತಿ	ಪತ್ತಿ	ವಂಡು	ಬೆಂಡು
ಮಾಗಾಣಂ	ಮಾಗಣಿ	ಕೊಂಡೈ	ಕೊಂಡೆ
ತಿನ್ಱಿ	ತಿಂಡಿ	ಶಂಬಳಂ	ಸಂಬಳಂ
ಎರುಮೈ	ಎರ್ಮೆ	ಇದಟ್	ಎಸಟ್
ಕರುಂಡೊೞ	ಕರ್ದೊೞ	ತಿನೈ	ತನೆ
ವರಗು	ಬರಗು	ಕನ್ಱು	ಕಱು

Tamil	*Kannaḍa*	*Tamil*	*Kannaḍa*
ವಯಿಱು	ಬಸಿಱು	ಪೊರುಳ್	ಪುರುಳ್
ತಂಗೈ	ತಂಗೆ	ಶಟ್ಟುವಂ	ಸಟ್ಟುಗ
ವೇಲ	ಬೇಲ	ತಂದೈ	ತಂದೆ
ವೇಡರ್	ಬೇಡರ್	ಅಲುಪ್ಪು	ಅಲಪು
ಕುದಿರೈ	ಕುದುರೆ	ಕಟುದೈ	ಕದೆ
ಪೈದರ್	ಹೈದಂ	ನಿಬರ್	ನೆಬರ್
ಪೆಟ್ಟೈ	ಹೇಟೆ	ನಿಲೈ	ನೆಲೆ
ಪುನರ್	ಪೊನರ್	ನುರೈ	ನೊರೆ
ಶೇಗು	ಚೇಗು	ಮುಗೈ	ಮೊಗೆ
ವಡಕ್ಕು	ಬಡಗು	ಕುಡಂ	ಕೊಡಂ
ತೇಕ್ಕು	ತೇಗು	ಶುಡರ್	ಸೊಡರ್
ಮರುಂಗುಲ್	ಮಗ್ಗುಲ್	ಕಡಲೈ	ಕಡಲೆ
ಕರುಂಬು	ಕಬ್ಬು	ಕುಡೈ	ಕೊಡೆ
ಕಟುತ್ತು	ಕತ್ತು	ಕೊಡೈ	ಕೊಡೆ
ಉಟುಂದು	ಉದ್ದು	ಒಟ್ಟೈ	ಒಂಟೆ
ಮಾಮಱಂ	ಮಾವಂ	ಮುಟ್ಟೈ	ಮೊಟ್ಟೆ
ವಾಯ್ಕ್ಕಾಲ್	ಬಾಯ್ಕಾಲ	ಪಡೈ	ಪಡೆ
ಶಾಮೈ	ಸಾಮೆ	ತಟ್ಟು	ತಟ್ಟೆ
ಮುರುಂಗೈ	ನುಗ್ಗೆ	ನಿಣಂ	ನೆಣಂ
ಮಯಿರ್	ನವಿರ್	ಪಿಣಂ	ಪೆಣಂ
ಮುಟಂಗಾರ್	ಮೊಣಕಾರ್	ಶಿದಲೈ	ಗೆದಲ್
ವಲಂಬುರಿ	ಬಲಮುರಿ	ಮುದಲೈ	ಮೊಸಳೆ
ಪಱುವಿ	ಹಱುವಿ	ನುದಲ್	ನೊಸಲ್
ಕುರುಂಬೈ	ಕುರುಬೆ	ಮುದಲ್	ಮೊದಲ್
ಪುನ್ನೈ	ಹೊನ್ನೆ	ವೆದಿರ್	ಬಿದಿರ್
ಅಡೈಕ್ಕಾಯ್	ಅಡಕೆ	ಎದಿರ್	ಇದಿರ್
ಕಾರ್ವಾಯ್	ಕಾಲ್ವೆ	ಪೊದು	ಪುದು
ಅಡೈಪ್ಪಂ	ಹಡಪಂ	ಮೂಪ್ಪು	ಮುಪ್ಪು
ಅಣಿರ್	ಅಳಿರ್	ವದುವೈ	ಮದುವೆ
ವಿರಲ್	ಬೆರಲ್	ವಿತ್ತು	ಬಿತ್ತು
ಅಣ್ಣಂ	ಅಣ್ಣಂ	ತೊತ್ತು	ತೊಱು
ಅರಕ್ಕು	ಅರಗು	ಇಮೈ	ಎವೆ
ಅರುತ್ತಿ	ಅಟ್ಟಿ	ಪೆಯರ್	ಪೆಸರ್
ಅಱುವೈ	ಅಱುವೆ	ವಯಲ್	ಬಯಲ್
ಉಡರ್	ಒಡರ್	ಉಯಿರ್	ಉಸಿರ್
ಉಗಿರ್	ಉಗುರ್	ವೆಯಿರ್	ಬಿಸಿಲ್
ಪಗೈ	ಪಗೆ	ಇರಲೈ	ಎರಲೆ
ವಿಕ್ಕಲ್	ಬಿಕ್ಕಳ್	ಉರಲ್	ಒರಲ್

Tamil	*Kannaḍa*	*Tamil*	*Kannaḍa*
ಪೂರಿ	ಪುರಿ	ವೞಿ	ಬೞಿ
ವರಿಶೈ	ವರಿಸೆ	ತಡೈ	ತಡೆ
ಇರೈ	ಎರೆ	ಕಿಳಿ	ಗಿಳಿ
ಎಲಿ	ಇಲಿ	ವೆಲ್ಲಂ	ಬೆಲ್ಲಂ
ಕುಲೈ	ಗೊಲೆ	ತಿಱಂ	ತೆಱಂ
ಕೊಲೈ	ಕೊಲೆ	ಶಿಱುತ್ತೈ	ಚಿಱುತ
ವಲೈ	ಬಲೆ	ನನವು	ನನಸು
ಏರ್	ಬಿರ್	ಕಡುವನ್	ಗಡವಂ
ಕವಣೈ	ಕವಣೆ	ಕೞಂಜು	ಕಣಜ
ಶುಟಿ	ಸುಟಿ	ಕನ್ನಂ	ಕನ್ನ
ಇಳವೈ	ಎಳವೆ	ಕವಡಿ	ಕವಡೆ
ಅಳೈ	ಅಳೆ	ಕುಳಂಬು	ಕೊಳಗು
ವೆಳ್ಳಿ	ಬೆಳ್ಳಿ	ವೆಳ್ಳಂ	ಬೆಳ್ಳಂ
ಮುೞಂ	ಮೊೞಂ	ಶಿಱಪ್ಪು	ಚೆಱಪು
ಶೆಱೈ	ಸೆಱೆ	ಶಿಱಿದು	ಕಿಱಿದು
ಶೋಳಂ	ಜೋಳಂ	ಕನವು	ಕನಸು
ಕಱುಪ್ಪು	ಕರ್ಪು	ಮಾಱ್ಱಂ	ಮಾತು
ಕನ್ಱು	ಕಂದು	ತಾಡೈ	ತಾಡೆ
ಕುಳಂ	ಕೊಳಂ	ಪುನ್ನೈ	ಪೊನ್ನೆ
ತುಣೈ	ತೊಣೆ	ಏರಾಳಂ	ಹೇರಳ
ಪಿಳ್ಳೈ	ಪಿಳ್ಳೆ	ಈಚ್ಚು	ಈಚಲು
ಮಱವಿ	ಮಱವೆ	ನಾಂಜಿರ್	ನೇಗಿರ್
ಪಿೞೈ	ಪೞೆ	ತೊಟುತ್ತೈ	ತೊಟ್ಟು
ನಾಱ್ಱಂ	ನಾತಂ		

ಇತ್ಯಾದಿ

These examples in Tamil and Kannaḍa which contain only a selection of words may be enlarged to any extent. To give all the words that are more or less indentical in the two languages, we shall have to transcribe more than a half of the words given in the dictionaries of these tongues.

Tatsama and Tadbhava.

All the four Draviḍian languages of Southern India have Sanskrit words, both pure (tatsama) and corrupt (tadbhava) introduced into their vocabularies to a smaller or greater extent. The number of Sanskrit words in Tamil is comparatively small, in Kannaḍa and Telugu rather large and in Malayāḷam the largest. With regard to Tamil, it is stated that the works of Avvai—*Āttiśūḍi*, etc., contain altogether 2,020 words, of which only 156 are Sanskrit. Similarly, the Tamil work *Narundogai* which contains 600 words in all has only 24 Sanskrit words. As we go back, Tamil literature shows an increase in the number of Tamil words with a proportionate decrease in Sanskrit words. In Telugu, according to the *Śabdaratnākara* there are 12,337 dēśya words, 14,814 tatsama words and 2,000 tadbhava words. No such enumeration is found in any Kannaḍa work, though there is a large number of Sanskrit words in that language. According to Caldwell the reason why the amount of Sanskrit employed in the other Draviḍian languages is considerably larger than in Tamil and the use of it has acquired more of the character of a necessity is because the literatures of those languages have chiefly been cultivated by Brāhmaṇas, while in Tamil few Brāhmaṇas have written anything worthy of preservation. This is true only to a limited extent with regard to Kannaḍa, and probably Telugu also. We know for a fact that the best works in Kannaḍa have been written not by Brāhmaṇas but by Jainas who were strong advocates of purism in the use of Kannaḍa That it is possible to avoid the use of Sanskrit in Kannaḍa and Telugu is evidenced by the existence in those languages of works such as the *Kabbigarakāva* of Āṇḍayya and the *Yayāticharitra* of Ponnaganṭi Telaganna which contain no pure Sanskrit words though tadbhavas are freely admitted. It is, however, a well-known fact that almost all the early Jaina authors in Kannaḍa were good Sanskrit scholars and consequently, notwithstanding their advocacy of purism in the use of Kannaḍa, some Sanskrit words must have entered into the Kannaḍa vocabulary. Besides, Kannaḍa, in common with Tamil, has borrowed Sanskrit words to express abstract ideas of philosophy, science and religion. Later writers in all these languages have unhesitatingly introduced a pretty large number of Sanskrit words, though, in most cases, there was no necessity for doing so. These circumstances account for the presence of a large number of Sanskrit words in these languages, though the words in Kannaḍa and Telugu may be somewhat in excess of those in Tamil.

The occurrence of a large number of Sanskrit words in the Draviḍian languages of Southern India led some orientalists of a former generation, such as Colebrooke, Carey, Wilkins and others, to believe that these languages were derived from Sanskrit. But, now, such notions are known to be without any foundation. These orientalists did not, as Caldwell says, take into account the material circumstance that the pronouns and numerals of the Draviḍian languages, their verbal and nominal inflections, and the syntactic arrangement of their words —everything, in short, which constitutes the living spirit of a language—were originally and radically different from Sanskrit. Besides, the grammatical structure and system of sounds in Sanskrit and the Draviḍian languages are, as was amply shown before, essentially different. Further, it will be quite difficult to account for the existence of indigenous words which constitute the major portion of the vocabulary of each one of these languages. There is, moreover, the circumstance that the uncultivated Draviḍian dialects contain scarcely any Sanskrit words.

The first word *tat* in the compounds tatsama and tadbhava is taken in Kannaḍa grammars to denote Sanskrit, but in Telugu it is taken to denote Prākṛit also. So we have four classes of words: Samskṛita-sama, Samskṛita-bhava, Prākṛita-sama and Prākṛita-bhava. And this classification is desirable since there are instances of words which it is easier to derive from Prākṛit than from Sanskrit. Thus, the Kannaḍa word ಕಂಬಂ (Telugu ಕಂಬಮು) may be more easily derived from the Prākṛit ಖಂಭೋ than from the Sanskrit ಸ್ತಂಭಃ. I give below a few other instances of words in their Sanskrit, Prākṛit and Kannaḍa forms where it will be clearly seen that the Kannaḍa form is more alike the

Prākṛit than the Sanskrit form, and may therefore be called Prākṛita-bhava :—

ದಂಷ್ಟ್ರಾ	ದಾಢಾ	ದಾಡೆ	ಶೀಕರಃ	ಸೀಧರೋ	ಸೀವರಂ
ಶ್ರೀಃ	ಸಿರೀ	ಸಿರಿ	ಕಟುಃ	ಕಾರೋ	ಕಾರಂ
ವೃತ್ತಂ	ವಟ್ಟಂ	ಬಟ್ಟ	ವೈದ್ಯಃ	ವೇಜ್ಜೋ	ಬೆಜ್ಜಂ
ಕೂರ್ಪಾಸಃ	ಕುಪ್ಪಿಸೋ	ಕುಪ್ಪಸಂ	ರಾಜ್ಞೀ	ರಾಣೀ	ರಾಣಿ
ನಿರ್ಝರಃ	ಓಜ್ಝರೋ	ಒಜ್ಜರಂ	ಶ್ರದ್ಧಾ	ಸಡ್ಢಾ	ಸಡ್ಡೆ
ಪರ್ಯಸ್ತಃ	ಪಲ್ಲಟ್ಟೋ	ಪಲ್ಲಟಂ	ವಿಜ್ಞಾನಂ	ವಿಣ್ಣಾಣಂ	ಬಿನ್ನಾಣಂ
ಶಿಥಿಲಃ	ಸಢಿಲೋ	ಸಡಿಲ	ಹರಿದ್ರಾ	ಹಲದ್ದಾ	ಹಳದಿ
ಸ್ಥೂಲಃ	ಥೋರೋ	ತೋರ	ಶಯ್ಯಾ	ಸೆಜ್ಜಾ	ಸೆಜ್ಜೆ
ಆಳಿಃ	ಓಳೀ	ಓಳಿ	ಆಜ್ಞಾ	ಆಣಾ	ಆಣೆ
ಸ್ನುಷಾ	ಸುಸಾ	ಸೊಸೆ	ಜ್ಯೋತ್ಸ್ನಾ	ಜೋಣ್ಹಾ	ಜೊನ್ನಂ
ಸಾಕ್ಷೀ	ಸಕ್ಖೀ	ಸಕ್ಕಿ	ತ್ವರಿತಂ	ತುರಿಅಂ	ತುರಿಹಂ
ವಿದ್ಯಾ	ವಿಜ್ಜಾ	ಬಿಜ್ಜೆ	ಸಿಂಹಃ	ಸಿಂಘೋ	ಸಿಂಗಂ
ಯಜ್ಞಃ	ಜಣ್ಣೋ	ಜನ್ನಂ	ಮಲಿನಂ	ಮಇಲಂ	ಮಯಿಲ
ಅಂತಃಪುರಂ	ಅಂತೇಉರಂ	ಅಂತವುರಂ	ಪೃಥಿವೀ	ಪುಢವೀ	ಪೊಡವಿ
ತೀಕ್ಷ್ಣಂ	ತಿಖ್ಖಂ	ತಿಕ್ಕಂ	ಅಗ್ನಿಃ	ಅಗ್ಗೀ	ಅಗ್ಗಿ
ವಿದ್ಯುತ್	ವಿಜ್ಜೂ	ಬಿಜ್ಜು	ಮೂರ್ಖಃ	ಮುರುಹೋ	ಮುರುವಂ

There are again other words which are identical with the Prākṛit forms and may consequently be styled Prākṛita-sama. The following are a few instances of such words :—

ನಿಭ	ನೆಪ	ನೆಪ	ವಕ್ರ	ವಂಕ	ವಂಕ
ಸ್ನೇಹ	ನೇಹ	ನೇಹ	ಸದೃಶ	ಸರಿಸ	ಸರಿಸ
ಪ್ರತಿ	ಪಡಿ	ಪಡಿ	ಕಾರ್ಯ	ಕಜ್ಜ	ಕಜ್ಜ
ಸ್ಥಾನಂ	ಠಾಣಂ	ಠಾಣಂ	ನೂಪುರಂ	ಣೇಉರಂ	ನೇವುರಂ
ವ್ಯಾಖ್ಯಾನಂ	ವಖ್ಖಾಣಂ	ವಕ್ಖಾಣಂ	ಅಂಗಾರ	ಇಂಗಾಲ	ಇಂಗಾಲ

Such tadbhavas are also found in Tamil and Telugu.

In this connection, it may be mentioned that tadbhavas like ಅಚ್ಚುಕಟ್ಟು (ಅತ್ಯುತ್ಕೃಷ್ಟ), ಅಂಬಿಲ (ಆಮ್ಲ), ಗಾವುದ (ಗವ್ಯೂತ), ಪಕ್ಖ (ಪಕ್ಷ), ಪಸುಬೆ (ಪ್ರಸೇವ), ಸದ್ದು (ಶಬ್ದ), ಸಕ್ಕರೆ (ಶರ್ಕರಾ) are found in Pāli dictionaries; as also words such as ಓಲಗ, ಕಾವರ, ಫೋಟ (ಫೊಟ್ಟೆ) in Hēmachandra's *Dēśināmamālā*.

In the earliest period in Tamil, the changes introduced in adapting Sanskrit words are very irregular. The following examples will illustrate this point :—

Sanskrit	*Tamil*	*Sanskrit*	*Tamil*
ಶ್ರೀ	ತಿರು	ಪುಷ್ಯ	ಪೂಶಂ
ಜ್ಯೇಷ್ಠಾ	ಕೇಟ್ಟೈ	ಮಾರ್ಗಶೀರ್ಷ	ಮಾರ್ಗಟಿ
ಶ್ರವಣಂ	ಓಣಂ	ಪೂರ್ವಾಭಾದ್ರಪದಾ	ಪೂರಟ್ಟಾದಿ
ವೈಶಾಖ	ವೈಗಾಶಿ	ಆಶ್ಲೇಷಾ	ಆಯಿಲಯಂ
ಫಾಲ್ಗುಣ	ಪಂಗುನಿ	ಪೂರ್ವಾ	ಪೂರಂ
ಆಶ್ವಯುಜ	ಐಪ್ಪಶಿ	ಶತಭಿಷಕ್	ಶದಯಂ
ಅನೂರಾಧಾ	ಅನುಷಂ	ಮಾಘ	ಮಾಶಿ

It is worthy of notice that ತೈ is derived from ತೈಷ್, ಅವಿಟ್ಟಂ from ಶ್ರವಿಷ್ಠಾ and ಪುರಟ್ಟಾಶಿ from ಪ್ರೋಷ್ಠಪದೀ.

The old tadbhava of ಕರ್ಮನ್ was ಕನ್ಮಂ, its modern equivalent being ಕರುಮಂ which is quite regular. The omission of sibilants is a very common feature in the formation of tadbhavas in Tamil. ಸಂಧ್ಯಾ becomes ಅಂದಿ, ಶ್ರಾವಣ ಆವಣಿ, ಶ್ರಮಣ ಅಮಣನ್, ಸೀಸ ಈಯಂ.

Telugu tadbhavas are more or less similar to those in Kannaḍa. Compare ಅಸಡ್ಡ with ಅಸಡ್ಡೆ, ಅಂದಲ with ಅಂದಳ, ಪಿನ್ನಪ with ಬಿನ್ನಪ, ಆಗಿಸೆ with ಆಗಿಸ, ಅಚ್ಚೆರುವು with ಅಚ್ಚರಿ.

Some tadbhavas in Kannaḍa, such as ಅರಸು, appear to be derived directly from Tamil tadbhavas. The tadbhava of ರಾಜನ್ in Tamil is ಅರಶನ್ or ಅರಶು, where the introduction of the vowel *a* before a word beginning with *ra* is, as stated before, peculiar to Tamil. In Kannaḍa the tadbhava of ರಾಜನ್ would properly be ರಾಯಂ. So the forms ಅರಸಂ, ಅರಸು, ಅರಸಿ are directly derived from the Tamil ಅರಶನ್, ಅರಶು, ಅರಶಿ. The same appears to be the case with the Kannaḍa words ಏಣಿ, ದಾವು, ನೊಗ, ಬಿನ್ನಪ, ಕೆಲಸ and ಸೊಣಗ. The omission of sibilants being, as stated before, a peculiarity of Tamil, the tadbhava of ಶ್ರೇಣಿ would in that language be ಏಣಿ; but in Kannaḍa it ought to be ಸೇಣಿ. The word in Kannaḍa for a ladder is, however, not ಸೇಣಿ but the Tamil form ಏಣಿ. ನೊಗ is derived from ನುಗಂ, the Tamil tadbhava of ಯುಗ, a yoke. So also is ಬಿನ್ನಪ from ವಿಣ್ಣಪ್ಪಂ,

the tadbhava of ವಿಜ್ಞಾಪ್ಯ. ಕೆಲಸ is derived from ಕಿರಿಶ್ಶೈ, the Tamil tadbhava of ಕ್ರಿಯಾ. Similarly ದಾವು and ಸೊಣಗ appear to be nearer to the Tamil forms ತಾಂಬು and ಶುಣಂಗ than to the Sanskrit ದಾಮ್ರ and ಶುನಕ. On the other hand, the Tamil ಆಯಿರಂ is derived from the Kannaḍa tadbhava ಸಾಸಿರಂ.

In Tamil, the aspirate *h* is always omitted; *e.g*, ಹರಿ ಅರಿ, ಹಿತಂ ಇದಂ, ಹೋಮಂ ಓಮಂ, ಹೇತು ಏತು, ಹಾರಂ ಆರಂ; but in Kannaḍa and Telugu it is rarely that the aspirate is omitted, though Telugu omits it oftener than Kannaḍa; *e.g.*, ಅಡಪಮು, ಅರಿವಾಣಮು, ಅರಿಗೋಲು, ಅರುಸಮು (ಹರ್ಷ), ಅಲಂದಿ; ಉದ್ಧ, ಇಂಗು. In the first five examples given from Telugu, Kannaḍa retains the aspirate. ಉದ್ದ is for ಹುದ್ದ (ಪೂರ್ವ) and ಇಂಗು for ಹಿಂಗು.

It may be noted that in these languages there are a few cases in which an aspirate is inserted where it is not required; *e.g.*, ಹಾರತಿ for ಆರತಿ (ಆರಾತ್ರಿಕಂ), ಹಗ್ಗಿ for ಅಗ್ಗಿ (ಅಗ್ನಿ).

Anyadēsya.

Anyadēsya or foreign words have largely entered into Kannaḍa and other Draviḍian languages owing to various causes, such as, among others, commercial intercourse, geographical contiguity, administrative control and absence of indigenous words to express new things or ideas. A few of them have become naturalised, *i.e.*, look like native words, *e.g.*, ನಂಗೂರಂ or ಲಂಗರ್ for anchor; ರಾಂದರ್ for lantern; ದುಸ್ತು for dress; ತುರುಪು for trump or troop; ಬುರುಸು for brush; ಇಸ್ಕೂಲು for screw; ಸಾಬೂನು for soap; ಗಿಲೀಟು for gilt; ಪಿಟೀಲು for fiddle. These words may be arranged according to the languages from which they have been borrowed.

Portuguese.—ಅಲಮಾರು, ಜನ್ನರ್, ಪಾದಿರಿ, ಇತ್ಯಾದಿ.

Persian.—ಜಮೀನ್, ದಸ್ತಾವೇಜು, ಬಂದೋಬಸ್ತು, ಮೇಜಾ, ರಸ್ತೆ, ಸರಬರಾಯಿ, ಸಿಪಾರಸ್, ಸಿಬ್ಬಂದಿ, ಸೀಪಾಯಿ, ಸುಮಾರು, ಇತ್ಯಾದಿ.

Mahrāṭhi.—ಪಸ್ತಾನು, ಬಾಪು, ಧಳಿರೆ, ಮರು, ಇತ್ಯಾದಿ.

Arabic.—ಅನಾಮತ್ತು, ಅಲಾಕ್ಕು, ಅಸಾಮಿ, ಇರಾಖಾ, ಕಾಯ್ದೆ,

ಖಜಾನಾ, ಗಾಡಿಖಾನಾ, ಜಪ್ತಿ, ನಾಜೂಕು, ಮಾಮೂಲು, ವಸೂಲ್, ಸಾವಕಾರಿ, ಇತ್ಯಾದಿ.

Hindustāni.—ಅಂತಸ್ತು, ಅಂದಾಜು, ಅಂಬಾರಿ, ಅತ್ತರ್, ಅದುಬ್ಬು, ಅಮಾನಿ, ಅಮಾನತ್ತು, ಅರ್ಜಿ, ಅವರ್, ಅಸರ್, ಅಖೈರು, ಇನಾಮು, ಇರಾದೆ, ಇಸವಿ, ಇಸ್ತ್ರಿ, ಉಮೇದು, ಊದಾ, ಕಂತು, ಕಂದಾಯ, ಕಚೇರಿ, ಕಬೂಲು, ಕಮ್ಮಿ, ಕರಾರು, ಕಲಾಯಿ, ಕಸಬು, ಕಾಗದ, ಕಾಜಿ, ಕಾನೂನು, ಕಾಮಗಾರಿ, ಕಾರ್ಖಾನ, ಕಿಚ್ಚಡಿ, ಕಿಟಕಿ, ಕಿರಿಕಿರಿ, ಕಿಸ್ತು, ಕೀರು, ಕುಲಾವಿ, ಕೊಠಡಿ, ಕೊರಾಟ್, ಕೋಟಾ, ಖರೀದಿ, ಖರ್ಚು, ಖಾಲಿ, ಗಡಿಯಾರ, ಗಾಡಿ, ಗಾಬರಿ, ಗಿರಾಕಿ, ಗುಮಾಸ್ತ, ಗುಲಾಬಿ, ಗುಲಾಮ, ಗೋಲ, ಗೌಸು, ಚಕ್ಕುಬಂದಿ, ಚಡ್ಡಿ, ಚರ್ಲ್, ಚಾಕರಿ, ಚಾಲಕ್ಕು, ಚಾಳೀಸ, ಚಿರಂಡಿ, ಚಿಲ್ಲರೆ, ಚುಂಗಡಿ, ಚುನಾವಣೆ, ಚೂರಿ, ಜಂತಿ, ಜಮಖಾನ, ಜಮಾಬಂದಿ, ಜಮೆ, ಜಲ್ದಿ, ಜವಾನ, ಜವಾಬು, ಜಹಗೀರು, ಜಾಗ, ಜಾಪ್ತಾ, ಜಾಸ್ತಿ, ಜೋಡು, ಟಪಾಲ್, ಟೋಪಿ, ಠಾಣಾ, ಠೀವಿ, ಡಬ್ಬು, ಡವಣ್, ಡಾಬು, ಡೇರೆ, ಡೋಲ, ತಗಾದೆ, ತಂಟೆ, ತಯಾರು, ತರಕಾರಿ, ತಾರೀಖು, ತಾಲೂಕ, ತೊರಾ, ದಮಾಸ್, ದರ್ಜಿ, ದರ್ಬಾರ್, ದಲ್ಲಾಳಿ, ದಸ್ತು, ದಿನಸು, ದಿವಾನ, ದಿವಾಳಿ, ದುಪಟಾ, ನಗದು, ಪಂಚಾಯಿತಿ, ಪಂಜಾ, ಪಕ್ಕಾ, ಪಲ್ಲಕ್ಕಿ, ಪಸಂದ್, ಪಸಾರೆ, ಪಾರಾ, ಪೂರಾ, ಪೇಷ್ಕಾರ್, ಪೈಸರ್, ಬಂಗಲಾ, ಬಚಖಾನೆ, ಬಾಕಿ, ಬೇಡಿ, ಮಜಲು, ಮಜೂರಿ, ಮಸಾಲೆ, ಮಸೀದಿ, ಮಹಡಿ, ಮಿಠಾಯಿ, ಮೈದಾನ, ಮೊಹರಂ, ಮೊಹರು, ರಂಜಾನ್, ರಜಾ, ರಾಜಿ, ರುಜು, ರುಮಾಲು, ರೂಪಾಯಿ, ರೈತ, ರೊಕ್ಕ, ಲಂಚ, ಲಕೋಟೆ, ಲಾಡು, ಲಾಯ, ಲಾಳ, ಲೂಟಿ, ವಕೀಲ, ವರದಿ, ವಹಿ, ವಾಪಸು, ವಾಯಿದೆ, ಶಾಬಾಸ್, ಶಾಯಿ, ಶಾಲುವೆ, ಶಿಲ್ಕು, ಷೋದಾ, ಸರಕಾರ, ಸರಕು, ಸರದಿ, ಸಲಾಮು*, ಸವಾರಿ, ಸಾಮಾನು, ಸೀಸೆ, ಹಕ್ಕು, ಹದ್ದು, ಹಾಜರ್, ಹಾಜಿ, ಹುಂಡಿ, ಹುಷಾರ್, ಹೋಬಳಿ, ಇತ್ಯಾದಿ.

English.—ಅಪೀಲ್, ಆಫಿಸ್, ಇಂಕ್, ಇನೀಮಾ, ಇನ್ಷ್ಯೂರ್, ಎಕರೆ, ಎನ್ವಲಪ್, ಔನ್ಸು, ಕಂತ್ರಾಟು, ಕವರು, ಕಾಪಿ, ಕಾಮ, ಕಾರ್ಡು, ಕೇಸು, ಕೋರ್ಟು, ಕೌಲನ್, ಕ್ಯಾಂಡರ್, ಕ್ಯಾಮರಾ, ಕ್ಲಬ್ಬು, ಕ್ಲಾಸು, ಕ್ರಿಕೆಟ್ಟು, ಕ್ವೈನಾ, ಗೆಜೆಟ್, ಗೋಲ್, ಗೌನ್, ಗ್ಯಾಸ್, ಚೆಕ್ಕು, ಚಾರ್ಜು, ಚಿಮ್ನಿ, ಜಡ್ಜಿ, ಜ್ಯೂರ್, ಟನ್, ಟರಂ, ಟವರ್, ಟಾನಿಕ್, ಟಿಕೀಟು, ಟೀ, ಟೆಕ್ಸು, ಟೆನಿಸ್, ಟೇಬಲ್, ಟೈಂಪೀಸ್, ಟ್ರಂಕು, ಟ್ರೆಜರಿ, ಟ್ವೀಡ್, ಡಜನ್, ಡಾಕ್ಟರ್, ಡಿಗ್ರಿ, ಡಿಪಾಜಿಟ್, ಡಿವಿಡೆಂಡ್, ಡೆಪ್ಯು, ಡೆಲಿವರಿ, ಡೈರಿ, ಡ್ರಾಂ, ಡ್ರಿಲ್, ಥರ್ಮಾಮಿಟರ್, ನಂಬರ್, ನಾಟ್ಪೇಯ್ಡ್, ನೋಟಿಸ್, ನೋಟ್ಬುಕ್ಕು, ನೋಟ್ಸು, ಪಿಯಾನೊ, ಪೀರಿಯಡ್, ಪೆನ್ಸಿಲ್, ಪೆನ್ಷನ್, ಪೇನಾ, ಪೈಮೇಸ್ತ್ರಿ, ಪೊಲೀಸ್, ಪೋರ್ಟರ್, ಪೋಸ್ಟು, ಪೋಸ್ಟೇಜ್, ಪ್ಯಾಸ್, ಪ್ಯಾಂಸರಿ, ಪ್ರೋನೋಟ್, ಪ್ಯಾನಲ್, ಪ್ಲೀಡರ್, ಪ್ಲೇಗ್,

* This word is found in the Kannaḍa proverb ಕಂಕುಳಲ್ಲ ದೊಣ್ಣೆ ಕೈಯಲ್ಲ ಸಲಾಮು as given in Kittel's Dictionary, though ಶರಣಾರ್ತಿ usually occurs in place of ಸಲಾಮು. In Tamil, however, it has been used even in poetry by Aruṇagirinādar, a poet of about the 17th century :—

ಶುರಾದಿಪತಿ ಮಾಲಯನು ಮಾಲೊಡು ಶಲಾ ಮಿಡು
ಶುವಾಮಿ ಮಲೈವಾಯುಂ ಪೆರುಮಾಳೇ! (ತಿರುಪ್ಪುಗಳ್).

ಫಾರಂ-ಫೆಯಿರ್, ಫೋಟೋ, ಬನಿಯನ್, ಬರ್ನರ್, ಬಾಂಡ್, ಬಿರ್, ಬಿಸ್ಕತ್, ಬುಕ್ಪ್ವೇಸ್ಟ್, ಬೂಟ್ಸ್, ಬೆಂಚ್, ಬೆಲೂನ್, ದ್ಯೈಬರ್, ಬ್ಯಾಂಕು, ಬ್ರಾಂದಿ, ಬ್ರೆಡ್, ಮಿಕ್ಸಡ್, ಮಿನಿಮಂ, ಮೀಟರ್, ಮೆರೀನಾ, ಮೆಷೀನ್, ಮೇಸ್ತ್ರಿ, ಮೈಲ, ಮ್ಯಾಚ್, ಮ್ಯಾಪು, ರಬ್ಬರ್, ರಿಕಾರ್ಡು, ರಿಜಿಸ್ಟರ್, ರಿಪೋರ್ಟು, ರೂಲರ್, ರೂಲು, ರೈಲು, ಲಸ್ತರ್, ಲಾಂಗ್‌ಕೋಟು, ಲಾಕಪ್, ಲಾಯರ್, ಲೀವ್, ಲೆಟರ್‌ಪೇಪರ್, ಲ್ಯಾಂಪು, ವಾರಂಟ್, ವಾಲ್‌ಲ್ಯಾಂಪ್, ವಾಚರ್, ವ್ಯಾಗನ್, ಷರ್ಟ್, ಸಬ್ಜಕ್ಟ್, ಸಮನ್, ಸರ್ಜ್, ಸವರನ್, ಸಿಮೆಂಟ್, ಸಿರಿಂಜ್, ಸಿಲ್ಕ್, ಸಿವಿಲ್, ಸೋಫಾ, ಸ್ಕೂರ್, ಸ್ಕೋರ್, ಸ್ಟಾಂಪು, ಸ್ಟೂಲ್, ಸ್ಟೇಷನ್, ಸ್ಪಂಜ್, ಸ್ಪೂನ್, ಸ್ಪೋರ್ಟ್ಸ್, ಹಾರ್ಮೋನಿಯಂ, ಹಾಸ್ಟರ್, ಹೋಟರ್, ಹ್ಯಾಂಗಿಂಗ್ ಲ್ಯಾಂಪ್, ಇತ್ಯಾದಿ.

"In Modern Kannaḍa, even Sanskrit Avyayas or indeclinables have gained currency to spoil the elegance of the vernacular. The following are some of them :— ಬಹುಶಃ, ಪ್ರಾಯಶಃ, ಪ್ರಾಯೇಣ, ಏತೇನ, ಏವಂಚ, ಪರಂತು, ಸದ್ಯಃ, ಅಥವಾ, ಪುನಃ, ಮುಖತಃ, ಕ್ರಮೇಣ, ಅಗತ್ಯಾ, ಸ್ವತಃ, ಯದ್ಯಪಿ, ಇತ್ಥಂ, ಇತ್ಯಾದಿ.

In the interests of the purity of the language it is very necessary that strenuous attempts should be made to stop as far as possible the influx of unnecessary words from foreign sources.

NORTHERN AND SOUTHERN SCHOOLS IN KANNADA.

The expressions northern and southern schools occur in the *Kavirājamārga* of Nṛipatunga, the *Kāvyāvalōkana* of Nāgavarma II and the *Śabdānuśāsana* of Bhaṭṭākaḷanka. In the second chapter of the Kavirājamārga these expressions are used when treating of the ten merits of composition. This part of the chapter being, however, mostly a translation of the first chapter of Daṇḍi's *Kāvyādarśa* in which the expressions are used in the sense of the Gauḍa and Vaidarbha schools or styles in Sanskrit, whatever Nṛipatunga has written with regard to the merits of composition refers as in the original to the Gauḍa and Vaidarbha schools, and not to the northern and southern schools in Kannaḍa. Several examples of Nṛipatunga's translation of Daṇḍi's verses are given in the Kannaḍa Introduction (pp. 23-25) to Volume II of my *Karṇāṭaka-Kavicharite*. Nṛipatunga, however, gives in another place* what he con-

* II, 100–104.

siders to be the distinguishing characteristics of the northern and southern schools in Kannaḍa, which consist merely in the use of one of the recognised duplicate forms of certain verbs in preference to the other, *e.g.*, the forms ನೋಡುವೆಂ and ಬರಿಪೆಂ in the northern and ನೋಡ್ವೆಂ and ಬರಿಸುವೆಂ in the southern. He further gives three examples in poetry of the northern and southern styles* in Kannaḍa where it is not quite clear how they differ from one another. One example is given below, for examination :—

Verse 107.

ವಿದಿತಸುರಾಧಿರಾಜಮಕುಟಾಗ್ರಸಮರ್ಪಿತದೊಳ್ ಮುನೀಂದ್ರನಾ।
ಪದಯುಗದೊಳ್ ಮನೋಮುದದೆ ಬಾಗುವೆಂ (Northern)
ತ್ರಿದಶಗಣೇಶಮೌಳಿಮಣಿಪೀಠನಿಷೇವಿಗಳೊಳ್ ಮುನೀಂದ್ರನಾ।
ಪದಯುಗಳಂಗಳೊಳ್ ಮುದದೆ ಬಾಗುವೆಂ (Southern)

Whatever may have been the case during or previous to the time of Nṛipatunga in the matter of the use of the forms of verbs noted above, we find no such distinction observed by authors who came after him.

Let us see what Nāgavarma II says about the northern and southern schools. He has adopted the title of the first chapter of Daṇḍi's work, namely, Mārgavibhāga, for the first section, which treats of the same subject, of the third chapter of his *Kāvyāvalōkana*, and has closely followed Daṇḍi, like Nṛipatunga, in the treatment of the ten merits of composition. His verses 500 and 521 are merely a translation of verses 41 and 42 of the first chapter of the *Kāvyādarśa.*† So, the northern and southern schools men-

* II, 106–108.

† ಸಮಸಂಶ್ಲಿಷ್ಟಾರ್ಥವ್ಯಕ್ತಿಮಧುರಕಾಂತಪ್ರಸನ್ನಸುಕುಮಾರೋಜ।
ಸ್ಸಮಾಧಿಮತ್ತೋದಾರಾಷ್ಟಯ। ಸಮಾಧಿಗಳ್ ಕೃತಿಗುಣಂಗಳೀರಯ್ದುಕ್ಕುಂ॥
ಇವು ನಿಯತಂ ದಕ್ಷಿಣದೇಶವರ್ತಿಕವಿರಾಜಮಾರ್ಗದೊಳ್ ನೆಗಳ್ದುವು।
ತ್ತ್ರವಣ ವಿಪರ್ಯಯವೃತ್ತಿಯು। ಉಪರಿಸು ಗುಣಮುದೀಚ್ಯಮಾರ್ಗದೊಳ್ ಪ್ರಚುರತೆಯುಂ॥
— *Nāgavarma II*.

ಶ್ಲೇಷಃ ಪ್ರಸಾದಃ ಸಮತಾ ಮಾಧುರ್ಯಂ ಸುಕುಮಾರತಾ।
ಅರ್ಥವ್ಯಕ್ತಿರುದಾರತ್ವಮೋಜಃಕಾಂತಿಸಮಾಧಯಃ॥
ಇತಿ ವೈದರ್ಭಮಾರ್ಗಸ್ಯ ಪ್ರಾಣಾ ದಶಗುಣಾಃ ಸ್ಮೃತಾಃ।
ಏಷಾಂ ವಿಪರ್ಯಯಃ ಪ್ರಾಯೋ ದೃಶ್ಯತೇ ಗೌಡವರ್ತ್ಮನಿ॥
—*Daṇḍi.*

tioned by Nāgavarma II do not refer to any such schools in Kannaḍa but to the Gauḍa and Vaidarbha schools in Sanskrit.

Coming now to Bhaṭṭākaḷanka, we find that in his commentary on *Sūtra* 288 ಅದಃ of his *Śabdānuśāsana* he recognises the existence of the northern and southern schools in Kannaḍa and tells us that, of the two forms of the pronoun of the first person, *nān* is used by the poets of the north and *ān* by those of the south. But this dictum is not borne out by literature, since we find both the forms used indiscriminately by the poets of the north and the south.

The foregoing enquiry has led us to the conclusion that according to Nṛipatunga and Bhaṭṭākaḷanka there exist the northern and southern schools in Kannaḍa, their distinguishing characteristics being the use of one of the recognised duplicate forms of certain verbs and of the pronoun of the first person in preference to the other. But a study of Kannaḍa literature shows that these distinctions are more honoured in the breach than in the observance by the poets. It does not therefore appear to serve any useful purpose at present to make too much of what is evidently a distinction without a difference and quarrel about the northern and southern schools in Kannaḍa. It is not, however, denied that in Modern Kannaḍa there are local varieties due to geographical separation of the Kannaḍa speaking communities and their contact with people speaking non-Draviḍian languages.

The late Mr. R. Raghunatha Rao, B.A., wrote at considerable length about the above-mentioned northern and southern schools in Kannaḍa and expressed the opinion that they owed their origin mainly to the influence of Telugu and Tamil respectively. There do not, however, seem to be sufficient grounds for this opinion. Mr. Raghunatha Rao seems to have argued like this: Telugu does not possess the letter ೞ (ḻ); and according to Nṛipatunga the northern school in Kannaḍa does not use verbal forms with ೞ; consequently the northern school must have come into existence through Telugu influence. Though Telugu does not at present possess the letter ೞ, it had the letter even in the early part of the 10th century, about 50 years after the time of Nṛipatunga (815–877), as is evidenced by the Bezwada Telugu poetical inscription of the Eastern Chālukya king Yuddhamalla (927–934), in which the letter is used. Again, if the northern school in Kannaḍa arose through Telugu influence, Telugu ought to have only the form *nēnu* of the pronoun of the first person, but we find in it also the other form *ēnu* corresponding to the *ān* of the southern school. Further, if the southern school arose through Tamil influence, there is no reason for the existence in that language of *nān*, the form of the northern school. It is thus seen that there are no valid grounds for supposing that the northern and southern schools in Kannaḍa were brought into existence by Telugu and Tamil influence respectively.

There was a long controversy between Mr. Raghunatha Rao and myself about this matter. He challenged me to offer a rational explanation without having recourse to Telugu influence of these three points: 1. the disappearance of the letter ೞ from Modern Kannaḍa; 2. the use of ದರೆ for all tenses in the subjunctive mood in Modern Kannaḍa; and 3. the use of ಹಲು and ಅಲ for ಹಲ್ಲು and ಅಲ್ಲ. The following was the explanation given after some preliminary remarks which ran thus:—

It is unscientific to jump to conclusions by observing similarity of form in one or two instances. We must not be carried away by superficial resemblances but must try our best to trace effects to proper causes. These resemblances may be, for ought we know, "the result of like forces working independently in different languages," or they may be independent developments of tendencies commonly inherited. When the language itself does not afford a tolerably satisfactory explanation, it is then reasonable to postulate external influence. In these cases I shall try to show that the theory of extraneous influence fails miserably, and that the changes have been *ab intra*.

1. The disappearance of ೞ from Modern Kannaḍa.

As stated before, Telugu had ೞ in the first half of the 10th century, and must have lost it about the close of that century, since, according to Telugu scholars, the earliest extant Telugu work, which belongs to the 11th century, does not show any trace of it. In Kannaḍa the letter continued for two centuries longer and disappeared in the 13th century. We thus see that it took at least two centuries for the Telugu influence to take effect in Kannaḍa. Further, it is rather strange that Kannaḍa has lost the letter ಱ (ṟ) which is still in use in Telugu. Here Telugu influence has had no effect whatever on Kannaḍa. It will thus be seen that Telugu influence does not help us in the matter. The reason for the loss of the letter in Kannaḍa has to be sought in some other quarter. Philologists agree that in all languages the principle of laziness or phonetic decay is at work. According to this principle there is a tendency in all languages to soften down difficult sounds. And the sound of the letter in question being a difficult one, each Draviḍian language has tried to soften it down in its own way. Thus Telugu ordinarily substitutes *ḍ* for it, in some cases it uses *r*, *ṉ* or *ḷ* instead, sometimes it omits the consonant altogether without any substitute. In Tamil, the letter seems merging in most parts of the country either into *ḷ* or *y*; and the same is the case in Malayāḷam. In Kannaḍa it is changed into *ḷ* and in Tuḷu into *r*, *ṉ* and *ḷ*, so that we see the operation of a general principle in all these languages. The assumption of Telugu influence will not be of any use unless we are in a position to prove that it was the cause of similar changes in all these languages.

2. The use of ಡರೆ (dare) for all tenses in the subjunctive mood in Modern Kannaḍa.

Here there seems to be no connection whatever between the forms used in Kannaḍa and Telugu. In Kannaḍa the particle ಅರೆ a corruption of the Old

Kannaḍa ಒಡೆ, is affixed to the past relative participle. In Telugu, on the other hand, there are three ways of forming the conditional form—by adding the suffix ನ or ತೆ to the past verbal participle, ಚೇಸಿನ, ಚೇಸಿತೆ, and by adding ಏನಿ to the past tense of a finite verb, ಚೇಸಿತಿನೇನಿ. Not only are the particles different in the two languages but also the formation of the conditional forms.

If the idea is that ದರೆ, the past form, is used for all the tenses in Kannaḍa as the form with ತೆ is used in Telugu, it has to be stated that ದರೆ is not used for all tenses in Modern Kannaḍa; it is not used with verbs in the past tense—ಬಂದರೆ ಕೊಟ್ಟೆನು is an expression not commonly heard. The same is also the case in Telugu and Tamil. Again, there is also a future conditional form in Kannaḍa—ಮುಡಿವರೆ. Granting that ದರೆ is the suffix used for the present and future tenses in Kannaḍa, is it necessary to postulate Telugu influence to account for this? The past conditional form is used for the present and future tenses in Tamil also. Are we to postulate Telugu influence here too?

3. The use of ಹಲು and ಅಲ for ಹಲ್ಲು and ಅಲ್ಲ.

The 36th sūtra in the 2nd chapter of the *Āndhra-chintāmaṇi*, ಪ್ರಥಮಮುಲುಗಡಿ ದ್ವಿನುಲ್ಲೋಽ, says that in *compounds* the final double *nu* and *lu* of the first word may become single, but not when followed by a vowel. It will be seen that this rule is optional; it operates only in compounds in which the first words end in double *nu* or *lu*, and not when they are followed by a vowel. Mr. Raghunatha Rao thinks it necessary to press into his service a part of this optional rule to explain the form ಹಲು in Kannaḍa. The word ಪಲ್ or ಪಲ್ಲು is the common property of Kannaḍa and Telugu, as also of many other languages of the Draviḍian group. The forms in Telugu and Kannaḍa, though similar, have been arrived at in different ways. In Telugu, as the rule quoted above shows, the original form of the word was ಪಲ್ಲು. For metrical purposes the double ಲು was sometimes made single (*Brown's Grammar*, p. 296). But in Kannaḍa the original form was ಪಲ್, which is changed into ಪಲು or ಹಲು in compounds in *shaṭpadi* works. The principle according to which this change takes place is this: Sanskrit words are made tadbhava by separating conjunct consonants and adding some vowel, generally *u*, to the first letter to secure easy enunciation, *e.g.*, ಪದ್ಮ, ಪದುಮ ; ಫಲ್ಗುನ, ಫಲುಗುಣ. The same principle is at work in Modern Kannaḍa when dealing with Old Kannaḍa words, *e.g.*, ಹಲ್ಮುರಿದು, ಹಲುಮುರಿದು ; ಬಲ್ಜಾಣ, ಬಲುಜಾಣ.

With regard to ಅಲ್ಲ Mr. Raghunatha Rao dogmatically asserts ಇದು ತೆಲುಗಿನ ಪದ್ಧತಿ—this is the Telugu usage. We know that Telugu does not use ಅಲ್ಲ as a locative suffix, nor does it change it into ಅಲ. The locative suffix in Telugu is ಅಂದು to which the particle ಅಲ is sometimes added, but this ಅಲ is distinctly stated to be an augment used only in forming compounds. It answers to ಇನ of Kannaḍa—ಅಂದಲ, ಅಲ್ಲಿನ. Under the rule quoted above, the example of ತಲ್ಲಿ becoming ತಲ in compounds is also given. I do not see how this can prove Telugu influence. Let us see if we can account for this form in Kannaḍa. It is optional in Kannaḍa to use either of the forms ಬಂದಪಂ or ಬಂದಪ್ಪಂ, ತರ್ಪಂ or ತರ್ಪ್ಪಂ, ರಂಜಿಕುಂ or ರಂಜಿಕ್ಕುಂ. Metrical requirements are no doubt the cause of this option. The same appears to be the case with the locative suffix ಅಲ್ಲ. Its alternative form ಅಲ occurs in works and inscriptions of even the 11th century. Inserting or dropping a consonant for metrical purposes is very common in Tamil and Telugu. We therefore see even here the operation of a general law in all these languages and need not postulate the influence of one over another.

From what has been said above it is not to be inferred that Telugu has not exercised any influence whatever on the Kannaḍa language. Verbal roots ending in vowels, the addition of *u* to nouns ending in *i*, *u*, and *e*, and the use of the root *an* for *en* in Modern Kannada are only a few of the facts which bear testimony to Telugu influence. What was meant was that in the cases mentioned by Mr. Raghunatha Rao there was no reason at all to postulate Telugu influence.

Stages of the Kannada Language.

Primitive Old Kannada.

There are three stages of the Kannaḍa language, namely, Pūrvada Haḷagannaḍa or the Primitive Old Kannaḍa, Haḷagannaḍa or Old Kannaḍa and Hosagannaḍa or Modern Kannaḍa. Kittel, in the Introduction to his Kannada-English Dictionary, omits, however, Primitive Old Kannaḍa and gives Classical, Mediæval and Modern as the three stages of the language. Primitive Old Kannaḍa is said to have been in use to the end of the 7th century and seems to answer to the Paḷagannaḍa of Nripatunga. It is a very important stage in the language possessing several grammatical peculiarities which are not found in the succeeding or Haḷagannaḍa stage. As instances may be mentioned:—

1. The lengthening of the vowel of the conjugational suffixes of the 3rd person—ಸಂದಾನ್, ಏಱಿದಾರ್, ಪಡೆದಾನ್, ಪ್ರಸಾದಂಗೆಯ್ದಾರ್.

2. The very common change of this vowel into ō—ಸಂದೋನ್, ಅಪ್ಪೋನ್, ಕೊಂದೋನ್, ಕೊಟ್ಟೋರ್, ಸಲ್ವೋನ್.

3. The use of *uḷ* for the locative suffix—ವೆಟ್ಟದುಳ್, ಧರಣಿಯುಳ್.

4. The lengthening of the vowel in the suffixes of the negative mood—ತಪ್ಪಾದೆ, ಕುಡಾದೋನ್, ನಿಲಲಾಱದೆ.

5. The use of ಒದು and sometimes of ಅದು for the neuter suffix—ಇತ್ತೊದು, ಕೊಟ್ಟೊದು, ವಿಟ್ಟದು.

6. The use of *n* for bindu—ಅವನ್, ಆದಿತ್ಯನ್, ಇಂಬಿನನ್, ನೋನ್ಪಿ, ಅವನ್ಗೆ.

7. The lengthening of the vowel of the accusative suffix, even when not followed by a vowel—ಎಂಟುಮತ್ತರಾನ್ ಕೊಟ್ಟು, ಕೋಟೆಯಾನ್ ರೋಹಿಸಿ.

8. The lengthening of *a* the genitive and adjectival suffix—ದೇವನಾ, ಅವರಾ, ಏೞನೆಯಾ, ಕೀೞಯಾ.

9. The use of ಗ or ಕ as the suffix of the 3rd person of the imperative mood—ಕೊಳ್ಗ, ಕೆಡುಗ, ಪುಟ್ಟಲ್ಕ, ರಕ್ಷಿಕ. We have this suffix in Modern Kannaḍa also: ನಿನ್ನ ಮನೆ ಕಾಯುವಾಗ, ಅವನ ಮನೆ ಹಾಳಾಗಿ ಹೋಗ.

10. The use of *v* for *b*—ಎನ್ವ, ಉಣ್ಬ್ವೇರ್, ಇರ್ಪದಿನ್ವರ್, ಒಟ್ವ, ವರೆದೋಱ.

11. The use of the vowel *e* for *i*—ಎೞು, ಎನ್ಬರುಂ, ಎನೆತುಮಂ.

12. The use of double consonants for single ones—ತಡೆಕ್ಕಾಡು, ತಲೆಪ್ಪೋೞೆ, ಎೞುತ್ತನಂ, ಇತ್ಯಾದಿ.

As no works of this period have come down to us, a few inscriptions of the 6th, 7th and 8th centuries will be quoted to illustrate the points noted above.

1. Tagare Plates of Polavīra.* C. 550.

ಇದರ್ಕ್ಕೆ ನಲವೇಡುವ್ರೋಱ ಪುಣ್ಯಭಾಗಿ ಅಕೆ, ಕೇಡುವೇಡುವ್ರೋಱ ಪಞ್ಚಮಹಾ ಪಾತಕಱ ಅಕೆ.

2. Bādāmi Cave Inscription.† C. 575.

ಸ್ವಸ್ತಿ ಶ್ರೀಮತ್ ಪ್ರಿಥಿವೀವಲ್ಲಭ ಮಂಗಲೀಸನಾ ಕಲ್ಮನೆಗೆ ಇತ್ತೊದು ಲಂಜಿಗೇಸರಂ. ದೇವರ್ಕ್ಕೆ ಪೂನಿೞುವ ಮಾರಾಕಾರರ್ಗ್ಗೆ ಅರ್ದ್ಧವಿಸದಿ ಇತ್ತೊ ದಾನಟಿಪ್ರೋಱ ಪಞ್ಚಮಹಾಪಾತಕನಕುಂ ಏೞನೆಯಾ ನರಕದಾ ಪುೞು ಅಕುಂ.

3. Koppa 38 (Kadur District). C. 675.

ಆದಾನಟಿಪ್ರೋರುಂ ಮನದೆ ನೆನೆವ್ರೋರುಂ ಅೞಿವೆನೆಂದುಪಾದೇಶಂ ಕೊಡುವ್ರೋರುಂ ಪಞ್ಚಮಹಾಪಾತಕಸಂಯುಕ್ತರಪ್ಪಾರ್. ದೇವದಣ್ಡದಿನ್ದೞಿವೆ ಪ್ಪಡುವ್ರೋರುಮಪ್ಪಾರ್. ರಾಜದಣ್ಡಮುಮೆಯ್ದೆಪ್ಪಡುವಾರ್.

4. Koppa 37 (Kadur District). C. 690.

ಕೊಳ್ವೋರುಂ ಕೊಣ್ಡು ಉಣ್ಬೋರುಂ ಪೂತಿ ಎನ್ವ ನರಗಕ್ಕೆ ಸರ್ಗ್ಗ. ಧರ್ಮಮಾರ್ಱ ಕಾದೋರಾ ಕುಲಂ ಪೆಟ್ಟುಗೆ. ಇದಾಱ ಪೞಿನೊರ್ವಱ ಕೊಳ್ವೋನುಂ ಕೊಡುವ್ರೋನುಂ ಪಞ್ಚಮಹಾಪಾತಕನಕ್ಕುಂ.

5. Śravaṇa Beḷgoḷa 88, C. 700.

ಪರಮಾರ್ಥಂ ಮೆಚ್ಚೆನಾನೀ ಧರಣಿಯುಳಿರವಾನೆನ್ದು ಸನ್ಯಾಸನಂಗೆ ।
ಯ್ದುರುಸತ್ತ್ವಱ ನನ್ದಿಸೇನ ಪ್ರವರಮುನಿವರಱ ದೇವಲೋಕಕ್ಕೆ ಸನ್ದಾಱ ॥

6. Śravaṇa Beḷgoḷa 27, C. 700.

ಮಾಸೇನರ್ ಪರಮಪ್ರಭಾವರಿಷಿಯರ್ ಕಟ್ವಪ್ಪಿನಾ ಪೆಟ್ಟದುಳ್ ।
ಶ್ರೀ ಸಂಘಂಗಳ ಪೇೞ್ದ ಸಿದ್ಧಸಮಯಂ ತಪ್ಪಾದೆ ನೋನ್ತಿಮ್ಬಿನಱ ॥

---

* Mysore Archæological Report for 1918, 36.

† Indian Antiquary, x, 59.

ಪ್ರಾಸಾದಾನ್ತರಮಾರ್ೞ್ ವಿಚಿತ್ರಕನಕಪ್ರಜ್ವಲ್ಯದಿೞ್ ಮಿಕ್ಕುದಾೞ್ ।
ಸಾಸಿರ್ವರ್ ವರಪೂಜಿದಂದುಯಿ ಅವರ್ ಸ್ವರ್ಗಾಗ್ರಮಾನೇಱಿದಾರ್ ॥

7. Māchēnhaḷḷi Plates of Jayasangraha,* C. 700.
ಮೂನೂರ್ವರ್ರುಂ ರಕ್ಷಿಕ ಕಿಱಿಯ ಅರಸಂಗ' ಒಕ್ಕರ್ ಪೆಟ್ಟುಗೆ.

8. Inscription at Mahākūṭa near Bādāmi,† C. 720.
ದೇವನಾ ಪೀಠಮಾರ್ೞ್ ಕಿಸುವಿನೆ ಕಟ್ಟಿ ದಳ್ಳಿಯಾ ಕೊಡೆಯಾನೇಱಿಸಿ ಎ ಮಗ್ಗಲುಳ್ಳೆ ಅಷ್ಟಶತಂ ಕ್ಷೇತ್ರಗೊಟ್ಟೋರ್. ಇದಾನಟಿದೋೞ್ ಪಞ್ಚಮಹಾಪಾತಕನಕ್ಕುಂ.

9. Hoskōṭe 86 (Bangalore District). C. 725.
ಇದಟಿವೋೞ್ ವಾರಣಾಸಿಯುಳ್ ಸಾಸಿರ್ವ ಪಾರ್ವರುಂ ಸಾಸಿರ ಕವಿಲೆಯುಂ ಕೊಂದೋನ ಲೋಕಕ್ಕೆ ಸಂದೋೞ್.

10. Bowringpet 13 (Kolar District). C. 725.
ಪಾಲ್ಪಡುವಿಷುಳ್ ಪಡುವಣ ಕೆಱೆಯುಳ್ ತಾಮರೆಕಟ್ಟೞ್ ಕೆಟಗೆ ಕರ್ನಾಡು ಪ್ರಸಾದಙ್ಗೆಯ್ದಾರ್.

11. Dēvalāpura Inscription (Mysore District).‡ C. 750.
ಮದುಗರುಂ ಕೋನಬ್ಬರುಂ ಸಾಕ್ಷಿ ಆಗ ಕೊಟ್ಟದು. ವಾರಣಾಸಿಯಾ ಸಾಸಿರಕವಿಲೆ ಸಾಸಿರಪಾರ್ವರ್ ಕೊನ್ದ ಕೊಲೆ ಅಕ್ಕ. ಕೆಡಿಸಿದೋನುಂ ಕೇಡುವೇಡಿದೋನುಂ ಒತೋನುಂ ಒದವಿದೋನುಂ.

12. Agara Inscription (Mysore District).§ C. 750.
ನಾಲ್ವದಿನ್ವಕ್ಕರ್ಗಂ ಒನ್ದುನ್ಬಂಗಳೆ ವಿಟ್ಟ ಇರ್ಲೆ. ಎಬ್ಬುತ್ತಕೋಳ್ ಇರ್ಲೆ. ಇರ್ಪದಿನ್ವರಾ ಎಬ್ಬುತ್ತಕೋಳ್ ಇರ್ಲೆ. ತರೆಪ್ಪೂಱೆಯಕ್ಕರ್ ಸುಂಕಂ.

13. Pāvagaḍa 11 (Tumkur District). 754.
ಇತ್ತಾತ್ತರಕಳೆಸಮುದ್ರದುಳ್. ವಕ್ರವಪ್ಪೋೞ್ ಪಞ್ಚಮಹಾಪಾತಕನಕ್ಕುಂ, ರಕ್ಷಿಪ್ಪೋೞ್ ವೈಕೊನ್ತವಾಸಿಯಕ್ಕುಂ, ಲಱಟ್ಟಿದೋೞ್ ದಿವ್ಯನಾಮಾಕುಲೞ್.

14. Heggaḍadēvankōṭe 87 (Mysore District). C. 800.
ಸ್ವಸ್ತಿ ಶ್ರೀಮತ್ ಶಿವಮಾರಂ ಪ್ರಿಥುವೀರಾಜ್ಯಂಕೆಯೆ ವೆದಿರುೞ್ ಸ್ವರ್ಗತ್ತೆಱೆಯ ಮರಿಯಾದಿ ಕೊಟ್ಟಾೞ್. ಸೇದೆಗೆ ವಿಟ್ಟಾರ್. ಇದಾನಟಿತ್ತೋೞ್ ಪಞ್ಚಮಹಾಪಾತಕಸಂಯುಕ್ತನಪ್ಪೋೞ್. ಅನ್ದಿನಾ ತೆಱೆ ಎ ಕೊಳ್ಗ ಅನ್ದಿನಾಕೆಯ್ವೆಸನೆ ಕೊಳ್ಗ ದೇವಮಣ್ಣುವಾಂದಾರ ಎಱೆತ್ತನವೆ. ಅದಾನಟಿತ್ತೋೞ್ಸಾಸಿರ ಕವಿಲೆಯುಮಾರ್ೞ್ ಕೊನ್ದೋೞ್ ಅಪ್ಪೋೞ್. ಒಕ್ಕಲುಳೊಪ್ಪತ್ತಿನ್ತಕ್ಕಳ್ ಪುಟ್ಟೆಲ್ಕ. ಪುಟ್ಟಿದೊವುಂ ಪುರಿಗ.

---

* Mysore Archæological Report for 1908, 6.
† Indian Antiquary x, 104.
‡ Mysore Archæological Report for 1916, 37.
§ *Ibid.* for 1917, 31.

15. Ṣorab 10 (Shimoga District). C. 800.

ಆೞುವಖೇಡಮಱುಸಾಸಿರನುಮಾನ್ ಚಿತ್ರವಾಹನನಾಳುತ್ತುಂ ಬಾಯ್ಕೇ ೞದಿರೆ ಮುನಿದು ನೊಱಮ್ಬರಾದಿತ್ಯನ್ ವೆಸಸಲ್ ಪೆಗ್ಗಡೆಯ ಕೋಟೆಯಾನ್ ರೋಹಿಸಿ ಕಿಟ್ಟಿ ಕಾದಿ ಮಱುವಕ್ಕದವರ ಮೆಯ್ಮೆಯ್ಯಂಬಾಗೆ ಎಚ್ಚೋಡಿಸಿ ತಾನುಂ ಪಲವುಂ ಏಸುವೆತ್ತು ಕಣೆಪಣ್ದರದೊಳೆಱಗಿ ಭೀಷ್ಮನ್ ಎಬ್ದನ್ತೆ ನೆಲಮುಟ್ಟದೆ ಬಿದ್ದೋನ್ ದೇವಗಣಿಕ್ಕೆಯರ್ ಅಗ್ಗಮ್ಬಿಡಿದು ಬನ್ದಿದಿಗ್ಗೊಣ್ಡಿಯೆ ವೀರಲೋಕಕ್ಕೆ ಸನ್ದೋನ್. ಇನ್ತೀ ಎನೆಬ್ಬರುಂ ಶ್ರೀಕರಣಸಹಿತಂ ಬಿಟ್ಟಾರ್. ಇದನ್ ಕೆಡಿಪೋನುಂ ಕೆಡೆಬಾಪ್ದೋನುಂ ಪಞ್ಚಮಹಾಪಾತಕಸಂಯುಕ್ತನಕ್ಕುಂ. ವಾರಣಾಸಿಯೊಳ್ ಸಾಸಿರಕವಿಲೆಯನ್ ಕೊನ್ದೋನ ಲೋಕಕ್ಕೆ ಸನ್ದೋನುಮಕ್ಕುಂ.

Now, the forms ಸಂದಾನ್, ಬಂದೋನ್, ಒಕ್ಕಲುೞ್, ತಪ್ಪಾದೆ, ಪಿಟ್ಟದು, ನೋನ್ಪಿ, ಕೆಡುಗ, ವರೆದೋನ್, ಎಱು, ತಱಿಕ್ಕಾಡು, which are not found in Haḷagannaḍa, are identical or nearly so with the forms used in Tamil. It may be stated that as we go farther back to the early period of Kannaḍa literature we shall find the forms approximate more and more to the Tamil ones.

A few notes may be added on certain additional forms contained in the inscriptions quoted above. The numbers denote those of the inscriptions.

2. ದೇವಕ್ಕೆ. The suffix *ke* occurs where we should expect *ge*. Compare also ಮುತ್ತರಸಕ್ಕೆ in another inscription of C. 750. ಪೂನಿಱುವ. ನಿಱು as a verb is obsolete in Haḷagannaḍa, though the word ನಿಱುಗೆ occurs.

3. ಅಱಿಮಿನ್, the 2nd person plural of the imperative mood, is identical with the Tamil ಅಱಿಮಿನ್. The Haḷagannaḍa form is ಅಱಿಯಿಂ. The form ಕೊಡು occurs, which is identical with the Tamil ಕೊಡು, the Haḷagannaḍa form being ಕುಡು. It is interesting to note the passive forms ಎಱುವೆಪ್ಪಡುವೋರ್ and ಎಯ್ದುಪ್ಪಡುವಾರ್ in about 675.

8. ಏಱುಸಿ ಎ. The particle of emphasis *e* is not combined with the previous word as in Haḷagannaḍa. ಉೞ್ಳೆ answers to ಒಳ್ of Haḷagannaḍa.

10. ಕಟ್ಟಿನ್ಕೆಱಗೆ *Cp.* Tamil ಕಟ್ಟಿನ್ಕಿೞ್. The Haḷagannaḍa form would be ಕಟ್ಟಿನಕೆಱಗ್.

11. ಆಗ *Cp.* Tamil ಆಗ. In Haḷagannaḍa it would be ಆಗುಗೆ. ಕೆಡು is identical with the Tamil ಕೆಡು, the Haḷagannaḍa form being ಕಿಡು.

12. ಇಲ್ಲೆ *Cp.* Tamil ಇಲ್ಲೈ. In Haḷagannaḍa it is generally ಇಲ್ಲ.

13. ವೈಕೊನ್ಠ, the *tadbhava* of ವೈಕುಂಠ, may be compared with the Tamil ವೈಗುನ್ದಂ. ಲಬಿಚ್ಚಿದೋೞ್ may be compared with the Telugu ಲಬಿಂಚಿನವಾಂಡು and the Tamil ಲಭಿತ್ತೊೞ್. The Haḷagannaḍa form would be ಲಬಿಸಿದಂ.

14. ಅಱಿತ್ತೊೞ್ is identical with the Tamil ಅಱಿತ್ತೊೞ್. It would be ಅಱಿದಂ in Haḷagannaḍa. ಪುಟ್ಟಲ್ಕ (let them not be born) is the same as the Tamil negative verb ಪಿಱವಱ್ಕ, the Tamil root corresponding to ಪುಟ್ಟು being ಪಿಱ. ಅಲ್ is the negative particle in both the languages—ಪುಗಲ್ ಮಾಡಲಿಂ; ಶೆಯ್ಯಱ್ಕ. In Haḷagannaḍa it would be ಪುಟ್ಟದಿಕ್ಕೆ.

Haḷagannaḍa.

As stated before, Kittel omits Primitive Old Kannaḍa altogether, and mentions Classical or Ancient Kannaḍa answering to Haḷagannaḍa and Modern Kannaḍa with an intervening stage called Mediæval Kannaḍa. According to him Haḷagannaḍa is quite uniform and shows an extraordinary amount of polish and refinement. It has to the present time been preserved in several works written mostly by Jaina scholars, and appears to have been in common use for literary purposes from at least the 10th to the middle of the 13th century. Its principal characteristics are the elaborate and highly artificial *champu* composition, strict adherance to the use of now more or less disused case-and tense-signs and to the rules of syntax, the use of Sanskrit words in their unaltered form whenever desirable or necessary as an aid in composition and that of a conventionally received number of *tadbhavas*, the proper distinction between the letters ಱ ೞ ಳ ಲ and ರ—alliteration carefully based also on this distinction—and lastly pleasing euphonic junction of letters.

Mediæval Kannaḍa.

If the term Modern Kannaḍa is limited to the present Kannaḍa of prose writings and common conversation, as is done by Dr. Kittel, an intermediate stage between

Halagannaḍa and Modern Kannaḍa, styled by hin Mediæval Kannaḍa, is quite necessary. This, as contained in the poetry of Vīraśaiva authors, is written mostly in *shaṭpadi* metre, is negligent as to the use of suffixes and the rules of syntax, uses a few new suffixes, contains a number of *tadbhavas* not sanctioned by previous authors, has entirely lost the letter ಱ and frequently changes the letter *p* of the present or future verbal suffix and an initial *p* into *h*. Its period terminates at about the end of the 15th century.

From about the 16th century, according to Kittel, Mediæval Kannaḍa got the character of the language of the present day or of Modern Kannaḍa, which transition is seen especially in the poetry of the Vaishṇavas.

Several ancient verbs and nouns fell into disuse, the letter ೞ began to be discarded, words borrowed from Mahrāṭhi and Hindustāni came into use, and more frequent omission of suffixes took place.

Modern Kannaḍa.

Modern Kannaḍa, comprising the present Kannaḍa of prose writings and common conversation, is less particular in the choice of words, arbitrary about the use of suffixes and not sparing in the use of vulgarisms especially in ordinary talk. Many words are Sanskrit especially such as are abstract, religious or scientific terms, the ancient form of the present tense has been changed, most verbal suffixes have been somewhat altered, a few of the suffixes of nouns and pronouns have ceased to be used, many verbs, nouns and particles have become obsolete, and other verbs and nouns have been formed mostly based on existing roots. It is not uniform but varies more or less according to localities.

Some scholars are of opinion that only two stages need be recognised. A scholar says: "The language changed gradually, and no useful purpose is served by dividing its history into clearly defined periods. About A.D. 1100 Nayasēna spoke of a Hosagannaḍa, and it was extensively used 50 years later. That is the only dividing line which deserves recognition."

In this connection, it may be mentioned that what were condemned as ungrammatical and unidiomatic in one stage of the language have become approved forms in the next stage.

Forms once condemned have become current.

As instances may be mentioned, certain specific statements of Kēśirāja in his *Śabdamaṇidarpaṇa* about the use of certain forms and words which were not strictly followed by writers who came after him. (1) He lays down the rule that *ḷ* ought not to be used in place of *l* in words such as ಬೆರಲ್ (sūtra 28). (2) He condemns the use, as *śithila*, of an initial letter compounded with *rēpha* following a short letter (sūtras 59 and 60); *e.g.*, ಮಿಱುಗುತ್ತಿರ್ಪ ತ್ರಿಶೂಲದಿಂ. (3) He says that verbs in the present tense ought not to be used as declinable *kṛillingas* (sūtra 73)*, *e.g.*, ಮಾಡಿದಪನಂ. (4) He states that nouns ending in consonants, except ಅಗಳ್, ಈಗಳ್, ಪಗಲ್ and ಇರುಳ್, do not add the augment *in* before the genitive suffix *a* (sūtra 109); *e.g.*, ಬೆಮರಿನ. (5) He disapproves of the use of the suffix *ike* after roots ending in consonants, *e.g.*, ಕಾಣಿಕೆ, and of the suffix *tana* after Sanskrit words, *e.g.*, ಆರೋಹಕತನ (sūtra 211)†. (6) For *sati-saptami*, which refers to two subjects or nominatives he prescribes the use of the suffix *e* and does not allow the use of *al* (sūtra 249). (7) Finally, he states that when both the words forming a compound are capable of being used as *tadbhavas*, it is wrong to use only one of them as a *tadbhava* and leave the other in its Sanskrit form; *e.g.*, ಮಾಣಿಕ್ಯ ಭಂಡಾರ (sūtra 289). Most of the forms disallowed by Kēśirāja have subsequently been looked upon as correct.

Explanation of Kēśirāja's 60th sūtra.

A word in explanation of sūtra 60 in which Kēśirāja condemns the use as *śithila* of an initial letter compounded with rēpha (see 2 above), may be said

* Bhaṭṭākaḷanka allows this. See his sūtras 447, 448 and 544.

† Bhaṭṭākaḷanka allows forms like ಉಸ್ವತತನ. See his sūtra 431.

here, as the terms ಸತ್ಯಣಾಭ್ಯವಹಾರಿ and ಅರೋಚಿ used by him in it do not appear to have been properly understood. Kittel wrongly translates the sūtra. I give below the sūtra and his translation :—

ಬಗೆಯದೆ ಸತ್ಯಣಾಭ್ಯವಹಾ'ı ರಿಗಳುಸಿರ್ವರ್ ಗದ್ಯಕಾವ್ಯದೊಳ್ ನಿರ್ಬಂಧಂ ।
ಪುಗದೆಂದರೋಚಿಗಳದಂ । ತೆಗದೆಂದಾಗದ್ಯಪದ್ಯಕಾವ್ಯದೊಳಿಕ್ಕರ್ ॥

Some (grammarians or poets) who are fond of a practice that is connected with grass (satriṇābhyavahārigaḷ), do not consider that abnormity does not enter in poetical prose (and use a short letter followed by an initial letter which is a compound with rēpha, as śithila); such disgustful persons (arōchigaḷ) do put it in poetical prose without calling it a blame (tegaḷ)*.

The terms ಅರೋಚಿ and ಸತ್ಯಣಾಭ್ಯವಹಾರಿ are taken by Kēśirāja from Vāmana's *Kāvyālankārasūtra* (I, 2, 1-3) where they are used in the sense of "the wise" and "the foolish" :—

ಅಧಿಕರಣ I, ಅಧ್ಯಾಯ 2.

ಅಧಿಕಾರಿ ನಿರೂಪಣಾರ್ಥಮಾಹ—

ಸೂತ್ರಂ ॥ ಅರೋಚಕಿನಃ ಸತ್ಯಣಾಭ್ಯವಹಾರಿಣಶ್ಚ ಕವಯಃ ॥ ೧ ॥

ಇಹ ಖಲು ದ್ವಯೇ ಕವಯಃ ಸಂಭವಂತಿ—ಅರೋಚಕಿನಃ ಸತ್ಯಣಾಭ್ಯವಹಾರಿಣಶ್ಚೇತಿ. ಅರೋಚಕಿ ಸತ್ಯಣಾಭ್ಯವಹಾರಿ ಶಬ್ದೌ ಗೌಣಾರ್ಥೌ. ಕೋಽಸಾವರ್ಥಃ—ವಿವೇಕಿತ್ವಮವಿವೇಕಿತ್ವಂ ಚೇತಿ. ತದಾಹ—

ಸೂತ್ರಂ ॥ ಪೂರ್ವೇ ಶಿಷ್ಯಾಃ । ವಿವೇಕಿತ್ವಾತ್ ॥ ೨ ॥

ಪೂರ್ವೇ ಖಲ್ವರೋಚಕಿನಃ ಶಿಷ್ಯಾಃ ಶಾಸನೀಯಾಃ—ವಿವೇಕಿತ್ವಾತ್ ವಿವೇಚನಶೀಲತ್ವಾತ್.

ಸೂತ್ರಂ ॥ ನೇತರೇ । ತದ್ವಿಪರ್ಯಯಾತ್ ॥ ೩ ॥

ಇತರೇ ಸತ್ಯಣಾಭ್ಯವಹಾರಿಣೋ ನ ಶಿಷ್ಯಾಃ—ತದ್ವಿಪರ್ಯಯಾತ್ ಅವಿವೇಚನಶೀಲತ್ವಾತ್—ನ ಚ ಶೀಲಮಪಾಕರ್ತುಂ ಶಕ್ಯಂ.

ಸತ್ಯಣಾಭ್ಯವಹಾರಿ would be a man who eats food mixed with straw, *i.e.*, a man devoid of the power of discrimination, in other words, a fool. Similarly ಅರೋಚಿ or ಅರೋಚಕಿ would be a man who does not relish food until

* *A Grammar of the Kannaḍa Language* (1903), preface IV.

he has completely examined it, *i.e.*, a man endowed with the power of discrimination.

The correct rendering of the sūtra would be—

Some fools, without reflection, use such a śithila thinking that no restriction applies to prose; but the wise, looking upon it as a blemish, will use it neither in prose nor in poetry.

CHAPTER V.

Changes in the language. Changes in form. Phonetic decay. Emphasis. Prosthesis. Compensation. Analogy. Assimilation. Metathesis. Changes in meaning. Extension. Contraction. Amelioration. Deterioration. Decency. Euphemism. Freemasonry in words. Extension by metaphor. Changes in form of Old Kannaḍa words when becoming Modern Kannaḍa. Mistakes committed by authors. Some general remarks on the language. Disappearance of old and entry of new words. Words not found in classical literature but current in common speech. Some lost words that deserve restoration. Some words which are seemingly correct. False etymology. Forms given in Kannaḍa grammars. Tamil rules of euphonic combination adopted in Kannaḍa. Help of Tamil in the derivation of some Kannaḍa words. Words about whose derivation Grammarians differ. Reform of the language. Advancement of the language.

Changes in the Language.

If there can exist a fixed and stable society, cut off from close intercourse with its neighbours and handing down unchanged its customs and institutions, it is likely to have a more or less fixed and stable language. For language is the mirror of the society that uses it, and where the society alters but little, the language, too, will alter but little. But this state of things is very rare indeed. Language requires uninterrupted intercourse between the whole body of speakers to keep it uniform; this is not, however, possible beyond a certain area, and consequently language tends to split up into dialects. Differences have also arisen from difference in climate, food and education. A language which has no manner of contact with any other resembles a stagnant pool of water and is liable to decay, while a language which does not refuse help from other languages as necessity arises resembles a flowing river and is capable of attaining a high development.

Changes are constantly going on in a language. They are so gradual that the speakers of the language are unconscious of them. As civilisation increases language changes somewhat rapidly and words become corrupt; but grammar affords a check to this variability. In languages which have no grammar the changes go on unchecked, till they become almost unintelligible to the speakers themselves.

There are certain principles regulating the changes in a language which are of two kinds, namely, changes in form and changes in meaning. They are :—

Changes in form. Phonetic decay.

1. Laziness (or Phonetic decay) which means economy of effort, *i.e.*, a desire to do what is to be done with the least expenditure of energy. It is due to this principle that words become clipped and shortened in the course of time, until it may happen that nothing is left of the original. Rapid speaking, an imperfect ear or pronunciation, and the common desire to save time and trouble are the causes of the wearing away of words in daily use. As instances may be mentioned ಹೊಸಲು corrupted from the Old Kannaḍa ಪೊಸಂತಿಲ್ ; ಚಾಟಿ from ಚಮ್ಮಟಿಗೆ, a *tadbhava* of ಚರ್ಮಪಟ್ಟಿಕಾ ; ತಂಗಳು from ತಣ್ಗೂಳ್. Cp. ಅರುಮಂದಪಿಳ್ಳೈ for ಅರುಮರುಂದನ್ನಪಿಳ್ಳೈ, ಶೀಮಾರಾವ for ಶ್ರೀನಿವಾಸರಾಘವ in Tamil. Cp. also ಬಂತು for ಬಂದಿತು. ನಿಂತು for ನಿಂತಿತು in Kannada, and ಅಚ್ಚು for ಅಯ್ಚ್ಚು in Tamil.

Emphasis.

2. Emphasis is the striving after clearness and distinctness. It works in the contrary direction to phonetic decay and counterbalances it. It is according to this principle that new letters are added to words. Cp. the words *sound* and *lend* in English with the additional letter *d*; the Tamil word ಪೆಂಡು for ಪೆಣ್ and the Kannada word ಪೆಂಡತಿ.

Prosthesis.

Prosthesis or the insertion of a vowel before a word beginning with a double consonant, or as is specially the case in

Tamil, before a word beginning with *y*, *r*, *l*, also comes under this head. ಇಸ್ಕೋಲು, ಇಸ್ಪ್ರಿಂಗ್ ; ಇಯುಕ್ಕರ್, ಅರಂಗಸಾಮಿ, ಅರಶ ಅರಸಂ, ಇಲಕ್ಕಣಂ, ಉಲೋಕಂ.

What are now suffixes were once independent words with a definite meaning. But owing to carelessness, forgetfulness, laziness, economy of effort and wrong pronunciation on the part of the speakers of the language, in other words, owing to phonetic decay, they have now become mostly meaningless particles. In a literary language every syllable is watched with jealous care; but in spoken dialects phonetic decay reigns supreme. It is owing to changes such as these that the earliest written documents of a language become obscure in course of time and at last unintelligible.

Compensation.

In compensation, which means that the loss of a sound is compensated by the lengthening of the adjoining syllable, both phonetic decay and emphasis are at work; *e.g.*, ಮಯೂರ ಮೋರ, ಖದಿರ ಕ್ಕೈರ ; ಪೊೞುದು ಪೋದು, ಪೆಯರ್ ಪೇರ್ ; ಅದಿನಿ ದಾನಿ, ಇದಿನಿ ದೀನಿ ; ಕೆಸಱು ಕೇಱು, ಕೆಸವು ಕೇಂಬು ; ಉಗುರು ಗೋರು, ಒರಲ್ ರೋಲು.

Analogy.

3. Analogy means the mistaken application of a rule to cases to which it does not apply. According to Sayce, it is a main element of change in the signification as well as in the outward form of words; and just as phonetic decay wastes and destroys, so analogy repairs and reconstructs. The one is the agent of destruction, the other of construction, though they both spring from the same root of human laziness. The principle of analogy may be ultimately traced partly to the desire of saving trouble, partly to the natural instinct of imitation. It is easier for the vocal organs to repeat the same sound than to attempt a new one, while the repetition of the same idea or the expression of an analogous one, involves less exertion on the part of the mind. Habit is a ruling power in life, and sounds or ideas to which we are accustomed rise uncalled for to the intelligence and

the lips. A few instances of false analogy may now be given. ಹೊದ್ದು is the colloquial past participle of the root ಹೊದಿ (more correctly ಹೊದೆ). Similarly ಕದ್ದು is taken to be the past participle of a root ಕದಿ which has no existence in literary Kannaḍa, the correct root being ಕಳ್. ಕದ್ದು is only a corrupt form of ಕಳ್ದು, just as ಬಿದ್ದು is of ಬಿೞ್ದು. Again, on the analogy of ನಿಂತು a curious form ಕುಂತು is made use of in place of the correct form ಕುಳಿತು. Roots ending in a double consonant such as ಕಟ್ಟು, ಕುಟ್ಟು, ಮುಕ್ಕು, ನಕ್ಕು, ಕಚ್ಚು, ಮುಚ್ಚು add the suffix *itu* to form the neuter singular of the past tense: ಕಟ್ಟಿತು, ಕುಟ್ಟಿತು, ಕಚ್ಚಿತು, etc. The same suffix is also added to the past participles of verbs, which end in a double consonant: ಕೊಟ್ಟಿತು (from ಕೊಡು), ಬಿಟ್ಟಿತು (from ಬಿಡು), ಮಿಕ್ಕಿತು (from ಮಿಗು), etc. The suffix in these cases ought to be *udu*. Cp. ಪೌರ್ವಾತ್ಯ on the analogy of ಪಾಶ್ಚಾತ್ಯ; ವನಸ್ಪತಿ on the analogy of ದಿವಸ್ಪತಿ, etc.

Assimilation.

Among other causes of changes in form may be mentioned assimilation and metathesis. In assimilation a vowel or consonant in a word becomes similar to another vowel or consonant in the same word; *e.g.*, ಕಳುಹು for ಕಳಿಪು, ಉಸುರು for ಉಸಿರು, ಎತ್ತು for ಎೞ್ತು, ಬಿದ್ದು for ಬಿೞ್ದು. Metathesis is the euphonic displacement of consonants and vowels; *e.g.*, ಅಲರ್ ಅರಲ್, ಎಲರ್ ಎರಲ್, ಮಲರ್ ಮರಲ್, ಮಱಲ್ ಮರಳ್; ತಶ್ಶೈ ಶದ್ವೈ, ಕೊಪ್ಪುೞ್ ಪೊಕ್ಕುೞ್ ಪೊಕ್ಕುಲ, ಪದರ್ ಹರದು.

Metathesis.

Changes in meaning.

Generally speaking, there are four ways in which the meanings of words undergo change, namely, extension, contraction, amelioration and deterioration. By extension is meant that words which once denoted only a few special objects have their meaning extended so that they now denote more things than they did before; *e.g.*, ಎಣ್ಣೆ, ಒರೆ, ಚೆಂಬು, ಯಜಮಾನ. ಎಣ್ಣೆ (ಎಳ್ +

Extension.

ನೆಯ್) once denoted the oil derived from ಎಳ್, the sesamum seed, *i.e.*, gingely oil. But now it is applied not only to oils derived from various other seeds, but also to those derived from wood, etc., *e.g.*, ಬೇವಿನೆಣ್ಣೆ, ಕೈಯೆಣ್ಣೆ or ಹರಳೆಣ್ಣೆ, ಹಿಪ್ಪೆಯೆಣ್ಣೆ, ಹೊಂಗೆಯೆಣ್ಣೆ, ಸಾಸವೆಯೆಣ್ಣೆ, ಗಂಧದೆಣ್ಣೆ, ಕೊಬರಿ ಯೆಣ್ಣೆ, and so forth. The derivation of ಎಣ್ಣೆ was forgotten and we now have ಅಚ್ಚೆಳ್ಳೆಣ್ಣೆ and ಹುಚ್ಚೆಳ್ಳೆಣ್ಣೆ. ಓಲೆ once meant an ear ornament made of palm leaf, but now it means not merely an ear ornament made of palm leaf, but also one made of gold or any other material; *e.g.*, ಚಿನ್ನದ ಓಲೆ, ವಜ್ರದ ಓಲೆ, ಕೆಂಪಿನ ಓಲೆ, etc. ಚೆಂಬು was once applied to a copper vessel, but now it denotes in addition a vessel made of any metal or even of wood or stone; *e.g.*, ಬೆಳ್ಳಿಯ ಚೆಂಬು, ಚಿನ್ನದ ಚೆಂಬು, ಹಿತ್ತಾಳೆಯ ಚೆಂಬು, ಮರದ ಚೆಂಬು, etc. ಯಜಮಾನ once meant a man who performed and bore the expenses of a sacrifice, but now it means besides a head of a family, a respectable or elderly person. Cp. ಮರಕ್ಕಾಲ್ originally a measure made of wood; but now applied to measures made of metal, etc., also. Cp. also ಯತ್ತೇ ಅಗ್ಗೇ.

Contraction. On the other hand, contraction limits the use of words which were once of a wider application to some special things, *e.g.*, ನೆಯ್. This word which was formerly applied even to the oils extracted from the margosa and *hippe* seeds, as also to honey (ಜೇನೆಯ್), is now restricted in its use to the ghee of cows and buffaloes. ಆಡು in Old Tamil meant both victory and sheep, but now it means only sheep.

Amelioration. Words which once conveyed a bad sense come to be used in a good sense according to the process known as amelioration; *e.g.*, ಕೆಂದು, ಹೊಂದು. ಕೆಂದು once meant to cohabit; it now means to develop. The meaning of ಹೊಂದು was to die; it now means to obtain. In the latter sense the word is probably a corruption of ಪೊರ್ದು. Cp. the Tamil word ಕಳಿಪ್ಪು, which once denoted the pleasure derived from drinking, but is now used in the sense of pleasure in a general way.

Deterioration.

On the other hand, deterioration tends to make words which once conveyed a good sense convey a bad sense; *e.g.*, ಒಜ, ಕಂಪು, ದೆವ್ವ, ದೇಗುಲ. ಒಜ once denoted a teacher; it now means a carpenter. ಕಂಪು which once meant fragrance now means bad smell. ದೆವ್ವ meant at one time a god, but now means an evil spirit. ದೇಗುಲ once denoted a temple; now, however, it means an unwieldy deserted house. As additional instances may be given ಹಾರುವ, ಕವಳ, ನಾತ, ತೀಟೆ, ಬಸ್ತಿ, ಅಮ್ಮ, ಬಿನ್ನಾಣ, etc.

Decency.

Decency and euphemism also contribute to change in the meaning of words. In civilised society, whatever is indelicate is expressed in some disguised form, *e.g.*, to go to stool is denoted by such expressions as washing the feet and going to the backyard. This is known as ಇಡಕ್ಕರಡಕ್ಕರ್ in Tamil. ಪವ್ವೀ is usually given as an example. It means *ī* added to *p* and denotes fæces. Similarly, whatever is considered inauspicious is ex-

Euphemism.

pressed in such a way that the inauspiciousness does not obtrude itself on one's mind; *e.g.*, death is called ದೀರ್ಘನಿದ್ರೆ, (long sleep); a widow is styled a ದೀರ್ಘ ಸುಮಂಗಲಿ; ಅವಲಕ್ಷಣ is denoted by the Tamil expression ಎಟ್ಟೇಕಾರ್ ಲಕ್ಷಣಂ where ಎಟ್ಟೇಕಾರ್ indicates the symbols அ *a* (8) and வ *va* (¼); the ephemeral body is called ಮೆಯ್ as if it were a permanent thing; ಅಮಂಗಲವಾರ is known as ಮಂಗಲವಾರ; the year ಕ್ಷಯ is named ಅಕ್ಷಯ. There is also a sort of freemasonry in words, *i.e.*, a secret meaning attached to

Freemansonry in words.

some words by certain communities or societies, which is not understood by others; *e.g.*, ದ್ವಯಾಕ್ಷರ ಸಂಖ್ಯೆ means 25 among the Śrīvaishṇavas; ಗುಣಪೆಕ್ಕೆ ೩ means 3 rupees among merchants; and ಕೊರ್ವಿಳಂಬಿ means ಕಳ್ (toddy). This is called ಕುಱೂಉಕ್ಕುಱಿ in Tamil.

Extension by metaphor.

We spoke of extension of meaning, and this extension is mostly by metaphor and transference of meaning. Such transference is known as *lakshaṇā* in Sanskrit—an indirect application of a word as distinguished from its literary meaning or the substitution of the name of one thing for that of another connected with it, answering in a manner to the figure metonymy. This transference is known as ಅಗುಪೆಯರ್ in Tamil. It is of several kinds and answers in a way to the figures synecdochy and metonymy. To give a few examples:—

(1) The part is put for the whole or the whole for the part,—ವೀಳೆಯದೆಲೆ ನಟ್ಟನು, the name of the leaf is put for the creeper; ತಾವರೆವೂಗ, the name of the creeper is used for that of the flower.

(2) The container for the contained and *vice versa*,—ಊರೇ ಬಂದು ಸೇರಿಬಿಟ್ಟಿತು, the village for the inhabitants; ದೀಪ ಒಡೆದು ಹೋಯಿತು, the flame for the lamp.

(3) The cause for the effect and *vice versa*,—ಕುಱಳ್ ಮುಗಿಯಿತು, the metre ಕುಱಳ್ for the work composed of it; ಹೊತ್ತು ಹುಟ್ಟಿತು, ತಿಂಗಳು ಮೂಡಿತು, time and month for their cause the Sun and Moon.

(4) Measure for the thing measured,—ಒಂದು ಸೇರು ಕೊಡು, a measure of grain, etc.; ಒಂದುಮೊಳ ಬೇಕು, a cubit of cloth, etc.; ಕಾಲು ನೋಯುತ್ತದೆ, $\frac{1}{4}$ for the limb which forms that much of the body. Cp. also ನಡು; the Sanskrit ಪಾದ and ಮಧ್ಯ, and the Tamil ಅರೈ and ಇಡೈ.

(5) Season for the crop of the season,—ಕಾರು ಕೊಯ್ಯಿತು, the rainy season for its crop.

(6) Quality for the thing possessed of it,—ಬಣ್ಣ ಉಟ್ಟಳು, colour for cloth possessed of it.

(7) Word for its meaning,—ಮಾತು ತಿಳಿಯಿತು, the meaning of the word.

(8) Author for his work,—ಮಾಘವನ್ನು, ಅಮರವನ್ನು, ಓದು, the work of ಮಾಘ, of ಅಮರ.

(9) One thing for another resembling it,—ದಬ್ಬ, means a piece of wood which is flat like the *darbha* grass.

Here also may be mentioned a few of the Sanskrit words which are used in Kannaḍa in a sense quite different from the one they bear in Sanskrit. For instance, ಕ್ಷಾಮ which means emaciated in Sanskrit means famine in Kannaḍa. Similarly—

ಅಭಿಮಾನ means in Sanskrit pride and in Kannaḍa affection.

ಅವಸರ means in Sanskrit opportunity and in Kannaḍa haste.

ಅಸಹ್ಯ means in Sanskrit unbearable and in Kannaḍa disgustful.

ಭದ್ರ means in Sanskrit auspicious and in Kannaḍa safe.

ವಿಪರೀತ means in Sanskrit contrary and in Kannaḍa excessive.

As further examples may be given ಚಾಳೀಸ, ಸಧ್ಯ, ವ್ಯವಹಾರ, ಪ್ರಾಯ, ಖಂಡಿತ, ಬುದ್ಧಿ, ದ್ರೋಹ, ಆಗ್ರಹ, ಬ್ರಾಹ್ಮಣಾರ್ಥ, ಬ್ರಹ್ಮಾಂಡ, ಆತುರ, ಸಂಭ್ರಮ, ವರ್ತಮಾನ, ಸಮಾಚಾರ, ಅಪರೂಪ, ನಿಜ, ಮರ್ಯಾದೆ, ನಿದಾನ, ವಿಶ್ವಾಸ, ಕ್ರೋಧ, ಸರಾಗ, ಶಿಕ್ಷೆ, and so forth.

Changes in form of Old Kannaḍa words when becoming Modern Kannaḍa.

As further instances of changes in form dealt with before may be mentioned some of the changes which Old Kannaḍa words undergo when becoming Modern Kannaḍa. These changes are somewhat similar to those which Sanskrit words undergo when becoming *tadbhava*.

(1) *I* becomes *e*—

Sanskrit.	*Tadbhava.*	*Old Kannaḍa.*	*Modern Kannaḍa.*
ಇಳಾ	ಎಳೆ	ಬಿಸು	ಬೆಸೆ
ವಿನಾಯಕ	ಬೆನಕ	ಇಸು	ಎಸೆ
ಬಿಲ್ವಪತ್ರ	ಬೆಲ್ಲವತ್ತ	ನಿನ್ನೆ	ನೆನ್ನೆ

(2) *U* becomes *o*—

Sanskrit.	*Tadbhava.*	*Old Kannaḍa.*	*Modern Kannaḍa.*
ತುಲಸಿ	ತೊಳಸಿ	ಕುಡು	ಕೊಡು
ಮುಖ	ಮೊಗ	ತುಡು	ತೊಡು
ಸುಧಾ	ಸೊದೆ	ಪುಗು	ಪೊಗು

(3) Conjunct letters are separated by the insertion of a vowel:—

Sanskrit.	*Tadbhava.*	*Old Kannaḍa.*	*Modern Kannaḍa.*
ರತ್ನ	ರತುನ	ನುಣ್ಪು	ನುಣುಪು
ಹರ್ಷ	ಹರುಷ	ಅಳ್ಕು	ಅಳುಕು
ಯತ್ನ	ಜತನ	ಪೇಳ್ದು	ಹೇಳಿದ
ವರ್ಷ	ಬರಿಸ	ನಿಳ್ಕು	ನಿಲುಕು

(4) In conjunct consonants the first letter is assimilated to the second:—

Sanskrit.	*Tadbhava.*	*Old Kannaḍa.*	*Modern Kannaḍa.*
ಶುಕ್ತಿ	ಸುತ್ತಿ	ಪೊಱ್ತು	ಹೊತ್ತು
ಬ್ರಹ್ಮ	ಬೊಮ್ಮ	ಬಿಱ್ದು	ಬಿದ್ದು
ರತ್ನ	ರನ್ನ	ಪುರ್ಬು	ಹುಬ್ಬು
ವರ್ಣ	ಬಣ್ಣ	ಪೊರ್ಕುಳ್	ಹೊಕ್ಕುಳು

(5) A *bindu* is added in some cases:—

Sanskrit.	*Tadbhava.*	*Old Kannaḍa.*	*Modern Kannaḍa.*
ದಾಡಿಮ	ದಾಳಿಂಬ	ಪೊಱಮಟ್ಟು	ಹೊರವಂಟು*
ಕ್ರಮುಕ	ಕವುಂಗು	ಎಲಹಕ್ಕ (ಇರ್ಕೈಪ್ಪಾಕ್ಕಂ)	ಎಲಹಂಕ
ವೋಧಿ	ವೋಂಟಿ	ಒಟ್ಟೆ	ಒಂಟೆ
ಕೂಷ್ಮಾಂಡ	ಕುಂಬಳ	ಸುಟ್ಟುರೆ	ಸುಂಟುರೆ
		ಬಾಸುಳ್	ಬಾಸುಂಡೆ
		ಪಡಿಸಣಿಗ	ಹಡಿಸಂಡಿ

Among other changes which old Kannaḍa words undergo when becoming Modern Kannaḍa are:—

(1) Words ending in consonants add *u*.—ಕಲ್ ಕಲ್ಲು, ಮಣ್ ಮಣ್ಣು, ತಿನ್ ತಿನ್ನು, ನಿಲ್ ನಿಲ್ಲು, ಕೊಳ್ ಕೊಳ್ಳು, ಕಾಣ್ ಕಾಣು, ಪೇಳ್ ಹೇಳು, ಕೇಳ್ ಕೇಳು, ಮೀನ್ ಮೀನು, etc.

* Cp. Also the words ಎಂಟು, ಹೇಂಟೆ, ಬೇಂಟೆ, ಕೋಂಟೆ, ತೋಂಟ with the corresponding Tamil words ಎಟ್ಟು, ಪೆಟ್ಟೈ. ವೇಟ್ಟೈ, ಕೋಟ್ಟೈ, ತೋಟ್ಟಂ.

(2) Change of *p* into *h*.—ಪಂಜರ ಹಂಜರ, ಪಾಗುಕೆ ಹಾವುಗೆ, ಪಿಪ್ಪಲ ಹಿಪ್ಪಲಿ, ಪಾಲ್ ಹಾಲು, ಪಾವು ಹಾವು, ಪೆಸರ್ ಹೆಸರು, ಬರ್ಪ ಬಹ, ಅರ್ಪ ಅಹ, ಇರ್ಪ ಇಹ.

It may be mentioned here that the aspirate was unknown in the original Draviḍian languages.

(3) Omission of *bindu*.—ಅಡಂಗು ಅಡಗು, ದಾಂಟು ದಾಟು, ಬೇಂಟೆ ಬೇಟೆ, ತುಱುಂಬು ತುರುಬು, ಕರದಿಂದಂ ಕರದಿಂದ, ಮಾಡುತ್ತಂ ಮಾಡುತ್ತ, ಮಧುಪಿಂಗೆ ಮಧುಪಿಗೆ, ಭಯದಿಂ ಭಯದಿ, ನೋಡಿಂ ನೋಡಿ, ರಾಮಂ ರಾಮ, ಬಂದೆಂ ಬಂದೆ, ವನಂ ವನ.

(4) *Bindu* is changed into *nu* or *vu*.—ಅವಂ ಅವನು, ರಾಮಂ ರಾಮನು, ಬಂದಂ ಬಂದನು, ತಂದೆಂ ತಂದೆನು, ತಾಂ ತಾವು, ನೀಂ ನೀವು, ನೆಲಂ ನೆಲವು, ಗುಣಂ ಗುಣವು.

(5) Change of the suffix *chu* into *isu*.—ಅಮರ್ಚು ಅಮರಿಸು, ಸಡಿಲ್ಚು ಸಡಿಲಿಸು, ಉರುಳ್ಚು ಉರುಳಿಸು, ಬೞಲ್ಚು ಬಳಲಿಸು, ತೀರ್ಚು ತೀರಿಸು.

(6) Change of *ṟ* and *ḻ* into *r* and *ḷ*.—ಅಱಿ ಅರಿ, ಪೊಱೆ ಹೊರೆ, ಮೀಱು ಮೀರು, ಕಾಱು ಕಾರು, ಸುೞಿ ಸುಳಿ, ಬಾೞೆ ಬಾಳೆ, ಪೊಗೞ್ ಹೊಗಳು, ಬಾೞ್ ಬಾಳು.

Even in Tamil Buddhamitra, the author of the Tamil Grammar *Vīraśōḻiyam*, who flourished in the 11th century, wanted to do away with the distinction between *ḷ* and *ḻ* like Harīśvara and Bhaṭṭākaḷanka in Kannaḍa. See his examples ಪುಗೞ್ + ದೀಪಂ = ಪುಗಡೀಪಂ, ಪಾೞ್ + ನರಗು = ಪಾಣರಗು, where the combination applying to *ḷ* is prescribed for *ḻ* also.

Mistakes committed by authors.

There are a few instances of words acquiring a wrong meaning owing to the carelessness of authors. Decipherment of old writing in palm leaf manuscripts is a rather difficult matter not only because the forms of letters are different but also because there is no distinction made between short and long *e* and *o*, and especially in Tamil, between a consonant and the same combined with *a* [*e.g.*, க் (*k*) க (*ka*) ர் (*r*) ர (*ra*)] owing to the absence of the upper dot, and between *ra* and the sign for the long *a* (ர and ா). The Telugu method of marking the short and long *e* and *o* does not appear till the 17th century. The same is the case with Kannada also even till much later. The famous Jesuit C. J. Beschi (1704–1744) is credited with the introduction into Modern Tamil orthography of the distinction between the short and long *e* and *o*. Maṇḍalapurusha, the author of a Tamil lexicon called *Chūḍāmaṇi*, mistook the Sanskrit word śalalam, a porcupine or its quill, for śallam and śaragam a bee* for śāgam—ಶಾಗಞ್ಜಾಕಿನಿ ವೆಳ್ಳಾಡು ತೇಕ್ಕನುಂ ತರುವು ತೇನೀ. In the first instance *ḷa* was taken for *l* and in the second *ra* was taken for the sign of long *a*. So much for Tamil.

Tirumalārya, author of the *Chikadēvarājavijaya* and other works, has wrongly taken the word ಉಕ್ಕವ in the sense of ಉತ್ಸವ (a festival), supposing ಉಕ್ಕವ to be a *tadbhava* of ಉತ್ಸವ. But ಉಕ್ಕವ, as found in the works of Nāgachandra and other old Jaina authors, means deceit. The *tadbhava* of ಉತ್ಸವ is ಉಚ್ಚವ. In Old Kannaḍa writing it requires some experience to distinguish between the letters *bha* and *cha* and the lack of this experience on the part of some writers of the close of the last century accounts for the form ಕಾಲಭೂರ್ಯ for ಕಾಲಚುರ್ಯ found in some books on Indian History.

Some general remarks on the language.

Language may aptly be compared to the sea owing to the ceaseless change that it undergoes, though the speakers may not be quite conscious of it. The sea is constantly losing water by evaporation but is at the same time being supplied with it by rivers, springs and clouds. In the same way, language gets rid of old words and is supplied with new ones. One of the *sūtras* in the Tamil grammar *Nannūl* lays down the rule that obsolete forms have to be rejected and new ones received in consonance with the progress of the times.† It is not possible to say

Disappearance of old and entry of new words.

---

* ಸರಘಾ ಮಧುಮಕ್ಷಿಕಾ.

† ಪೞೈಯನ ಕೞಿದಲುಂ ಪುದಿಯನ ಪುಗುದಲುಂ.
ವೞುವಲ ಕಾಲವಗೈಯಿನಾನೇ—Sūtra 462.

exactly when old words disappear and when new ones enter the language. Just as coins worn out by use lose currency, so do words in a language. Nṛipatunga says in his *Kavirājamārga* * that Oḍd Kannaḍa words were appropriate in old works (ಪುರಾಣಕಾವ್ಯ), but were insipid in works of his own time. He compares their use in contemporary works to an unnatural union with an old woman.† Words with which old people were familiar in their boyhood have gone out of use and words of which they had not heard then have now become current. Words not found in lexicons are creeping even into literary works. Such being the case, nothing need be said about their free entry into ordinary speech. The following are some of the words that are not found in classical literature but are current in ordinary speech :—

Words not found in classical literature but current in common speech.

ಅಕರಾಯ, ಅಂಚು, ಅಡವು, ಅಲ್ಲಾಡು, ಉಗ್ರಾಣ, ಊಟೆ, ಐಪಾರ್ಡು, ಒತ್ತಾಸೆ, ಕುಳ್ಳ, ಕೆನ್ನೆ, ಕೊಸರು, ಗಿಡ್ಡ, ಗೀಟು, ಗೋಂದು, ಚಟುವಟಿಕೆ, ಚಾಳಿ, ಚಿಲುಕ, ಚೀಲ, ಜವಳಿ, ಜಿಪುಣ, ಜುಟ್ಟು, ತುಂಟ, ತೊಂದರೆ, ದಪ್ಪ, ದವಸ, ದನ, ದುಡುಕು, ನೀಸು, ಪಿಕ್ಕರಾಟ, ಬೊಂಬೆ, ಮುಂಜಾನೆ, ಮಷ್ಟು, ಮೂತಿ, ಮೋರೆ, ಯೋಚನೆ, ವಟ್ಟ, ವಾಡಿಕೆ, ಬಾಡಿಗೆ, ಪೆಚ್ಚ, ಸಪ್ಪೆ, ಹಾವಳಿ, ಹೀಚು.

Some lost words that deserve restoration.

Some of the lost forms and words such as the following, which are terse and expressive, may with advantage be restored :—ಸುಖಮಿರ್ದಂ, ಆಯಿರ್ಪಗಿಳಿ, ಬೆನ್ನನೆ, ಐವುದು, ಕದಪು, ನಿಟ್ಟಿಸು, ನರುಗಂಪು, ಸೂಳು, ತೀಡು, ಅಲಂಪು, ಅದಟು, ನೇರ, ಪಾಂಗು, ಪೆಂಪು, ಬಿಣ್ಪು, ತನಿ, ನಿಡು, ನೆಗಳ್ತೆ, ಸೈಪು, ಕೂರ್ಮೆ, ಕಡುಪು, ತರಿ, ಸಲ್ಲು, ಬಿಸವಂದ.

There is, however, a sort of natural selection in language according to which whatever is useless is got rid of and whatever is conducive to the advancement of the language is freely admitted.

---

* I, 50.

† In my introduction to the revised edition of *Karṇāṭaka-Kavicharite* Vol. I (p. XVII) I have wrongly given this comparison in connection with the mixture of Sanskrit and Kannaḍa words.

Some words have the appearance of being correct forms, but are not really so, though they can claim the authority of long usage. As instances may be mentioned ವಾಯ್ಕ್ಕಾಲ್ for ಕಾಲ್ವಾಯ್, ವಾಯಿಲ್ for ಇಲ್ವಾಯ್, ಮುನ್ಱಿಲ್ for ಇಲ್ಮುನ್, ತುಡಿಮರಂ for ಮರತುಡಿ, ಪುಱನಗರ್ for ನಗರ್ಪ್ಪುಱಂ. ಬಾಯ್ಕ್ಕಾಲ್ is met with in Kannaḍa inscriptions in the sense of ಕಾಲ್ವಾಯ್, now corrupted into ಕಾಲ್ವೆ. ಕಾಲ್ವಾಯ್ means the mouth (ಬಾಯ್) of a stream (ಕಾಲ್), *i.e.*, a channel from a river. Similarly, ವಾಯಿಲ್ (ಬಾಯಿಲ್), corrupted into (ಬಾಗಿಲ್) stands for ಇಲ್ವಾಯ್, the mouth (ಬಾಯ್) of a house (ಇಲ್), *i.e.*, the door of a house. Such forms are given in Tamil grammar as examples of ಇಲಕ್ಕಣಪ್ಪೋಲಿ.

Some words which are seemingly correct.

A word may be said here about the etymology of some words. In all these languages mistakes are committed with regard to the derivation of words, mistakes which are mostly attributable to a lack of knowledge of the sister languages and ignorance of the science of language. In Tamil the word ನಾಕ್ಕು (tongue) is derived from the root ನಕ್ಕು to lick. This is plausible enough; but when we consider the words used in cognate languages for the tongue, namely, ನಾಲಗೆ in Kannaḍa, ನಾಲುಕ in Telugu and ನಾಲಯಿ in Tuḷu and Koḍagu, we cannot but feel a doubt as to the correctness of the Tamil derivation. The Tamil word seems to have lost the letter *l* which forms an integral part of the words in the other languages. We may therefore presume that the word is not derived from the root *nakku* to lick but from the root *nāl* or *nēl* to hang. Again, the word ಅಮೈಚ್ಚು a minister, is derived by some Tamil scholars from the root ಅಮೈ to arrange, but the word is clearly a *tadbhava* of the Sanskrit word ಅಮಾತ್ಯ, a minister. Some derive the Kannaḍa word ಮಾತು from the Sanskrit ವಾರ್ತಾ but ಮಾತು is a pure Kannaḍa word answering to ಮಾಱ್ಱಮ್ in Tamil and ಮಾಟ

False etymology.

in Telugu. It is derived from ಮಾಱು and meant originally something said in reply.* ಕಡವೆ is written by some as ಕಡಿವೆ on the supposition, perhaps, that the word is derived from the root ಕಡಿ. But compare the Telugu ಕಡವು remainder, and ಕೊದವ deficiency or remainder (ಕಡಿಮಿ in Telugu means valour or increase). The correct form ಕಡವೆ occurs in verse 89 of the Jaina work ರತ್ನಾಕರಾಧೀಶ್ವರ ಶತಕ (ಸು. 1600).

Forms given in Kannaḍa grammars.

We shall now consider some of the forms given in Kannaḍa grammars. In the compound ಅಂಗಯ್ the first word ಅಂ is stated to be a substitute for ಅಡಿ.† But it is more likely that ಅಂ in a contraction of ಅಗಂ (inner portion) as stated in Tamil grammars. The nouns ಏತಂ and ಓತಂ are derived from ಏಱುತಂ and ಓದುತಂ by the elision of the syllables ṟu and ḍu.‡ The real explanation of these forms is this: the ṟu of the root ಏಱು and the du of the root ಓದು are doubled and the suffix *am* is added. Compare the Tamil equivalents ಏಱ್ಱಂ and ಓತ್ತು. ಓತ್ತು in Tamil for the Kannaḍa ಓತಂ may be compared with ಮಾತು in Kannaḍa for the Tamil ಮಾಱ್ಱು. In ಅಡುಂ ಬೊಲಂ and ಇಟಿಯುಂಬೊಟ್ಟು, *bindu* is laid down for the final portion of the first words ಅಡುವ and ಇಟಿವ, and it is further stated that in the second instance *u* has crept in as an increment.§ The proper explanation appears to be that in both cases *um*, the Tamil future relative participle suffix, is used. In all Kannaḍa grammars there is a special rule enunciated for the formation of the compound ಜೇನೆಯ್ in which it is presumed that ಜೇನ್ has become ಜೇ by the elision of its final letter.‖ According

* ಮಾಱ್ಱಮುಂ ತಾರಾರೋ ವಾಶಲ್ ತಿಱವಾದಾರ್—*Tiruppāvai.*

† *Śabdamaṇidarpaṇa*, sūtra 166 : *Śabdānuśāsana*, sūtra 348.

‡ *Śabdamaṇidarpaṇa* sūtra 209.

§ Ibid., sūtra 170 ; *Śabdānuśāsana*, sūtra 333.

‖ Ibid., sūtra 176 ; *Śabdānuśāsana*, sūtra 332 ; *Kāvyāvalōkana*, sūtra 54 ; *Bhāshābhūshaṇa*, sūtra 148.

to the rules of euphonic combination in Tamil, this is a very ordinary change.

Tamil rules of euphonic combination adopted in Kannaḍa.

When n following a long letter or two short letters is combined with a word beginning with n the first n disappears. ಕೋೝ+ನಲ್ಲೝ=ಕೋನಲ್ಲೝ ; ತೇೝ+ನೆಯರ್=ತೇನೆಯರ್ ; ಕಲೝ+ನಲ್ಲದು=ಕಲನಲ್ಲದು ; ಪದಿೝ+ನಾನ್ಗು=ಪದಿನಾನ್ಗು. The Kannaḍa ಪದಿನಾಲ್ಕು is formed on the same plan as the Timil ಪದಿನಾನ್ಗು, though the Kannaḍa grammars say that the first word here is ಪದಿ and not ಪದಿೝ. Another rule in Tamil says that when l following a long letter or two short letters is combined with a word beginning with n, the l disappears. ಕಾರ್+ನೆಡಿದು=ಕಾನೆಡಿದು ; ನಾರ್+ನೂಱು ನಾನೂಱು. ನಾನೂಱು in Kannaḍa is formed on the same principle. As other instances of compounds formed according to the Tamil rules of combination may be mentioned ಕತ್ತಾಱ and ಚೆಪ್ಪೋಡು. A Tamil rule states that when l following a short letter is combined with t of the following word, both the letters are changed into $\underline{r}\underline{r}$ (ṭṭra); *e.g.*, ಕರ್+ತೀದು=ಕಱ್ಱೀದು ; ಕರ್+ತಾದ್ಕೈ=ಕಱ್ಱಾದ್ಕೈ. The sound corresponding to $\underline{r}\underline{r}a$ being *tta* in Kannaḍa, we have the form ಕತ್ತಾಱ. Another rule in Tamil enjoins the change of a sonant preceded by its nasal into a double surd in composition ; *e.g.*, ಕರುಂಬು+ಏರ್=ಕರುಪ್ಪುಏರ್ ; ಮರುಂದು+ಪೈ=ಮರುತ್ತುಪ್ಪೈ ; ಶೆಂಬು+ಏಡು=ಶೆಪ್ಪೇಡು. The Kannaḍa word ಚೆಪ್ಪೋಡು is a corruption of ಚೆಪ್ಪೇಡು corresponding to the Tamil ಶೆಪ್ಪೇಡು which means a copper plate—ಶೆಂಬು copper and ಏಡು a plate. There are also some other forms in Kannaḍa such as ಕೈದು, ಏನಾನುಂ which require the help of Tamil to be properly understood.

Help of Tamil in the derivation of some Kannada words.

ಕೈದು a weapon is ಕೈಯುದು in Tamil, *i.e.*, what is held in the hand (for defence). ಆನುಂ in ಏನಾನುಂ, ಎತ್ತಾನುಂ, ಎಂದಾನುಂ, ಎಲ್ಲಿಯಾನುಂ is only the Tamil ಆಯಿನುಂ (ಆದೊಡಂ) from the root ಆಗು. The modern equivalent of ಆನುಂ is ಆದರೂ. Again, ನೇರೆ in

Kannaḍa seems to be a corruption of the Tamil ಕೇರಂಗ್ಗ which explains itself. There are likewise some other Kannaḍa words which require some explanation as regards their etymology, *e.g.*, ಅಟ್ಟಿಂದು, ಬೆಕ್ಕಸಮುತ್ತು and ರಾಗಿ. ಅಟ್ಟಿಂದು as a past participle is frequently met with in literature in the sense of having chased. Its root, which is not generally known, is ಅಟ್ಟರ್ *. The form ಬೆಕ್ಕಸಮುತ್ತು has puzzled some scholars. It is made up of the two words ಬೆಕ್ಕಸಂ surprise, and ಉತ್ತು, the past participle of ಉಱು (compare ಪೆಱು ಪೆತ್ತು, ಪೊಱು ಪೊತ್ತು) to feel, and means having become surprised. ರಾಗಿ is said to be derived from ರಾಘವ, a name of ರಾಮ, and is styled ರಾಮಧಾನ್ಯ by Kanakadāsa in his *Rāmadhānyacharitre*†. The spelling, ರಾಘಿ given in inscription 172 (*l*, 11) of the Muḷbāgal Tāluk, dated 1496, lends some support to this derivation.

Words about whose derivation Grammarians differ.

I shall close this section by giving two examples of words about the derivation of which the grammarians Kēśirāja and Bhaṭṭākaḷanka differ. These are ಹಗ್ಗ and ದಮ್ಮಾಣಿ. Kēśirāja derives ಹಗ್ಗ easily enough from the Sanskrit ಪ್ರಗ್ರಹ by postulating the elision of the final syllable *ha* of the Sanskrit word‡. The first syllable loses the *rēpha* (compare ಹದಿಟೆ from ಪ್ರತಿಷ್ಠೆ) and in the second syllable the *rēpha* is assimilated to the letter ಗ. On the other hand, Bhaṭṭākaḷanka's way of getting ಹಗ್ಗ from ಪ್ರಗ್ರಹ is rather clumsy. He says under sūtra 160 that in ಪ್ರಗ್ರಹ the first syllable disappears, the *rēpha* of the second syllable is assimilated to ಗ and then the third syllable and the second interchange their places! Kēśirāja derives ದಮ್ಮಾಣಿ from ಧರ್ಮಪಾನೀಯ, § which probably means water

* Pampa-Bhārata, xii, 18 Pr.—ಅಟ್ಟರ್ದಂದು; Mallinātha-purāṇa, i,-ಅಲೆದಾಟಕೆ; Shikārpur Taluk Inscription 136, *l*. 3-ಅಟ್ಟರ್ದ'; Do–Inscription 149, *l*. 43–ಅಟ್ಟರ್ದಂಗೆ.

† Karṇāṭaka-Kavicharite, ii, 239.

‡ Śabdamaṇidarpaṇa, sūtra 280.

§ Śabdamaṇidarpaṇa, sūtra 293.

supplied as an act of charity. Bhaṭṭākaḷanka, however, derives it from a word ದ್ರಮ್ಮಣ್ which, according to him, means a mint, *dramma* being the name of a coin. But no explanation is forthcoming of ಅಣ್, the second part of the word.

Reform of the Language.

The development of Kannaḍa has not kept pace with the growth of civilisation among the Kannaḍigas. When the language is properly developed, there will be no difficulty in finding words for expressing new ideas. These words have to be got either by suitably altering existing words, or by coining new ones or by borrowing from other languages.' Change in ideas is reflected in the words used. The language of authors must not be allowed to differ greatly from that of polite conversation. Otherwise, the two are likely to become two different languages altogether. Authors must be prevailed upon to avoid archaic forms and constructions and to use *sandhi* or euphonic combination as sparingly as possible. Special attention has to be paid to perspicuity of style which must never be allowed to become either pedantic or enigmatic. Writers will do well to bear in mind that their works are not intended for Pandits alone but for ordinary people who have neither time nor inclination to solve riddles as they go on reading. The style must be simple and easily intelligible, characteristics which are denoted by the term perspicuity. By perspicuity, according to Quintillian, care is taken, not that the hearer may understand, if he will, but that he must understand, whether he will or not. The marks of punctuation used in English may with advantage be adopted in Kannaḍa as far as they are deemed necessary. Present day writers must see that in giving expression to new thoughts they do no violence to the genius of the language. Some writings of the present time, which abound in foreign words and idioms needlessly introduced, cannot but tend to denationalise and deprave the language. From this it is not to be understood that foreign words are to be tabooed altogether. When found absolutely necessary, it is nothing but wisdom to welcome them. If foreign terms are more easily understood than any Kannaḍa or Sanskrit equivalent, it would be mere affectation not to use them. But every attempt should be made to maintain the purity of the language. I cannot do better than quote a writer in the New York "*Round Table*" in this connection. He says, "The corrupter of a language stabs straight at the heart of his country. He commits a crime against every individual of the nation, for he throws a poison into a stream from which all must drink. He wrongs himself first, and afterwards every man and woman whose native speech he mars. It is the duty of every educated man to guard zealously the purity of his native tongue. He who hunts down and pillories a slang phrase, a vulgarism, a corruption of any kind, is a public benefactor. In the fulfilment of the sacred trust which rests on him as an educated man, he adds a stone to the bulwark of his nation's safety and greatness."

I must also utter a word of caution. The growth of a language being natural and unconscious, reforms ought not to be forced but must be introduced with care at the proper time.

Advancement of the Language.

The advancement of Modern Kannaḍa began in the first half of the 19th century during the reign of the Mysore king, Krishṇarāja Oḍeyar III, who was a munificent patron of all kinds of literary merit and afforded special encouragement to the production of Kannaḍa versions of all the more important Sanskrit works. The last quarter of the century may be said to have witnessed a revival of Kannaḍa learning. Under the late Chāmarājēndra Oḍeyar of Mysore, encouragement was given to the production of dramatic works of a high order, which supplanted the rude dramas known as *Yakshagānas*. In 1889 a school called the Karṇāṭaka-

Bhāshōjjīvini was started for imparting a high standard of education in Kannaḍa. It was subsequently converted into a Government Normal School, and has now become the Training College. The Trustees of the Dēvarāja Bahadur Charities have been encouraging the higher study of Kannaḍa by giving suitable rewards to authors of good works. The Karṇāṭaka-Vidyāvardhaka-Sangha of Dharwar has likewise done good service in this line. The first Kannaḍa monthly journal in Mysore, the *Hitabōdhini*, was started in 1881. It contained articles on scientific and other subjects of general interest and did important service to the Kannaḍigas during its career of about 10 years. Of the journals subsequently started, the most important from the point of view of the advancement of the language are the *Kāvyamañjari*, styled later on the *Kāvyakalānidhi*, and the *Granthamāle*, devoted, respectively, to the publication of old and modern Kannaḍa works. The former did excellent service to the country by bringing to light rare Kannaḍa works of great literary merit; it is however to be deplored that it has ceased to exist owing chiefly to the withdrawal of Government support. The latter affords facilities for authors to publish their works and brings within the reach of the Kannaḍa public works in English or Sanskrit by means of translations and adaptations. Even this journal is in a moribund condition owing mostly to the same cause mentioned in connection with the other. Under the fostering care of our beloved sovereign, Śrī Krishṇarāja Oḍeyar Bahādur, considerable literary activity is observable on all sides. Educated men have begun in earnest to enrich Kannaḍa literature and promote the study of the language by supplying dainty pabulum in the shape of original works, translations and adaptations. In 1915 an association named the "Kannaḍa Sāhitya Parishat" or "Kannaḍa Academy" including representatives from all parts of the Kannaḍa country, was formed, having for its objects not only the study of past literature and the encouragement of present writers of merit, but also the cultivation and improvement of the language by the unification of dialects, the fixing of scientific terminology and the formation of a common literary style. The Parishat publishes a quarterly journal which contains useful articles bearing on the language and its literature. The Mysore University, which came into existence in 1916, has been doing something in the way of encouragement to Kannaḍa studies and authors. The Karṇāṭaka Sanghas attached to the constituent colleges of the University and other similar ones have also been trying to do some thing in this line. Finally, H. H. the Maharaja, with his keen interest in the revival of Kannaḍa learning, has graciously instituted an annual poetical competition in Kannaḍa with suitable prizes to the first three of the successful competitors.

With all this it has to be stated that the encouragement afforded to the advancement of the language of the country is very inadequate. Some years ago, there used to be a decent sum in the educational budget earmarked for the encouragement of authors. We do not hear of it now. The interest of the University, too, in the promotion of the language appears to have diminished in some degree, judging from the continual decrease in the budget allotments made for this purpose. Encouragement of students and authors is a *sine qua non* for the advancement of the language. It is therefore absolutely necessary that liberal sums should be allotted in the budgets of the University and the Education Department for the encouragement of authors. It is, indeed, a curious anomaly that the business of the courts and offices in Mysore should all be mainly transacted in a foreign tongue and not in the language of the country. The sooner this anomaly is got rid of the better. The State of Mysore has a special mission to discharge in relation to the learned world of Orientalists in general, and to Karṇāṭaka and South India in particular, in vindicating the claims and promoting a healthy revival of the culture of its pithy and expressive language.

WORKS CONSULTED.

BHATTAKALANKA : Ŝabdānuŝāsana.
BROWN, C. P. : Telugu Grammar.
BUDDHAMITRA : Vīraŝōḷiyam.
BURNELL : South Indian Palaeography.
CALDWELL : Comparative Grammar of the Dravidian Languages.
CHELVAKESAVARAYA MUDALIAR : Tamil.
COWELL : Short Introduction to Prākrit.
CUST : The Modern Languages of the East Indies.
,, Linguistic and Oriental Essays.
FLEET : Dynasties of the Kanarese Districts.
GRIERSON AND STEN KONOW : Linguistic Survey of India, Vol. IV.
KITTEL : Kannada Grammar.
,, Kannada-English Dictionary, Introduction.
KESIRAJA : Ŝabdamaṇidarpaṇa.
MAX MULLER : Science of Language.
,, Selected Essays.
NAGAVARMA II : Kāvyāvalōkana.
,, Bhāshābhūshaṇa.
NANNAYYA BHATTA : Āndhraŝabdachintāmaṇi.
NARAYANA RAO, H. : A Short Story of Kanarese.
NRIPATUNGA : Kavirājamārga.
OPPERT : Classification of Languages.
PAVANANDI : Nannūl.
PIELE : Philology.
RAGHUNATHA RAO : Vyākaraṇōpanyāsa-manjari.
SAYCE : Principles of Comparative Philology.
,, Introduction to the Science of Language.
SESHAGIRI SASTRI : Aryan and Dravidian Philology.
,, Tamil Philology.
,, Telugu Philology.
SRINIVASA IYENGAR, M. : Tamil Studies.
STEN KONOW : The Aryan Gods of the Mitāni People (Royal Frederick University Publications of the Indian Institute) Kristiania 1921.
SUBBA RAO : Telugu Literature.
SURYANARAYANA SASTRY : History of the Tamil Language.
SWEET : The History of Language.

VAMANA : Kāvyālankāra-sūtra.
WHITNEY : Language and the Study of Language.
Journal of the Royal Asiatic Society.
Indian Antiquary.
Journal of the American Oriental Society.
Modern Review.
Mysore Archæological Series.
Travancore Archæological Series.
Cambridge History of India.
Prākritaŝabda-pradīpikā.
Ŝambhurahasya, etc.

INDEX.